THE REFUSED

The AGONY of the INDOCHINA REFUGEES

by
Barry Wain

SIMON AND
SCHUSTER
New York

SIMON AND SCHUSTER and colophon are trademarks of
Simon & Schuster
Designed by Irving Perkins Associates
Manufactured in the United States of America

10 9 8 7 6 5 4 3 2 1

Library of Congress Cataloging in Publication Data

Wain, Barry.
  The refused.

  Includes bibliographical references and index.
  1. Refugees—Indochina.   I. Title.
HV640.5.I5W3   362.8'7'09597   81–16554
ISBN 0-671-42236-7   AACR2

The author is grateful for permission to quote from the following:
Murder of a Gentle Land by John Barron and Anthony Paul,
copyright © 1977 by The Reader's Digest Association, Inc.,
Reader's Digest Press, New York, 1977;
Giai Phong: The Fall and Liberation of Saigon by Tiziano Ter-
zani, John Shepley, ed., St. Martin's Press, 1976;
Decent Interval by Frank Snepp, copyright © 1977 by Frank W.
Snepp, III, Random House, 1977.

FOREWORD

THE OPTIMISTS SAID it could not happen. The suggestion that there would be a bloodbath if the revolutionary forces took over in South Vietnam, Laos and Kampuchea seemed to them an easy line of propaganda spread by the Americans to justify and perpetuate an increasingly unpopular war.

The skeptics, including some Western correspondents who had witnessed the ferocious cruelty and inhumanity on both sides, for the most part stayed silent. They lived in hope. The prospect of peace at last was understandably appealing as America's anti-Communist crusade in Indochina inched inevitably to defeat.

Even when the tales of atrocities began to seep out of Kampuchea, which had been effectively sealed off by the victorious Khmer Rouge, they were for a long time largely discounted. The source, usually a refugee, was always suspect. Refugees tell their rescuers what they want to hear, it was said, and they exaggerate events to justify their flight.

The optimists were wrong. We now know that something

5

terrible did happen when Communist-led movements seized control of Indochina in 1975. The starkest evidence is in the story of the Indochina refugees to be found in the following pages. In the first five years under Communist rule in Vietnam, Kampuchea and Laos, nearly 1.3 million people decided to forsake their homes, an outflow of permanent refugees on a scale the globe had not witnessed since World War II.

It is true that Indochinese had been driven from their homes in vast numbers during thirty or forty years of conflict; by 1975, an estimated 11 million of them could be considered displaced within the three countries—settled in permanent slums on the edge of cities, in camps, on roads without shelter, even across national boundaries. But they had not chosen the extreme course of abandoning Indochina forever.

In Kampuchea, the Khmer Rouge under Pol Pot terrorized an entire population in one of the bloodiest experiments in human engineering ever recorded. They sought nothing less than instant reversion to an agrarian society without trace of foreign influence or modernization. Phnom Penh and other cities were emptied in the first of several extraordinary migrations. Mass executions, starvation and disease took an appalling toll.

Despite the barbarism—or, perhaps, because of it—relatively few Kampucheans managed to escape to neighboring countries. They found it almost impossible to evade security patrols and survive the overland trek through forest and mountain. Those who made it to Thailand received, at first, little publicity as they recounted their experiences to disbelieving reporters. The majority, including Khmer Rouge defectors and intended victims of purges, found sanctuary in Vietnam, while a few took shelter in Laos.

In Laos, the takeover meant much the same thing for the Hmong, a minority hill tribe. One faction of the Hmong, with a history of collaboration with the U.S. Central Intelligence Agency, was marked for annihilation. Vietnamese and Pathet Lao forces attacked them in their mountain villages, ambushed them as they fled and pursued survivors all the way to Thailand.

For other Laotians, including lowlanders, the socialist transformation was not fatal, but deeply traumatic. Thousands were packed off to remote reeducation camps. Vestiges of Westernization were eliminated abruptly, and all personal liberties were severely restricted. Private enterprise was strangled, but no alternative system was developed to produce needed goods.

The lowlanders found it easier to escape than the hill tribes. For the most part they had only to cross the Mekong River to Thailand. Some were shot by armed patrols, but a combination of bribery and stealth ensured for most a safe passage. More a steady hemorrhage than a visible bloodbath, the outflow just as surely drained the life from Laos.

In Vietnam, by contrast, the victors liked to boast that the American predictions of bloodletting had proved false. Indeed, after the frantic scramble at the time of the takeover, it seemed that the transition was going to be accomplished with a minimum of dislocation. Reports from foreign correspondents who stayed to witness events spoke initially of a spirit of elation, tolerance and forgiveness.

In time, however, the result was the same as in Laos. As tens of thousands were dispatched to reeducation camps, where many were to stay for years, reforms were introduced to bring the rip-roaring South into line with the closely controlled North. Economic conditions deteriorated, and the authorities cracked down on dissidents. Vietnamese in droves looked for a chance to escape.

Their way out was by sea. The "boat people," as the world came to call them, often took enormous risks, long before setting foot in a boat. As they slipped past police and military patrols, they risked being shot, or at the very least arrested and jailed. Those who did get to boats set out in flimsy, overcrowded fishing vessels unsuited to ocean travel. Usually they headed for Thailand or Malaysia, but they often landed elsewhere, between Hong Kong and Australia.

An untold number of lives were claimed by the sea.

Ultimately, the flight of the Indochina refugees came into focus as an exodus of biblical proportions. But for several years while it was building, the picture was not quite so clear to many of us in Asia, including myself. By 1978, I had been working as a newsman in the region for seven years, most recently as correspondent in Malaysia for *The Asian Wall Street Journal*. The big issues on my beat were the questions of economic and political development. I was aware that the number of boat people arriving in Malaysia was rising at an alarming rate, but the story was not one that I, or my editors, perceived as urgent.

This changed sharply one day in November 1978, when *The Asian Wall Street Journal*'s correspondent in Indonesia, Raphael Pura, phoned seeking help on what he warned could turn into a major story. The Indonesian government, he said, was investigating reports that a large freighter carrying 2,500 refugees from Vietnam had appeared in the South China Sea. According to his sources in Indonesia, the ship had gone to Vietnam by arrangement to collect the refugees, mainly ethnic Chinese, who had paid in gold for the one-way trip.

My contacts in Malaysia, where the United Nations headquartered its Southeast Asian refugee operations, confirmed most of the details and were able to fill in the background of the vessel. It soon became clear to both Pura and me, as well as our editors, that a new and ominous development was taking place as fast as we could keep up with it. We filed late into the night, piecing together the story of the voyage of the *Hai Hong*. The following morning, the page-one headline in the *Journal*'s Hong Kong edition summed up our finding: "EVIDENCE IS GROWING OF VIETNAMESE ROLE IN EXODUS OF REFUGEES. JOURNEY OF THE HAI HONG OFFERS BEST PROOF YET OF ACTIVE ASSISTANCE."

It had been known for some time that refugees often bribed police and security forces to escape. But the *Hai Hong*'s trip showed that officials "and perhaps the Hanoi government itself," as the article put it, were accepting payment to facilitate the departure of ethnic Chinese. What made this so ominous was the background of internal politics in Vietnam and the growing tension between Vietnam and China, which, during the war against America, had once stood as "close as lips and teeth."

Indeed, as early as late 1977, there were rumors within Vietnam's Chinese community of an imminent war between the two countries. Peking and Hanoi had already been trading bitter verbal assaults, and by 1978, large numbers of Sino-Vietnamese had been streaming overland to China. Hanoi's decision to nationalize business in southern Vietnam, largely in the hands of ethnic Chinese, added to the panic. On the assumption that the Sino-Vietnamese could act as a fifth column for Peking, Hanoi was prepared not only to allow them to become refugees but to help them leave—while confiscating most of their wealth.

The implications of the *Hai Hong*'s trip were thus enormous, but still just a beginning. The following month, Vietnam invaded Kampuchea and toppled the Khmer Rouge government, aggravating nationwide turmoil and famine. China retaliated in behalf of its ally Pol Pot by staging a limited invasion of northern Vietnam. This move, in turn, spelled genuine disaster for Vietnamese of Chinese extraction. Fearful of a second Chinese attack, Hanoi set about systematically evicting ethnic Chinese from northern and central Vietnam, forcing them to take their chances by sea.

The editors of *The Asian Wall Street Journal* assigned me to cover this story in all its breadth. I was given carte blanche to travel anywhere, and so the story took me to the farthest and most fetid refugee camps in Southeast Asia, to the rarefied atmosphere of the United Nations in Geneva, and finally—in several trips in 1980—to the sad towns, villages and countryside of Vietnam, Kampuchea and Laos.

The overpowering and lasting picture in my mind is of people in flight, gathering in establishments that shared the common name of "refugee camps" but varied widely, from brick and concrete shelters amid the tenements of Hong Kong, to barbed-wire enclosures near the surf in Malaysia, to sprawling dusty enclaves in Thailand. One such camp, Pulau Bidong, is etched indelibly in my memory: a waterless, previously uninhabited island 10 miles off the Malaysian coast where 40,000 people shared little more than a square mile and built high-rise, thatched-roof slums to survive.

As a newspaper story, the agony of the Indochina refugees was an important one for what it told of the present and for what help it could be in the public policy decisions that had to be made immediately. But the story could not be fully or satisfactorily told within the limitations of daily newspaper space. It warrants telling in its full context, and at book length, not simply because it is compelling in itself, but for what it might suggest about the future. We live in an age of refugees, and coming to terms with them remains a baffling but unavoidable challenge.

The situation in Indochina in the second half of the 1970s was made for the generation of refugees. There had been the long years of foreign intervention and destructive wars. Then there was the hasty, haphazard and humiliating withdrawal of the Americans who, following the French, had tried to resist the incoming Communist tide in collaboration with anti-Communist local forces. The Americans did not have time to wrap up their affairs and ensure the safety and protection of compromised allies.

Since the creation of the refugees obviously is linked to the installation of Communist governments throughout Indochina, some people want to lay the blame entirely on "communism." Certainly the decision to flee represented in large part a rejection of the socialist system and its failure to deliver a tolerable daily existence. It might also say something about the attitude of socialist governments toward their people. But to hold communism solely responsible for what happened is simplistic and misleading.

This is nowhere so clearly illustrated as in Communist Vietnam's falling-out with both Communist China and Communist Kampuchea. Here was a situation in which hundreds of thousands of refugees fled from one Communist country to another. They were victims of complex factors and events—some of which originated in the dim past long before Marx was born—that came together with cataclysmic results in the 1970s. Ideology was an element, but only one of many.

In the end, however, the story of the Indochina refugees is the story of people refused—refused first and most painfully by their own governments, refused too often by neighboring countries where they sought temporary asylum and refused, initially at least, by the West and Japan, the only nations with the capacity and the heart to save them.

One sensitive, articulate woman among 42,000 who were forced back at gunpoint into Kampuchea from Thailand spoke for all refugees. She described an inch-by-inch death crawl down a steep slope and through a minefield to a stream two miles away. Thousands were forced to do it en masse. The bodies of earlier mine victims, decomposing in the burning sun, lined the way. Flies and worms had begun their work. The wounded moaned next to the dead. "The tears I thought were exhausted mounted to my eyes," she said, "less at the horror of that scene than at the idea that these innocent beings had paid with their

10

lives for their attempt to find a place in a world too selfish to receive them."

The displaced Indochinese were not, of course, the first to be treated as a burden and a nuisance; history has assigned most refugees that fate. But there was something particularly disturbing about the events that simultaneously created their predicament and swept them aside. And there was something chilling in what these events did to quite ordinary people. One day in Thailand, a Westerner engaged in refugee work noticed some village boys playing soccer. As he approached, he was horrified to discover that the ball they were kicking was a human head. Recently severed, it still bore the unmistakable features of a Khmer male, who no doubt had come from nearby Kampuchea.

As one of many gory incidents, it was sad but unexceptional. And yet, as few others did, it distilled much of the Indochina story. The victim not only had died unknown and unmourned but evoked so little sympathy that he was denied peace in death. The tormentors of his soul, though excusable to some extent by their age, were all too much like people everywhere who reacted to the refugees with indifference or hostility. As for the game, it seemed most appropriate. The Indochinese were kicked back and forth as player nations sought to score points in what became little more than political football.

At the same time, some themes of hope weave into and out of this story as well, for the agony of the Indochina refugees eventually moved millions to contribute to what was one of the great rescue efforts in history. It led to relatively happy endings for some hundreds of thousands of refugees who might have met a much crueler fate than being separated from family and nation.

In recording events, I have approached the subject thematically rather than chronologically. The book opens with the voyage of the vessel *Hai Hong*, which signaled the massive and chaotic departure of ethnic Chinese from Vietnam. It examines the factors that stimulated this exodus and other outflows from the three countries, details the Vietnamese government's activist role and explains how Hong Kong sought to deter racketeers—and Hanoi—from running refugees in *Hai Hong*-style freighters.

Subsequent chapters deal with the burden imposed on

11

neighboring countries and the making of a tragedy as they closed their doors to refugees in the face of grudging and inadequate support from the industrial democracies. The refugees are also set in a political framework: they helped polarize Southeast Asia into two hostile blocs—the non-Communist Association of Southeast Asian Nations and Vietnam-dominated Indochina.

Because Vietnam has consistently denied ejecting its people, the evidence is scrutinized in a separate chapter. My finding is, I believe, a solid and damaging one: apart from authorizing the departure of boat people and charging them exit fees, Hanoi expelled for profit Sino-Vietnamese and other unwanted elements in an exercise that reminded many of Hitler's treatment of the Jews.

The closing sections of the book, tracking developments leading up to a U.N. conference in Geneva in July 1979, show an international community unprepared, unwilling or unable to fashion a lasting solution to the refugee crisis. Diplomatic pressure forced Vietnam to stop the evictions along with the departure of all refugees, but it did not compel Hanoi to treat its people any better. It left untold numbers trapped unhappily behind a bamboo curtain.

I am indebted to numerous people for their help in the preparation of this book—so many that it would be impractical to acknowledge my debt to each individually. But Wayne Gibbons, who was based in Kuala Lumpur as regional coordinator of Australia's Indochinese-refugee resettlement program, was especially helpful. With his assistance, it was possible for me to gain access to remote refugee camps and insight into particular events.

I am grateful to the *Far Eastern Economic Review* for permission to excerpt freely from its weekly magazine and annual Yearbook, especially from articles by its diplomatic correspondent and Indochina specialist Nayan Chanda.

The Office of the United Nations High Commissioner for Refugees was responsive to requests for information, both from its headquarters in Geneva and from many officers in the field, despite the fact that several of my articles were critical of the agency. A number of journalistic colleagues were kind enough to share with me their extensive knowledge of Indochina.

Special thanks are due to Dow Jones & Co., which publishes *The Asian Wall Street Journal* in Hong Kong and *The Wall Street Journal* in the United States. Its editors recognized early the size and importance of the refugee story and, in years during which everyone on the Asian edition was working double time to get out the paper, arranged for me to be able to take the time off to write this book. Carol Currie, the paper's office manager, arranged the logistics of assembling and typing the manuscript while I was traveling. Seth Lipsky, managing editor of the Asian edition during these years, provided the advice and encouragement of a friend when it was needed.

Barry Wain
Bangkok
April 13, 1981

N.B. The terms Vietnamese, Laotians and Kampucheans are used to refer to residents of those countries and are not meant to connote their racial origin or nationality. Where ethnicity is intended, people are identified as Khmer, ethnic Vietnamese, Sino-Vietnamese or ethnic Chinese, Lao, Hmong, and the like.

ONE

Nguyen Dinh Thuy did not think there was any chance of the Communists' conquering South Vietnam, and by the time he realized he was wrong it was too late. He believed his friends in the government of President Nguyen Van Thieu, who said the threat had passed when the guerrillas spent themselves on the bloody Tet offensive in 1968. Besides, the Americans were still around and they would not let it happen.

The truth hit home about April 20, 1975, just ten days before the end. With cities falling like dominos to the North Vietnamese advance, Thuy panicked. He wanted to escape. His preference was for Australia, where he had met and married a fellow Vietnamese student and their first child was born. "But I was prepared to go anywhere, even the Congo," he said. Middle-class civilians such as himself might be slaughtered, he feared.

With his wife and their two young children, Thuy

*rushed to Saigon's Tan Son Nhut airport on April 24, along
with thousands of others trying to get out. A friend who was
a senior officer in the U.S. Army had put them on an evacuation list. But the officer got into trouble for trying to help too
many Vietnamese, and his list was not accepted.*

*Thuy had only one more opportunity. It came on April
29, just twenty-four hours before the government surren-
dered. A South Vietnamese navy lieutenant would try to get
him past the guard post and onto a departing military ship.
Thuy and his uncle rounded up 33 family members, including his mother, his stepfather, two stepbrothers and his children. His wife, Nguyen Thi Phi Yen—Phi Yen means "flying swallow"—was conspicuously absent. She had decided
not to leave. Her father had died fighting for the Viet Minh
against the French, and she had a certain amount of sympathy for the Communists.*

*In the end, none of them made it. All 33 had to be fer-
ried to the naval base in Thuy's small Toyota sedan and the
uncle's Citroën. Crammed with 10 persons at one stage and
sitting waiting for Thuy's mother in the hot sun, the Toyota
overheated and refused to start. The passengers pushed, but
to no avail. The uncle waited too long for them: by the time
the Citroën reached the base, the gate was shut.*

Thuy was trapped in Vietnam . . .

ON OCTOBER 15, 1978, an aging coastal freighter named the *Hai
Hong* steamed out of the bustling port of Singapore heading
north, ostensibly bound for Hong Kong. At the wheel was Susun
Serigar, an Indonesian captain, who had been hired along with
15 of his countrymen as crew specifically for the voyage. The
only passengers were Lee Sam and Lee Kian Yap.

The 1,586-ton vessel was empty. Sold thirteen days earlier
for $125,000 by Guan Guan Shipping (Pte.) Ltd., an established
line, it was being delivered to the new owner, Rosewell Maritime Co., a small Hong Kong trading concern. Rosewell had
purchased it through Singapore-based Vitimex Import & Export,
using Seng Bee Shipping (Pte.) Ltd. as its agent for the transaction in Singapore. Vitimex, run by Tay Kheng Hong, a 51-year-
old Singaporean businessman with maritime connections, ap-

plied for a temporary Panamanian flag in order to take it to Hong Kong, explaining that it was to be scrapped. For a fee of $4,600, the Panamanian Consulate-General in Singapore issued a one-month registration certificate valid from October 9.

The newly renamed freighter aroused little attention as it made its way out of Singapore harbor. Built thirty years earlier to carry general cargo, it was a familiar sight in Southeast Asia as Guan Guan's *Golden Hill*. But once at sea, away from prying eyes, the *Hai Hong* changed course and switched roles. Instead of holding to a direct tack that would take it to Hong Kong, it made for the coast of Vietnam.

The *Hai Hong* never had any intention of completing an empty run. If it ended its voyage in Hong Kong, it would be only after picking up a cargo that was promising to become the hottest property in regional trade: Vietnamese refugees.

The economics of it was compelling. Tens and perhaps hundreds of thousands of people no longer wanted to remain in Vietnam now that the Communists had control of the country, and they were prepared to pay, in gold and hard currency, to leave. A growing number of refugees had been finding their way independently in small boats to neighboring countries since South Vietnam was taken over in 1975, just as they had been leaving Kampuchea and Laos by land since the Communist victories there the same year. If a large number of paying Vietnamese could be shipped out in a single operation, it would be infinitely more lucrative than hauling timber, coconuts and other produce around Asia.

Nobody appreciated the potential of trafficking in refugees more than Tay Kheng Hong, an ethnic Chinese who had set up in business in South Vietnam in 1971 through his company, Vietnam Timber Manufacture Export, which was known as Vitimex. Tay had placed Lee Sam and Lee Kian Yap, two of his Singapore employees, aboard the *Hai Hong* to supervise just such an operation. He knew it was possible—and profitable—because he had done it before. Although only a few of his close associates were aware of it, Tay had masterminded the pioneering voyage of the *Southern Cross* a few weeks earlier. The *Southern Cross* had managed to collect 1,250 persons from Vietnam and pass them off as refugees, netting a cool $500,000 for a few weeks' work.

Although not yet recognized as such, the voyage of the *Southern Cross* was the first organized refugee movement involving a non-Vietnamese vessel. Arranged by Tay using overseas-Chinese contacts within Vietnam and outside, the *Southern Cross* affair also involved Chong Chai Kok, aged 30, managing director of Seng Bee Shipping, and Sven Olof Ahlqvist, a Finnish sea captain who carried a Singaporean employment pass. In return for a slice of the action, Chong and Ahlqvist had allowed Tay to use the *Southern Cross*, an 850-ton Honduras-registered freighter. Chong had provided the crew and arranged the bunkering. Tay had gone along when the *Southern Cross* set out from Singapore on August 24, accompanied by Allan Ross, a 36-year-old Singaporean seafarer and businessman dispatched by Chong and Ahlqvist to protect their interests.

Tay, who was married in Singapore, had not put the deal together for money alone. He hoped also to rescue a second wife and their two children he had left behind in Vietnam. The Communist conquest in April 1975 had trapped Tay in Saigon and required him to close his business there. He had not managed to return to Singapore until April 1978. Even then he had had to bribe Vietnamese immigration authorities with gold, and it still had not been possible to take his Vietnamese family with him. Just four months after boarding an Air France flight out of Vietnam he had headed back by sea, anxious to be reunited with his second wife and to recover $110,000 in cash he had entrusted to her.

Using the cover of a trip to Bangkok to collect a cargo of salt, the *Southern Cross* had sailed straight for southern Vietnam, making contact with an agent who appeared on the scene in a fishing boat flying the Vietnamese flag. The key to the connection was a coded sign draped over the side of the *Southern Cross*. After an overnight stop in Ho Chi Minh City, as the Communists had renamed the new administrative area that included Saigon, the former capital of South Vietnam, the *Southern Cross* had moved to the mouth of the Saigon River. It collected its human cargo, including Tay's wife clutching his $110,000 and their two children, along with four sacks of gold for its trouble. Then, performing an agreed ritual, it had sent a radio call for help from the South China Sea. Its message: hundreds of refugees had swarmed aboard in international waters from four large fishing junks. Later, Ahlqvist had taken a yacht from Singapore to rendezvous late at night with the *Southern Cross*. The idea was to collect Ross, Tay and the gold. The transfer had been accomplished without a hitch.

The rest of the *Southern Cross* operation had gone off fairly smoothly too, though there were some anxious moments for the organizers when the Malaysian government refused permission for the vessel to land at Mersing, near the Tengah Island refugee camp in the southern state of Johore. It had reached within a few hundred yards of the shore, and some refugees had been taken off for emergency medical treatment. But then a Malaysian naval patrol boat had escorted the *Southern Cross* out of territorial waters. Neighboring Singapore indicated it would not accept the vessel either. Ross hastily rejoined the *Southern Cross* with Ahlqvist, at the same time that Chong's Seng Bee Shipping had sent additional water, food and fuel for the vessel. With Ahlqvist in command, the *Southern Cross* had drifted into Indonesian waters and beached deliberately on Pengibu Island, a barren, uninhabited rocky outcrop southwest of the remote Anambas Islands. In good health and pleased to be back on firm ground, the Vietnamese scrambled ashore on September 21 and set about erecting makeshift shelters.

With the *Southern Cross* stuck fast and listing slightly about 50 yards from the beach, Ahlqvist had reported by radio that the ship had struck a rock and had been seriously damaged. He said there was almost no chance of its being refloated. In fact, he said, it might sink. Seng Bee Shipping, as agent for the *Southern Cross*, let it be known that the ship was believed to have been holed badly and that it was likely to be a total loss, though it said it had not received a full report from the vessel.

An aerial inspection had left Indonesian authorities with the feeling that the *Southern Cross* might not be heavily damaged at all, and that temporary repairs probably could be carried out on the spot. Indeed, the position of the *Southern Cross*, grounded on the seabed, made some Indonesians suspect that the ship's operators might have scuttled it in an effort to resolve their dilemma over the Vietnamese and at the same time collect insurance or salvage money for the vessel. But a trade in refugees never occurred to them—or to anyone else.

Representatives of the Office of the United Nations High

Commissioner for Refugees, known as UNHCR, had then pressed the Indonesian government to grant the Vietnamese temporary asylum so that arrangements could be made to find permanent homes for them in third countries. They stressed that the Vietnamese had enough food to last only a few days. The ship was unseaworthy, they believed, and the "refugees" should be moved quickly before the annual monsoon set in and made sea travel impossible.

Seng Bee Shipping again sent a trawler with relief supplies for the Vietnamese, this time, ironically, at the request and expense of UNHCR. It was followed within a day or two by an Indonesian Navy patrol boat, which resupplied the Vietnamese in another exercise underwritten by UNHCR. Australia undertook to start processing the refugees for resettlement as soon as they were transferred to a suitable location in Indonesia; it requested other resettlement countries to offer places as well. At this stage, Indonesia's acceptance of the Vietnamese as refugees was a foregone conclusion. They were moved soon after to Bintan, a more accessible island south of Singapore, and admitted to U.N. camps.

Back safely in Singapore, Tay, Chong, Ahlqvist and their aides had counted the proceeds. With the 560 children on the *Southern Cross* each paying one tael of gold for the voyage and adults two taels, the venture was extremely rewarding.* Chong and Ahlqvist together had received more than $184,000, Ross about $8,300, leaving Tay with a tidy bundle—and eager for more.

So it was that the *Hai Hong* set out on what Tay hoped would be a rerun of the *Southern Cross* affair. The Seng Bee Shipping connection again yielded a vessel, but this time Tay himself was the agent, having acted as broker in the sale of the *Hai Hong*. And with no family sentiment to cloud a purely business venture, the stakes were higher—much higher. If all went well, Tay planned to send the ship through to Hong Kong, offload the passengers once more as refugees rescued at sea, and deliver the *Hai Hong* to Rosewell Maritime, which had made a 10-percent down payment on it.

* A tael, a Chinese unit of weight equal to 1.21 troy ounces or 37.79 grams, was valued at about $250 at the time. Just over a year later, in November 1979, the price of gold had doubled to about $500 a tael.

If Tay had any doubts as to whether his second venture in refugee running would succeed, there was one thought to comfort him as the *Hai Hong* dropped anchor 40 miles off the port of Vung Tau on October 19: the Vietnamese authorities were on his side. Although the outside world did not realize it, Vietnam wanted potential refugees out as much as they wanted to escape the Communist system. Hanoi was prepared not only to let them go, but to assist them—for a fee.

For the *Southern Cross*, Tay had received a cable in June 1978 from Son Ta Tang, aged 54, a former business associate in Vietnam, saying the Vietnamese government had approved the departure of a large number of Vietnamese of Chinese origin and Tay's family. All Tay had to do was arrange transport for them. The refugees ended up each paying the Vietnamese authorities 6 to 8 pieces of gold, in addition to their boat fares of 1 or 2 taels. To Tay the price was well justified, because the *Southern Cross* had received red-carpet treatment when it went to collect its cargo. A Vietnamese government pilot launch came alongside; the pilot boarded the *Southern Cross* and guided it up the twisting Saigon River to a berth in Ho Chi Minh City. The ship was supplied with fresh water and vegetables, guarded by troops patrolling the wharf and guided by the same pilot to the collection point the following day. The pilot and three armed soldiers spent the night on board. In Ho Chi Minh City, Tay had been taken to a restaurant for a meal with civilian officials. On its departure, the *Southern Cross* was allowed to fly the red-and-yellow Vietnamese flag, had the benefit of the pilot's services until it was two hours into the open sea and was not challenged by Vietnamese security patrols.

In the case of the *Hai Hong*, Son Ta Tang had advised, again by cable from Vietnam, that 1,000 Vietnamese were ready to leave as soon as transport was provided. The organizers actually were expecting 1,200 as the ship neared Vung Tau. They were shocked when Vietnamese officials insisted the *Hai Hong* take an extra 1,300 passengers—free. The officials backed their demand with a threat: if the additional passengers were not accepted, Son Ta Tang and his assistants, all of whom planned to leave Vietnam on the *Hai Hong*, would be detained and the ship's exit would be blocked. Faced with that choice, the organizers gave way.

The pickup dragged on for days as the Vietnamese ferried aboard under armed escort—as they had done in the case of the *Southern Cross*—more refugees than had been agreed on and more than the ship could safely hold. It would be a cramped, uncomfortable passage at best in a vessel only 246 feet long and 34 feet at the beam. The ship was more suited to carrying cattle than human beings. The *Hai Hong* was scheduled to leave Vietnam for Hong Kong on October 22, but it was not ready until the evening of October 24. When the cramming exercise was done, it was packed to the gunwales with some 2,450 passengers, half of them under the age of 18, and including 125 aged persons. Another vital statistic: most were ethnic Chinese.

Son Ta Tang was handed 1,200 taels of gold by the Vietnamese officials, this being payment at the agreed rate of 1½ taels for each adult on the original 1,200-member passenger list, with children free. True to their word, the officials paid not a cent for the others they had foisted on the ship.

Things started to go seriously wrong as the *Hai Hong* resumed its original northward course. A typhoon, named Rita by meteorologists, roared into life in the South China Sea, making Hong Kong an increasingly risky destination for the overcrowded vessel. To make matters worse, the *Hai Hong* was having engine trouble. It took refuge for a few days in the Paracel Islands, off the coast of central Vietnam, and then, with food and water running low, turned around and headed for Indonesia, where Captain Serigar felt more at home. Distant parts of the far-flung Indonesian archipelago had provided the way out of a tight spot with the *Southern Cross*. The organizers would try it again.

Except for a call to Tay Kheng Hong in Singapore to advise of the change in course, the *Hai Hong* maintained radio silence until it reached Tarempa, the main port on Siantan, a large island in the Anambas group and not far from the final resting place of the *Southern Cross*.

On October 29, Captain Serigar again called Tay in Singapore, asking him to go to Siantan with $15,000. He said Indonesian authorities were demanding the payment for damage to the Tarempa jetty when the *Hai Hong* docked, and for the use of port facilities. Tay, who had advised Seng Bee Shipping's Chong when the *Hai Hong* altered course, flew to Indonesia on November 1 and chartered a fishing boat to take him to Tarempa. Tay boarded the fishing boat on Bintan Island, taking the opportunity to visit his second wife, who was still in a refugee camp there. After paying the Indonesians $12,500 compensation and port fees in Tarempa, Tay used the *Hai Hong*'s radiotelephone to call Seng Bee Shipping in Singapore, speaking to an employee named George Poay. He told Poay to advise Chong that he should arrange a rendezvous with the *Hai Hong* if he wanted to collect the gold.

Instead of contacting Indonesian authorities on his arrival, logical in the circumstances, Captain Serigar chose to direct his first outside radio message to the Eastern South Asia regional office of UNHCR in Malaysia. And he waited more than four days, until November 2, to send it. The line was faint and the connection was soon lost, but he managed to report that he was in Indonesian waters with more than 2,000 refugees on board. This was the first anybody had heard of a ship called the *Hai Hong*.

Later the same day, Captain Serigar had another radiotelephone conversation with UNHCR in Kuala Lumpur. He said the *Hai Hong* was Panamanian-registered, Singapore-owned. According to his story, it had been en route from Singapore to Hong Kong when, on October 23, it had developed engine trouble near Lincoln Island in the Paracels. The following day it had been boarded by more than 2,000 refugees from between 10 and 15 smaller boats. He gave his present location precisely: 106 degrees, 13 minutes east and 3 degrees, 13 minutes north. He said he was standing by for instructions from UNHCR.

Captain Serigar's comments and behavior provoked suspicion and set off investigations throughout Asia and much farther afield. It seemed curious, to say the least, that the *Hai Hong* had waited more than a week—until it berthed in Indonesia—before alerting UNHCR that it had picked up such a large number of refugees. And how had 2,000 Vietnamese managed to gather at one place in the middle of the ocean, 225 miles from the coast of Vietnam, as Typhoon Rita stirred the seas and sent much larger vessels scurrying for shelter?

Discrepancies surfaced. In a report compiled by Indonesian naval intelligence, Captain Serigar told a different story. He said the *Hai Hong* had been sheltering from Typhoon Rita off Lincoln Island when the refugees boarded on October 21. They had

23

forced him to turn the ship around and head for the northern Australian city of Darwin. In this version, engine trouble was no longer a factor, and the date of the crucial refugee transfer was advanced by three days.

Both explanations were full of holes. Why had the *Hai Hong*, which should have covered the 1,660 miles from Singapore to Hong Kong in about eight days, taken a week or more to reach the Paracel Islands, less than halfway? The ship should have been in Hong Kong by the time Captain Serigar claimed engine failure. Mention of the Paracels, well off the usual path taken by refugees fleeing southern Vietnam, also left investigators skeptical. Refugees preferred to make west and south toward southern Thailand or Malaysia. The Paracels would involve traveling north and east from most of the regular refugee departure points in southern Vietnam.

While inquiries continued, the Indonesians decided to take no chances. The government declared that foreign-registered commercial vessels could not stay in Indonesia, or discharge passengers, without good reason. An Indonesian naval officer boarded the *Hai Hong* in Tarempa, and the Ministry of Defense in Jakarta issued an instruction that no one was to leave the ship until further notice.

The *Hai Hong* received little publicity as it rode at anchor in the backwaters of Indonesia. But sketchy, low-key wireservice dispatches emanating from Jakarta, 650 miles away, belied the intense search being made by government and U.N. officials, diplomats and others into the background of the vessel and its strange voyage. In Singapore, after some initial confusion, it became apparent that the *Hai Hong* was the *Golden Hill* in different colors. Its recent sale was traced to Rosewell Maritime, whose proprietor, T. C. Wei, confirmed the purchase of the *Golden Hill* but denied all knowledge of a vessel called the *Hai Hong*. A Panamanian official confirmed its temporary registration. He also reported the declared intention of the ship's agent to scrap the vessel in Hong Kong. But why would businessmen have paid $125,000 for a decrepit ship that would bring less than that as scrap? Rosewell Maritime added to the mystery: T. C. Wei said he could not speak for others, but his intention had been to use the ship for more coastal trading.

A possible answer suggested itself when UNHCR received a

24

tip-off from a source in Ho Chi Minh City that a vessel believed to be Panamanian-registered had been anchored on October 24 off the coast of Vietnam while people were ferried to it from the mainland. It strengthened a confidential British report to the effect that arrangements had been made for a Panamanian-registered vessel to collect refugees off the Vietnamese coast beginning on October 24. The intention was for the loaded vessel to make for Hong Kong, the British report said, but if Typhoon Rita interfered with plans, Darwin would be the alternative destination.

These reports were deeply disturbing to UNHCR and the Western refugee-resettlement nations that shared the information. It indicated that the Vietnamese authorities, at least at a local level, might be involved in shipping their own people abroad. It had been known for some time that Vietnamese refugees often bribed their way past security officials, but an operation on the scale of the *Hai Hong* would put a different, more sinister complexion on the matter.

At the same time, the past was starting to catch up with Tay and company. Indonesian naval intelligence officers, after interrogating the crew of the *Southern Cross,* began to piece together the earlier voyage. They realized they had been duped. The *Southern Cross* had been no innocent ship fulfilling a mercy mission thrust upon it; it was a rogue that had gone to Vietnam specifically to traffic in refugees. Most galling of all to the Indonesians, Captain Ahlqvist, the master of the vessel, had been heard to remark that one more trip like that of the *Southern Cross* would complete his plans to retire to the Philippines.

The presence of so many ethnic Chinese on the *Hai Hong* also made the Indonesian military uneasy. The Indonesians saw Chinese as the villains in the unsuccessful coup attempt in Jakarta in 1965, which the military believed had been an attempted takeover by the Indonesian Communist Party with Peking's backing. Tens of thousands of ethnic Chinese in Indonesia had been hunted down and slaughtered in 1965 and 1966, and others had been detained for long periods without trial in the wake of the putsch. Relations between Jakarta and Peking had been on ice ever since, and the military remained deeply suspicious of any Chinese activity.

Determined not to be caught again, the Indonesians

escorted Tay aboard the *Hai Hong* and ordered it out of their waters. They would extend normal humanitarian assistance to passengers and crew, but the ship must leave. The Defense Ministry directed its personnel to make any necessary repairs to the engine and send the *Hai Hong* back to sea. Where it chose to go was not Indonesia's concern. So on November 6, the *Hai Hong* weighed anchor and resumed its voyage, maintaining a southwesterly course, apparently making for Singapore.

The following day, George Poay, in a tug named *Kalimantan,* pulled alongside the *Hai Hong* in international sea-lanes and collected 1,000 taels of gold from Tay. Tay retained 200 taels as an appropriate reward for himself.

Meanwhile, the voyage of the *Hai Hong* was being probed, unraveled and analyzed with concern. If it turned out that the *Hai Hong* was indeed trafficking in Vietnamese, it could jeopardize the entire Indochina refugee settlement program. As it was, the United States, Australia, France and a few other nations were not managing to provide enough permanent homes for the flow of refugees, which had quickened in recent months. Shiploads of 2,000 at a time—if one vessel could do it, others might follow—could swamp their efforts and stiffen the resistance of the Southeast Asian countries that were providing temporary asylum, an essential step in the process of rescuing and resettling refugees.

No nation was more alarmed than Australia. Darwin appeared to be an alternative landing site in the *Hai Hong*'s contingency plans. Officials in Canberra paled at the prospect. Direct arrival of small refugee boats in 1976, 1977 and again in 1978 had triggered an ugly public outcry in Australia, bringing together an odd coalition of leftist trade unionists, political conservatives and plain, old-fashioned racists demanding an end to the admission of Vietnamese refugees, whom they variously branded as former Saigon bar owners, drug pushers, brothel keepers and prostitutes. It was precisely to avoid a repeat performance that Australia had sent a permanent refugee team to Southeast Asia in early 1978. Based in Kuala Lumpur, it aimed to accept more refugees, speed up their interviewing and processing and facilitate their resettlement.

Although much of the information was unsubstantiated and

conflicting, Australia felt there were strong grounds for believing that the *Hai Hong* passengers had left Vietnam with the complicity of the Vietnamese authorities and that the boarding of the ship had been prearranged. It believed that if the *Hai Hong* were to attempt to land what Australia privately called "would-be refugees" in regional countries of first asylum or in Darwin, it could not only have a detrimental impact on established refugee programs but adversely affect the fate of "genuine" refugees already in camps in the area. Policy makers in Canberra concluded that the *Hai Hong* venture must fail and that its failure must stand as a deterrent to any similar enterprises in the future. The Australians argued privately to UNHCR that subject to clarification and evidence to the contrary, "governments concerned have clear grounds for taking the position that any claim the passengers might seek to advance to refugee status has been prejudiced."

In Kuala Lumpur, Rajagopalam Sampatkumar, Regional Representative of UNHCR, tentatively reached the same conclusion. He was discussing with UNHCR headquarters in Geneva the possibility of a statement that would lay the groundwork to classify the Vietnamese aboard the *Hai Hong*, if necessary, as illegal immigrants. The Australians said privately that they would welcome such a statement, regarding it as an essential first step in compelling those responsible for the *Hai Hong* to abandon the venture. They proposed an early ministerial statement in Australia endorsing the UNHCR stand.

Sampatkumar's short statement, issued on November 3, was the first public disclosure of a freighter carrying a large number of Vietnamese, and the mystery surrounding the vessel. Betraying the murky results of preliminary inquiries, the statement spelled the ship's name "Hi Hong" and gave "Hi Fong" as a possible alternative. UNHCR, Sampatkumar said, did not know the ship's movements after it had left Singapore on October 15, or how so many passengers had come to be aboard. Nor was it clear who the agent or owners were, though the ship's registration was valid for only a short time longer. If proved correct, he said, these factors "lead one to question the motive of the owners, agent and the captain of the ship concerned." Without explaining what he was getting at, Sampatkumar said the "activities of unscrupulous elements" would jeopardize UNHCR assistance and durable solutions for "genuine refugees." UNHCR was examining all available facts, he added, to determine whether there was a role for the agency in the affair.

Although the Australians were not entirely happy with the UNHCR text, because it was heavily qualified and omitted any reference to passengers' claims to refugee status being prejudiced if a plot were uncovered, they followed immediately as planned with a statement by Michael MacKellar, Minister for Immigration and Ethnic Affairs, reinforcing Sampatkumar's comments. MacKeller referred to reports that a business group had recently acquired the *Hai Hong* and arranged to collect several parties of Vietnamese and convey the impression that they were genuine refugees. "We now have the first clear indications that unscrupulous people are attempting to profiteer in the present Indochinese refugee situation," he said in part. ". . . Australia has played a major part in accepting many thousands of genuine refugees, but I give strong warning that we shall not accept cases involving subterfuge."

Approaching Singapore, Tay and Captain Serigar also were becoming anxious. Indonesia's decision to expel the *Hai Hong* almost certainly meant that other member countries of ASEAN, the Association of Southeast Asian Nations—Singapore, Malaysia, Thailand and the Philippines—would follow suit. Singapore was out anyway, because it had adopted a hard line from the outset against accepting Indochina refugees, even temporarily. As far as Tay and Captain Serigar were concerned, the danger was that the *Hai Hong* would be forced to continue its journey indefinitely, blocked at every port. Even opportunities to beach the ship illegally were fast disappearing as it attracted more and more attention.

With conditions on board deteriorating rapidly—1 woman had died, 2 babies had been born—the *Hai Hong* skirted Singapore, swung north and proceeded up the Straits of Malacca, which separate Peninsular Malaysia and the large Indonesian island of Sumatra. The passengers were becoming restive, demanding to know when the organizers were going to deliver on their promises of an early landing. Anticipating trouble, Tay took the precaution of depositing his Samsonite briefcase containing his 200 taels of gold in the captain's locker.

For his part, Captain Serigar, who had previously given inconsistent accounts, became more circumspect. When the UNHCR office in Kuala Lumpur contacted the ship by radiotelephone at 10:15 A.M. on November 8, two days after it departed Tarempa, Captain Serigar was prepared to give the *Hai Hong*'s position and course: 1 degree, 25 minutes north and 103 degrees, 7 minutes, 30 seconds east. This put it in Malaysian waters in the Straits of Malacca—heading northwest. But he refused to disclose his destination, and he would answer no further questions about the circumstances of the boarding.

At 1 P.M. on November 9, the ship dropped anchor 12 miles off Port Klang, the major sea outlet for Peninsular Malaysia, 25 miles west of Kuala Lumpur. The *Hai Hong*, which had been registered in the Malaysian island port of Penang when it was known as the *Golden Hill*, was once more flying the Malaysian flag. Whether it was still entitled to claim Malaysia as home was another matter. The ship's legal status was not at all clear, its temporary Panamanian registration having expired that day.

In any event, legalities were fast becoming unimportant. Royal Malaysian Navy and marine police vessels blockaded the *Hai Hong* to prevent it from entering the port area and to ensure that no one attempted to leave it. A police party, including members of the Special Branch, the security arm of Malaysia's law-enforcement agency, interviewed Captain Serigar and 5 representatives of the passengers. They found a grim scene: After more than two weeks at sea, subjected to severe storms and extreme heat with little food or water, many of the Vietnamese were dehydrated, listless and ill. Jammed together in ovenlike conditions belowdecks, some of them were too weak to stand. Children had open sores on their legs, arms and bodies. With minimal sanitation on the ship, the stench was vile.

There were certainly, as Captain Serigar had originally claimed, "more than 2,000" Vietnamese—a lot more. Indonesian naval intelligence had counted 2,518 persons all told when the *Hai Hong* was in Tarempa. The Indonesians passed the figure along to interested friendly governments. Births and deaths had since yielded a net gain of 1. The ship itself listed a captain, crew of 17 and 2,504 passengers—a total of 2,522 when the vessel set out from Tarempa and presumably 2,523 when it reached

Port Klang. But precisely how many were aboard when the Malaysian police began their inquiries it was impossible to say in the foul, overcrowded conditions.

Under pressure and close to panic, Captain Serigar fell back on his original story about an engine breakdown at Lincoln Island. Unable to prevent all 2,504 refugees from boarding, he said, he had decided to take the ship back to Singapore, but it had developed further engine trouble and had had to put into Siantan Island. When they reached the Straits of Malacca, the Vietnamese had ordered him to make for Port Klang.

Among the passengers, Malaysian police found Tay Kheng Hong, who claimed Singaporean nationality and said he had been the broker in the sale of the *Hai Hong* from Guan Guan to Rosewell Maritime. Tay said it was he who had hired Captain Serigar, 15 other Indonesians and 2 Singaporeans as crew to send the ship to Hong Kong.

Reflecting the spreading alarm over the *Hai Hong* and the implications of its voyage, Malaysia's National Security Council went into a huddle to decide what should be done. Its answer: the Indonesian solution. The *Hai Hong* could have food and water and the medical supplies Captain Serigar had requested, but it must leave. The reasons were given by Deputy Commissioner P. Alagendra, chief police officer of Selangor state, which includes Port Klang. "I find it difficult to believe the claim of the captain," he said in a prepared statement, "because without prior arrangement it is inconceivable for over 2,500 people to gather at one place in the South China Sea and to have succeeded in boarding the ship." He also thought it strange that the *Hai Hong* had bypassed Singapore when Captain Serigar maintained he was returning to Singapore. "It would appear, therefore, that the captain was trying to cover a planned migration of a sizable number of people from Vietnam," he added.

Information from Washington, conveyed officially to several other Western nations and filtered through to non-Communist Southeast Asian governments, deepened the fears of Malaysia and others. According to a senior official of the Carter administration quoting intelligence sources, the *Southern Cross* affair had been instigated on the initiative of authorities in Ho Chi Minh City with the involvement of the Vietnamese security agencies. It had been planned that the *Southern Cross* would

30

have engine failure in a designated area, he said, so that it could take on a large number of "refugees" who had paid about $2,000 each to be evacuated. The idea seemed to be to facilitate the emigration of ethnic Chinese, at a handsome profit.

Although direct evidence was still missing in the case of the *Hai Hong*, similar planning obviously could underlie other apparent escapes from Vietnam. The *Hai Hong* must be viewed with the deepest suspicion: guilty—on circumstantial evidence admittedly—until proved innocent. What it could portend was enough to put government officials and diplomats in a cold sweat.

For a start, it raised the question of whether the Vietnamese who left under such conditions should be classified as refugees and given care and protection at the expense of the international community through UNHCR. Indonesia had said no and had passed the buck. Malaysia, with the *Hai Hong* on its doorstep, was also turning thumbs down. Kuala Lumpur later formally justified its decision by saying government policy was to discourage refugees from entering the country. It also cited indications of a planned transshipment.

Malaysia's stand, as officially explained, was based solely on its national interests; the suspicious behavior of the *Hai Hong* made justification so much easier. Malaysia was able to adopt this policy, unfettered by broader considerations, because neither it nor any other country in Southeast Asia was a signatory to either the 1951 U.N. Convention Relating to the Status of Refugees or the 1967 Protocol Relating to the Status of Refugees. This was a key factor in the case of the *Hai Hong*, and it was to remain an important consideration as the Indochina refugee tragedy unfolded.*

Article 1 of the Convention defines "refugees" in general terms, as persons unable or unwilling to return to their country because of a well-founded fear of being persecuted for reasons of race, religion, nationality, political opinions or membership in a particular social group.[1] Some of the provisions of the Convention are considered so sacred that no reservations may be made to them. These include the definition of "refugee" and the so-called principle of nonrefoulment: no signatory nation shall

* The Philippines ratified the Convention and the Protocol in July 1981.

expel or return (*refouler*) refugees against their will to a territory where they fear persecution.

For UNHCR, charged with "promoting international instruments for the protection of refugees and supervising their application," deciding whether the *Hai Hong* passengers were refugees to be fed and sheltered clearly would not be easy. As signaled in the MacKellar statement, Australia, a party to both the Convention and the Protocol that updated it, was keen to draw a distinction between "genuine refugees" and those leaving by arrangement on foreign freighters such as the *Hai Hong*. UNHCR's Sampatkumar had not completed his investigations when the *Hai Hong* pulled out of Tarempa, but he was inclined to agree with the Australians by the time the ship reached Port Klang. After all, the thinking was, if the Vietnamese had left their homeland by open arrangement, they could hardly claim legitimate fear of persecution. Events in the next few days, however, persuaded him to adopt a different public posture.

In response to radiotelephone appeals from Captain Serigar, Sampatkumar visited Port Klang to determine whether UNHCR should become involved. But he was not allowed to board the *Hai Hong*. Malaysian authorities insisted the seas were too rough and there was also a danger he might be taken hostage, a danger that apparently did not exist in the case of 2 foreign correspondents who were permitted to climb over the vessel that day and interview the occupants freely.

Sampatkumar managed to speak to Captain Serigar and the 5 passenger representatives from a small boat that pulled alongside the *Hai Hong* under police escort. He arranged with police for food and medical supplies to be taken on board. But when he arrived the next day with the medicine and provisions in a three-ton truck, he was stopped and informed that orders had been received from Kuala Lumpur that no one was to board the ship. In the meantime, Malaysia had ordered the *Hai Hong* out and let it be known that if the ship proved obstinate the government would take all steps necessary to force it beyond territorial waters.

Alarmed at the poor health of some of the Vietnamese and at the same time responding to pressure applied by the United States, Sampatkumar chose to forget earlier concerns about "unscrupulous elements." Overnight he reversed his opinion. "We consider them refugees," he told newsmen. He wasted no time in informing the Malaysian government as well. Malaysia did not back down in response to UNHCR's decision, but neither did it attempt to tow the *Hai Hong* back out to sea immediately, encouraging the belief that the Vietnamese might yet be resettled as refugees if countries came forward to offer homes for them.

Sampatkumar's announcement was to have a profound effect not only on the fate of the *Hai Hong* passengers but on Vietnamese leaving their country in the future. In line with his definition, they would all be considered refugees by UNHCR, irrespective of how first-asylum countries and others treated them and regardless of the circumstances of their departure. As a result, the *Hai Hong* episode left a residue of distrust between UNHCR and host countries in Southeast Asia. It was to last for as long as they worked together. It also spread to include other U.N. agencies and international organizations. Relations fluctuated. But the feeling remained that the foreigners staffing the agencies were prone to emotionalism and given to making decisions that had much to do with humanitarianism and little regard for the harsher social, economic and political realities of the region.

It was not only the Malaysians who had second thoughts about UNHCR over the *Hai Hong*. The Indonesian military was not entirely convinced that UNHCR was an innocent party. It seemed odd to the Indonesians that only UNHCR had received radio messages from the *Hai Hong* and the *Southern Cross*. Before the navy reached Tarempa to take charge of the *Hai Hong*, Indonesian authorities had not been able to make contact with the ship. Nor had attempts to monitor radio traffic from it been successful. With personality clashes compounding the issue, some sections of the Indonesian military suspected that UNHCR had a special radio link to certain refugee ships. It did not, of course.

Sampatkumar's judgment went almost unnoticed at the time for the far-reaching ruling it was, as the standoff in Port Klang continued through November 1978. In any event, bigger trouble was brewing. Frantic government officials and diplomats, alerted by the *Hai Hong*, continued to receive a flow of intelligence that suggested the worst of the refugee influx was to come.

Although it would take weeks and months for much of the world to awaken to the implications, the enormity of the portents began to sink in immediately among those on the spot. Southeast Asia must go on red alert for the deluge that was likely to follow. If the Vietnamese government was really opening the back door and allowing its unhappy inhabitants to leave, millions might choose to run. At the seedy end of Asia's shipping industry there was no shortage of "unscrupulous elements" who would collaborate in a massive sealift with Hanoi. The glitter of the golden payoff that was apparently waiting would attract drug runners, smugglers and a host of entrepreneurs motivated by greed. Where would it end? Who could tell?

One thing was certain. Vast new numbers of refugees, if they materialized, would strain the facilities and patience of ASEAN members to the breaking point. Thailand, for one, was hurting already, and Malaysia demonstrably had had enough. The political fallout would be both internal, within each of the five member countries, and external, affecting their relations with Vietnam. Threatened at home were ambitious development programs that had helped make non-Communist Southeast Asia one of the fastest growing areas of the world. Abroad, it endangered the delicate task of working out an accommodation with freshly united Vietnam, the large Communist neighbor whose ultimate ambitions in the region were unclear.

All this could be put in jeopardy by the haphazard, wholesale dumping of Vietnam's misfits. The high proportion of ethnic Chinese in the refugee flow added a potentially explosive element to an already volatile mix. Their presence might upset delicate racial balances and stir latent anti-Chinese sentiment. Security was another acute concern in an area plagued by pro-China Communist insurgency. The bottom line was the very stability of Southeast Asia.

What of China itself, the spiritual motherland to the north that had always taken an interest in the welfare of persons of Chinese origin? It had already been accusing Vietnam of persecuting its ethnic-Chinese residents before there was any suggestion that they were being singled out and shipped out. China's repeated denunciation of Vietnam inevitably invited the Soviet Union into the fray, intensifying Sino–Soviet rivalry in the region. The refugees would be mere pawns in this kind of big power play. And where did China draw the line? It might be tempted in the future to step in to protect the rights of Chinese minorities elsewhere. To Southeast Asian governments, the prospect was frightening.

And so it was that the voyage of the *Hai Hong* opened one of the great human dramas of the generation. The rusting vessel itself traveled no farther than Port Klang. The voyage ended happily enough for its passengers. Once resettlement places were guaranteed for them in the West, they were all allowed ashore to await processing and transport. The Vietnamese end of the syndicate managed to get resettled along with the other passengers. Son Ta Tang went to West Germany. One of his assistants, accompanied by 14 family members, made a new life in France. Even Lee Kian Yap, one of the two Singaporeans of Chinese ancestry on Tay's payroll, passed himself off as a refugee from Vietnam and was given a home by Canada before he could be questioned by Malaysian police; Tay slipped him 122.22 taels of gold before he left the ship.*

But the bigger drama was just beginning. It was one that gripped Southeast Asia in political crisis, helped trigger a brief but bitter war and played in nearly all the capitals of the world.

* UNHCR eventually registered 2,449 refugees on the *Hai Hong*.

TWO

Some four decades of war have turned many of the people of Vietnam, Cambodia* and Laos into refugees. No estimate of the number can be regarded as accurate, but it is certain that the total over these years must amount to several million. Many Indochinese have become refugees twice or even more often as the fortunes of war or politics have on occasion frightened them into flight, lulled them into efforts at peaceful return to their homes or persuaded them to attempt resettlement else-

* Kampuchea was known as the Kingdom of Cambodia from its independence in 1953 until the ouster of Prince Norodom Sihanouk on March 18, 1970. Proclaimed the Khmer Republic on October 9, 1970, by Marshal Lon Nol and his supporters who overthrew Sihanouk, it was renamed Democratic Kampuchea by the Khmer Rouge revolutionaries who took Phnom Penh on April 17, 1975. Heng Samrin's forces, who toppled the Pol Pot government with Vietnamese backing on January 7, 1979, settled on the People's Republic of Kampuchea, though by early 1981 it had not been recognized by the United Nations.

36

where. During the decade of the 1970s, it is estimated, most years have had at least a half million Indochinese living as refugees or displaced persons.[1]

Even before the *Hai Hong* dropped anchor in Indonesian waters in October 1978, Southeast Asian governments, Western resettlement countries and UNHCR were studying disturbing trends in the refugee flow from Vietnam. No longer did the refugees consist mainly of small groups of rural ethnic Vietnamese, as had been the case at the outset. Now larger boats—while nothing like the *Hai Hong*—carried more urban ethnic Vietnamese, mostly officials of the former government or those associated with U.S. and other foreign companies. Leaving too were a growing number of intellectuals and the formerly wealthy. Many of these refugees admitted bribing government officials for permission to leave. They reported booking passage in advance, having land transport provided, being assigned vessels and meeting no opposition from security patrols.

By mid-1978, it was clear that something dark and frightening had been brewing in Indochina in the three years since the Communist victories. In southern Vietnam this was not surprising. The long and bitter years of war had deeply divided Vietnamese of all walks of life. The temptation to settle old scores and seek retribution and revenge was presumed to be strong—so strong that as South Vietnam crumbled, the U.S. President, Gerald Ford, like others before him, warned of a bloodbath in the event of its being taken over by northern forces. That prospect was sharpened by the failure of the United States to evacuate many Vietnamese whose lives were considered in danger because of their association with the American war effort.

The rapid disintegration of the South Vietnamese Army, beginning early in March 1975, caught the Americans off balance. An emergency airlift ordered by Ford culminated in an 18-hour nonstop operation by dozens of helicopters that plucked people from rooftops in Saigon and the U.S. Embassy compound, while Marine guards beat back hysterical mobs trying to escape. Most Americans were rescued and flown to U.S. naval vessels offshore, along with thousands of Vietnamese. But in the confusion and disarray, large numbers of Vietnamese designated "high risk" were left behind. They included hundreds of senior Communist defectors, several thousand direct operatives of the American Central Intelligence Agency and up to 30,000 agents trained by the CIA for the Phoenix program, which had been designed to capture or kill underground South Vietnamese Communists.[2] In addition, there were 1.5 million soldiers, police and civil servants of the defeated Nguyen Van Thieu regime who might be victimized.

Altogether, about 32,000 Vietnamese made their own way out of the country in small craft, barges and rafts and on floats, as the flag of the Provisional Revolutionary Government of South Vietnam was hoisted over the presidential palace on April 30, 1975. U.S. rescue operations were terminated on May 1.

In the following days, Vietnamese refugees appeared at ports throughout Asia. Early in May, 26 South Vietnamese Navy vessels arrived at Subic Bay, the big U.S. base in the Philippines, with 30,000. South Vietnamese civilian ships carried 3,000 others to Singapore, while 3,743 were rescued from a sinking vessel by a Danish container ship and put in at Hong Kong. About 700 turned up in Pusan, South Korea, aboard two navy ships that Seoul had dispatched to collect several hundred Koreans in South Vietnam. Most Vietnamese were channeled into the U.S. refugee operation, which took them first to Guam, a U.S.-administered territory in the Pacific, later to receiving centers at military bases in the United States itself.

Back in Vietnam, Hanoi Radio announced that thousands of Vietnamese who had attempted to flee during the takeover had been picked up and returned. But there was no immediate bloodbath, no wholesale massacres and reprisals so confidently predicted by White House occupants. Indeed, Communist troops and militia went out of their way to befriend Saigonese, even to the extent of allowing South Vietnamese soldiers who had fired on them a few minutes earlier to go free after surrendering.[3]

It turned out to be part of a moderate, pragmatic and reconciliatory approach adopted by the northern leaders toward absorbing the South. As the massive task of reconstruction got under way and unification of the two zones went ahead, the emphasis was put on restoring production quickly and trying to solve the problem of widespread unemployment.

38

Hanoi faced immense difficulties. Emerging from more than thirty years of almost continuous warfare, Vietnam was what its leaders called a "poor and backward" country dependent on food imports for survival and with a per capita income of only $150 a year. During the American phase of the war, apart from human destruction, bombs and chemical defoliants had turned once-fertile fields into a lunar landscape.

Vietnam's Second Five-Year Development Plan (1976–80) gave clear priority to agriculture, first of all to meet the population's basic food requirements and then to provide raw materials for industries and for export. "The main objective is to be self-sufficient in food grains by the end of the plan period," a confidential World Bank survey commented in 1977.

No immediate attempt was made to suppress the flourishing free-enterprise system based in the newly renamed Ho Chi Minh City, though the state began to supervise private business and industry and urged joint ventures with the government as a transitional measure. The enduring differences between the northern and southern economies were reflected in the continued use of separate currencies. Socialist transformation south of the 17th Parallel was to take place gradually, over the full five-year-plan period.

However, if the North Vietnamese were initially forgiving, they still had to face the problem of reforming, or at least neutralizing, South Vietnamese steeped in anti-Communism who might work against the new order.

The answer was *hoc tap*, or reeducation, a process of critically examining one's past and absorbing the new standards and values. For most of the population, *hoc tap* came fairly easily— on the job, in school or at street meetings near home. Enlisted soldiers and lower-level civil servants sometimes had to attend a perfunctory reeducation course lasting a few days. But for army officers, senior civil servants, political leaders and espionage, Phoenix and other so-called pacification agents of the fallen regime, it meant long periods in army-run camps in remote areas, often mosquito-infested and without electricity and running water. While performing manual labor and learning trades, they were fed a steady diet of politics as the authorities closely investigated what they had done under U.S. occupation. The idea was

39

to release inmates progressively as they confessed their mistakes in siding with the Americans and were judged unlikely to join "counterrevolutionary organizations" when they were set free.

Conditions in reeducation camps were grim and uncomfortable. It proved too much for some detainees who were softened by years of city life and unused to physical exertion. A number became emaciated on their meager diet and died. Others who were slow to repent remained interned, or were tried by people's courts. Foreigners who visited some of the sites agreed they were certainly not holiday camps. Some observers maintained they were not nearly as bad as South Vietnamese prisons under the Thieu regime, in which tens of thousands of civilians had been held, often without trial, tortured and maimed. But before long, reeducation had acquired a reputation as part of a concentration-camp system termed by *Le Monde,* the French newspaper that had long championed Hanoi's cause, "a Vietnamese gulag."

To take care of some of the 7 or 8 million persons displaced during the war, the government mapped out a strategy for another return to the countryside. Driven from their fields by the fighting and bombing, or attracted by the bright lights as part of a natural urban drift, many southern residents had flocked to the major towns. In 1960, 85 percent of the population of South Vietnam had lived in rural areas; in 1975, it was down to 35 percent. Hanoi set out to reverse the flow in order to relieve pressures on swollen cities, boost agricultural output and reduce unemployment. For those who could not return to their native villages, planners devised New Economic Zones, new villages to be set up in depopulated regions or in uninhabited areas. But the scheme in time would generate more dissatisfaction.

In the first year, 1976, 1.4 million people were relocated in the South: 1 million returned to their villages, while 400,000 settled on reclaimed acreage. About 700,000 of them left Ho Chi Minh City, many to carve farms out of virgin areas. The incentive to settle on the land was lack of opportunity in the city and a slim rice ration for those without an approved job.

But the program ran into severe difficulties and came almost to a halt within eighteen months. Some would-be farmers drifted back to the city complaining of severe hardship, blaming the government for reneging on a promise to supply water, food,

40

tools and building materials. Some areas were expanses of nothing but jungle, or bare earth too barren to yield crops. Unexploded mines and shells added to the hostility of the environment. Plans to thin Ho Chi Minh City's population to 2.5 million by 1979 from 4 million in 1975 faltered as the official figure for net departures failed to increase for three years.

The authorities moved to correct the situation by sending teams of volunteers, skilled workers and soldiers to clear the land, build access roads, peg out lots, dig wells and erect temporary thatched houses before the settlers arrived. Still, for some, trying to scratch out an existence in a New Economic Zone was no different from doing time in a reeducation camp.

While mismanagement and lack of resources caused some setbacks in Vietnam, Hanoi also had to grapple with events beyond its control. Prolonged cold spells, interspersed with serious drought and topped by several destructive typhoons, caused crop failures in 1976 and 1977, necessitating large-scale grain imports. The rice ration—the number of kilograms each Vietnamese was permitted to buy at fixed prices—was reduced, and recipients had to take an increasing portion of it in subsidiary crops such as wheat, flour, sweet potatoes and manioc. Food became extremely expensive on the free market. As the economic crisis deepened, the government cracked down harder on dissidents, declaring it would "deprive all rights of freedom to those who look at socialism with a grudging eye," as *Quan Doi Nhan Dan*, the army daily, put it.

A sustained dispute between Vietnam and Kampuchea also had serious domestic consequences for the Vietnamese. As differences that had been kept in check surfaced soon after the Communist victories in Ho Chi Minh City and Phnom Penh, the two sides immediately began fighting each other. To outsiders it seemed to be a revival of ancient fears and animosities between the racially hostile Khmers and Vietnamese, their Marxist affiliations notwithstanding.

Kampuchea, which had always feared domination by Vietnam, resisted all Hanoi's overtures. Instead, the Khmer Rouge under Premier Pol Pot spread fear among border Vietnamese with their brutality from 1977. They entered Vietnamese villages and towns, raped and disemboweled women, and slaughtered others with bullets, clubs and rocks. It reached the point of no return when Kampuchea made the feuding public in December 1977 and broke diplomatic relations following a large-scale Vietnamese incursion into its territory.

For Vietnam, the clashes meant the initial displacement of 750,000 villagers along the length of its ill-defined border with Kampuchea. Hanoi said the total rose eventually to 1,235,000. Their withdrawal from frontier regions further disrupted the New Economic Zone program. To cover the western front, Vietnam eventually widened its military draft, a far cry from the ten thousand years of peace promised in the first flush of victory in Ho Chi Minh City.[4]

It was against this background of deteriorating economic conditions, personal sacrifice and increasing political repression that a growing number of Vietnamese thought of getting out. A letter from a Vietnamese doctor to a Western embassy in Hanoi summed up the desperation in broken English. *"I must leave Vietnam, for lack of food and with impossibility to earn my livelihood, I must die by hunger,"* he wrote in part.

To escape, Vietnamese left by the back door, risking being apprehended or shot if discovered. They took to the water in a variety of craft, many of them completely unsuited to the open sea, giving rise to the term "boat people." In fact, the refugee movement that started in a panic-stricken scramble in April 1975 never really stopped. Excluding escapees from the immediate Communist takeover, 378 boat people, according to UNHCR, landed on neighboring shores in 1975.[5] After that the trickle became a regular flow, the number increasing almost fourteenfold to 5,247 in 1976, and swelling to 15,690 in 1977.

The refugees included a number of prominent political figures from the old days, as well as businessmen, property owners and former bureaucrats and servicemen. But many were simple folk—fishermen and the like—who decided to pull out because conditions were becoming too tough and the future looked bleak. Extended family groups of 20 or 30 would take a small wooden boat and slip into the night, sometimes paying local officials to look the other way. Reflecting the racial composition of the country, most of the refugees were ethnic Vietnamese.

For a start, the boat people headed for southern Thailand, the nearest landfall. But the pattern changed when Thai pirates

42

regularly began to attack and rob refugee boats, sometimes raping and killing the occupants. By mid-1977, most boat people were avoiding Thailand and instead making for Malaysia, despite the additional mileage and longer time at sea. Sometimes they would trace an arc, pushing slightly eastward out to sea to avoid the pirates before tacking southwest to Malaysia.

Other Southeast Asian countries continued to receive most of the remaining direct arrivals. Although few refugees intended to attempt the dangerous voyage eastward across the exposed South China Sea, they often made navigational blunders, were blown off course or had engine trouble. As a result they ended up in the Philippines, Brunei and the East Malaysian states of Sabah and Sarawak. Others bypassed Malaysia, accidentally or otherwise, and touched land in Singapore or Indonesia.

Merchant ships picked up some refugees who floundered at sea, dropping them at such scattered points as Japan, the United States, Saudi Arabia, Italy and the Ivory Coast.

Weather also was a factor. Large parts of eastern Asia are vulnerable to typhoons that originate in the South China Sea and the Pacific Ocean east of the Philippines from April to October. They sweep Vietnam, the Philippines and north past Hong Kong. A devastating mixture of wind and rain generating speeds of up to 150 miles an hour, typhoons can make playthings of the largest ships. Caught in a typhoon, flimsy refugee boats were like leaves in a torrent, incapable of struggle.

The Vietnamese refugees, mostly boating novices, also tended to be wary of the northeast monsoon, which brings torrential rain, strong winds and squalls to southern Vietnam, Malaysia and south to Indonesia, from October to March. It made the crossing to Malaysia or Thailand particularly perilous in November, December and January. The northeast monsoon gives way in May to the southwest monsoon, which also produces strong winds and is capable of whipping up fury at sea. A storm could blow up suddenly at the best of times. The gamble of the voyage was captured in verse by one anonymous refugee:

> . . . we are the foam
> floating on the vast ocean
> we are the dust
> wandering in endless space

our cries are lost
in the howling wind . . .[6]

A sense of desperation propelled the boat people. Nguyen Van Phong, a 51-year-old small-business man from Gia Dinh in Ho Chi Minh City, took three months to assemble a drum raft with the help of his three sons. It consisted of two parallel rows each of eighteen empty oil drums lashed together with metal chains and wooden rods. A floor and cabin were built over the drums. The raft was powered by two small motors, giving it an average speed of little more than 6 miles an hour. It left the Saigon River in September 1975 carrying 14 people including a baby of 3 months. They were 175 miles off the coast when a Japanese vessel picked them up four days later.[7]

In another case, shipping-company employees drugged 3 armed Communist cadres on the steel-hulled *Song Be 12*, were joined by the crew and their families and friends, and sailed 3,000 miles to Australia. The 120-ton vessel arrived in November 1977, after collecting 8 Vietnamese from a Malaysian camp and refueling in Indonesia, with 181 refugees—and the 3 cadres.

Casualties were high. Dao Van Ky, a former noncommissioned officer in the South Vietnamese Navy, was on a 30-foot boat carrying 30 persons, including his wife and 3 children, which slipped out of Vung Tau in June 1976. Another boat of the same length, carrying 60 people, accompanied it. Two nights later a larger fishing vessel pulled alongside and asked where they were headed. "We didn't know that they were actually Viet Cong," Ky said, using the old term for southern Communists, until the "fishermen" pulled out M-16 rifles and other weapons. They forced everyone to board the fishing boat.

At 2 o'clock the next morning, the escapees offered one of their guards a bribe of gold in exchange for his M-16. He proved receptive. In fact, he and another guard joined the flight. In the ensuing battle, the rest of the Communists were either killed or thrown overboard. The 92 refugees then piloted the larger boat to Songkhla in southern Thailand.

Some voyages were nothing short of miraculous. A U.S. congressional subcommittee was told of 25 Vietnamese men, women and children who made a 1,000-mile trip to southern Malaysia in

44

a 30-foot boat that had only 2 feet of freeboard above the waterline. Their sole navigational aids were an old rusty U.S. Army–issue pocket compass 2 inches in diameter and a fragment of a map of the world torn from a geography textbook. "That fragment is a little less than four inches long," testified Leo Cherne, cochairman of the Citizens Commission on Indochinese Refugees, an influential private organization. "It covers the Pacific area from the Bering Sea to the Antarctic Ocean. The portion of the journey that they were navigating with this map covers . . . the size of an aspirin tablet."

Others were not so lucky. Nguyen Thanh Dung, a former South Vietnamese military officer who worked with American intelligence, paid in gold for two boats to escape. He left on one, his family on the other. The boats were supposed to rendezvous at sea, but for some reason they did not. "I've been here for two months, and I have no idea where my family is," he told a visitor to Songkhla in 1977. "Sometimes I am like a crazy man without them."

Many failed to clear Vietnam. A lawyer who had not been allowed to practice after the Communist takeover made numerous attempts before getting out. In July 1975, she set out from Nha Trang, but the captain was afraid their destination in the Philippines was too distant and turned back. In 1976, she was about to leave on someone else's boat when she had the feeling it would not work and pulled out; it didn't work. On her third try, in 1977, she was arrested in Rach Gia and jailed there for eight months. After her release, she paid for an escape but it turned out to be a swindle.

With money running low, the lawyer joined some others in buying a 30-foot boat. For months they sent a small craft down the Saigon River, studying the frequency and location of police patrols. When they eventually set out from Ho Chi Minh City in May 1978, they knew of seven river checkpoints and changed the appearance of the boat before each one so that it would not match reports of boats heading downriver and would seem to have entered just above each point. The boat had two engines, one 5 horsepower, the other 20. When near police, they would shut down the large engine and use only the small one, which was plainly too weak to power the boat out to sea.

The meticulous planning paid off and they made it to the ocean—only to discover that they had forgotten to take a map. Their luck held, however, and though they got lost, a ship directed them to Malaysia.

Tran Hue Hue's escape was as harrowing as one could imagine. The 17-year-old was among 50 refugees who fled Can Tho in panic in September 1978 as police closed in on them. Those who got left behind included her parents and the skipper of the 36-foot boat. After five days at sea, the boat ran aground on a coral reef south of Palawan Island in the Philippines. Living in the rusting hull of an abandoned ship, she watched the others die as their diet of sea gulls, shellfish and oysters proved inadequate. After almost five months, a 14-year-old boy was her only companion. He died ten days before Filipino fishermen rescued her.

A Soviet vessel intercepted a refugee boat off Rach Gia in May 1976 and forced it back into the port. Local police, who had accepted payment from the refugees and supervised their departure only hours earlier, promptly jailed them all and confiscated their possessions.

About 60 Vietnamese trying to sneak out of Danang for Hong Kong early in 1977 were intercepted by a government patrol craft after being betrayed by a crewman on their boat. They too were thrown into jail without charge or trial. It is known that one 30-year-old man remained there for more than two years until his sister, who lived abroad, visited Vietnam and arranged for his release.

It seemed to be entirely up to local authorities to hand out what punishment they liked. As far as anyone could tell, no comprehensive records were kept of escape attempts.

Despite the exodus of boat people, the Socialist Republic of Vietnam, as the unified country was renamed in July 1976, represented a safe haven for many more refugees than those departing. They began streaming in from Kampuchea as soon as Pol Pot's Khmer Rouge captured Phnom Penh in April 1975 and imposed radical and ultranationalist policies. That Vietnam was a chosen country of asylum for displaced Indochinese struck some as ironical. "That shows that there is a pecking order even in hell," commented Leo Cherne.

In fact, Cambodians were leaving their country months before the inept and corrupt Lon Nol government was crushed by the Communists. Ethnic-Chinese merchants pulled out in favor of a new life in Hong Kong and elsewhere, while senior Khmer military and civilian officials headed for France, the former colonial power. Plane bookings were heavy, and only those with the means to pay the exorbitant departure fees, both official and unofficial, reached the top of the queue. They were usually the ones with the most to lose and most to fear.

Indeed, Cambodia had been a nation on the move since war came to the once-tranquil Buddhist society in 1969: American aircraft began secretly bombing eastern border areas in an effort to cut the movement of Communist supplies to South Vietnam. As the North Vietnamese and Viet Cong moved their sanctuaries farther inside Cambodia, the B-52s followed them and the war spread.

Soon after Sihanouk was overthrown by Lon Nol in March 1970, ostensibly in protest against the continued presence of the Vietnamese Communists on Cambodian soil, Cambodian marines vented their spleen on longtime ethnic-Vietnamese residents. Many of the Vietnamese, or their forebears at least, had been imported by the French to staff the colonial ministries in Phnom Penh. Others had emigrated from Vietnam of their own accord and settled as farmers and fishermen.

Contrary to official propaganda, most of the 600,000 ethnic Vietnamese in Cambodia were not Communists or even sympathizers—especially the more than 350,000 who made up half Phnom Penh's population. Nevertheless, in a frenzy of racial hatred, the military set upon them in the capital and at other centers to the south and east. As many as 3,000 to 4,000 were killed and their bodies thrown into the Mekong River.

It was like an eviction order. Tens of thousands of ethnic Vietnamese, most born in Cambodia, reacted by fleeing to Vietnam. They abandoned their homes, farms and shops where many were working at a range of skilled jobs. After protests by Saigon, an organized evacuation got under way by air and sea. River convoys, mainly large barges, carried military supplies from South Vietnam to the Cambodian Army and returned with refugees.

In retaliation for the assault, South Vietnamese forces that invaded Cambodia with the Americans in April 1970 went on a similar binge of racially motivated plunder and killing. They were supposed to be pursuing Vietnamese Communists, but they welcomed all Vietnamese they encountered, among them, no doubt, some who were supporting the North Vietnamese and Viet Cong. Instead, they concentrated on looting Khmer villages, driving off farm animals and extorting money for the return of possessions.

If it was not already apparent, ethnic-Vietnamese residents could see they had little future in Cambodia. Within a year the Vietnamese population of Phnom Penh had fallen to perhaps 30,000. The drift continued for years, groups of 20 or 30 moving out at a time. Saigon kept no check on them: most went to live with relatives, or just moved to villages in South Vietnam without notice and set up house. In 1975, an estimated 400,000 had gone to South Vietnam, leaving about 200,000 still in Cambodia.

Some of Cambodia's more than 500,000 ethnic Chinese pulled out too. Although they did not come under attack until 1971—and even then they were subject more to government rhetoric than to actual harassment—a few decided that conditions were too uncertain. They emigrated to Thailand, Taiwan and other countries where their commercial skills could be employed. Unlike the Vietnamese, they were able to take their time, selling their businesses before they went.

Meanwhile, the widening war uprooted the bulk of the remaining Cambodians. Foreign correspondents estimated that in five years of fighting at least 5 million of the total population, put at just over 7 million in 1970, were displaced. The Khmer Rouge guerrillas established a pattern of capturing villages and marching the peasants off to previously "liberated" areas that they held more securely. Other Khmer, uprooted by the bombing from small towns and farms in eastern Cambodia, made for the cities. Several hundred thousand settled in Phnom Penh, where they replaced the departing Vietnamese as small shopkeepers and performed a multitude of other jobs. The population of the capital had swollen fivefold to about 3.5 million when Pol Pot's black-clad revolutionaries entered it in April 1975, five days after the last Americans were evacuated.

Without warning, the little-known Khmer Rouge implemented one of the most ruthless revolutions on record. The bloodbath feared in Vietnam truly befell Cambodia. The old society was shattered overnight; whole classes of the population were systematically killed and the renamed Democratic Kampuchea turned into one vast work camp. Family life was destroyed, religion banned, the traditional land system eliminated. Many pagodas were razed and the rubble used to pave roads. Currency was replaced with a system of barter and dole. Telephones, postal services, public transport, schools and universities were abolished.

Cars, trucks, machines and equipment were abandoned in what became graveyards of imported technology. Books, manuscripts and printed records were burned and other symbols of education and learning vandalized and discarded. All vestiges of Western influence and modernization were eradicated. The country was returned to its primitive condition of centuries ago, theoretically dependent on nothing and no one but its own hard toil.

Everything was done in the name of Angka, the mysterious but omnipresent "Organization" that was the chosen faceless front for the Communist Party of Kampuchea. Criticism of Angka was forbidden; those who dared were killed. When a person was invited "to visit Angka," he disappeared; it was a euphemism for the death sentence.

To smash traditional frameworks and head off any opposition, the Khmer Rouge began emptying Phnom Penh within hours of conquering it "by arms and not by negotiation," as they put it. Everyone was driven out, including the sick, the elderly and hospital patients who had just undergone major surgery or were awaiting operations. Those who hesitated were threatened and sometimes shot. Most left on foot, some on bicycles, a few pushing cars. They crowded the major highways leading out of town, carrying a little food and a few pathetic possessions. It was to be a temporary measure, they were assured, though they were not told where they were expected to go or what to do.

But the assurances were only to deceive in order to minimize objections. There were to be no cities in the new Kampuchea; cities were the font of great evil. Within a week, the major

49

provincial towns were also deserted, their inhabitants force-marched into the countryside. The crude evacuation left tens, perhaps hundreds of thousands dead from starvation, sickness, accidents and exposure—and just as many others determined to desert the country at the first opportunity.

That opportunity presented itself immediately for some of the more skeptical residents herded out of Phnom Penh on April 17 and the following days. Sensing catastrophe, they thought of escaping to South Vietnam, where the Thieu government was battling a Communist onslaught but was not thought to be in imminent danger of collapse. They took Highway 1, which runs 100 miles southeast to Ho Chi Minh City, or Highway 2, which leads south into Takeo province, passing close to the Vietnamese border.

Naturally enough, their ranks included ethnic Vietnamese who were still living in Kampuchea, as well as Vietnamese married to Khmer. They were joined by ethnic Chinese with commercial and family links in Cholon, the Chinese quarter of Saigon. Other mixed-marriage families—Chinese and Vietnamese, Chinese and Khmer—were well represented, as were many ordinary Khmer who simply had escape in mind.

South Vietnam was the logical refuge. Kampuchea's other extensive land frontier is with Thailand, which was much farther distant for the residents of Phnom Penh and held few ties for them.

Kampucheans who ran doggedly for South Vietnam were lucky. Although Saigon crumbled, no attempt was made by the Vietnamese Communists to stop the influx from Kampuchea. As for the Khmer Rouge, they were not well enough organized at first to stem the outflow. Their attitude toward departing ethnic Vietnamese was good riddance. They let them cross to Vietnam, often providing an added incentive by robbing them of all their possessions. Haphazardly, the Khmer Rouge tried to stop Khmer from leaving, but some who spoke Vietnamese bluffed it out. Others bribed their way through, used subterfuge or simply evaded security forces.

Within about six weeks, however, the Pol Pot government was methodically blocking escapes. Soldiers patrolled the border region and hunted Kampucheans making for Vietnam. Although it was not known until much later, they even harassed and shot some ethnic Vietnamese trying to leave. Many an escape was made with the People's Liberation Armed Forces, the Communist army of South Vietnam, firing over the heads of the refugees at pursuing Khmer Rouge. This extraordinary scene—the Vietnamese forcefully disputing the actions of their supposed Communist allies in Kampuchea—was played out not only for ethnic-Vietnamese escapees but for Khmer and others as well. It was not publicized at the time because Hanoi and Phnom Penh were maintaining the facade of unity.

By the time the Khmer Rouge attempted to seal the border, around the end of May, at least 8,000 Kampuchean refugees were clustered in Ho Chi Minh City. They were housed temporarily in two large pagoda complexes and in four or five informal camps in the city. People arriving from the border said a further 20,000 were sheltering just inside Vietnamese territory, opposite Svay Rieng province, where most were crossing.

The nightmare for the people of Kampuchea that began with the death march from the towns and cities continued with numerous other barbaric reforms. The population was divided broadly into three categories: those who had been in Communist-held areas before April 17, 1975, were called "old people"; most others were called "new people," though in between was a candidate group on trial. The old people were trusted and privileged to some extent. The new people almost had to justify their right to live.

Members of the former military and civilian establishment were considered beyond reeducation. Where they were persuaded to declare themselves under one pretext or another, they were summarily executed. Those who tried to hide their identity were pursued relentlessly.

Students, intellectuals, professionals and foreign-trained personnel often met the same fate, though the circumstances differed from one part of the country to another. Learning was cause for suspicion. Power passed to youngsters in their early teens and to illiterate peasants.

The bulk of the population was put to work growing rice, digging irrigation canals and building dams. They worked long hours with little food and only brief breaks for meals. The slightest resistance or complaint met with death, usually by bludgeoning. Some were shot and toppled into mass graves. The

51

massacres continued far beyond the initial takeover period. Disease and starvation also took a heavy toll.

In addition to extreme revolutionary practices, widespread purges within the Khmer Rouge army, administration and Communist Party induced Kampucheans to flee. Pol Pot and his close associates rid their ranks of Sihanouk followers, those trained in Hanoi whose loyalty was considered doubtful and other rivals. The ruling clique also faced a series of rebellions and uprisings, which it answered with more purges and killings.

Exactly how many of Kampuchea's 7 million people died in the three and a half years of blood-soaked Khmer Rouge rule is not known. The country cut itself off from most international contact, and little verifiable news seeped out. Vietnam later claimed that 3 million people had been eliminated or had died, while some official U.S. estimates put it at up to 2 million (compared with an estimated 600,000 dead and perhaps as many wounded during the 1969–75 war).[8]

The victims included two small minorities: Cham, the Moslem survivors of the once-great kingdom of Champa that was centered on the lower central coast of Vietnam, and ethnic Thai. Khmer Rouge brutality was the end of centuries of periodic victimization and violence for the Cham, thought to number under 100,000, and would just about eliminate them as a community. Like everyone else, they fled if and when it was possible. For the 20,000 to 30,000 ethnic Thai scattered through the western provinces and concentrated on Kong Island, which until French colonial times had been part of Thailand, it was also just another round of discrimination. They headed for Thailand's Trat province, a favorite destination since the 1950s when confrontation between the two countries started to make their life in Cambodia miserable.

Only the ethnic Vietnamese were allowed to leave Kampuchea in any sort of order. Evidence suggests that Hanoi and Phnom Penh, despite their differences, were able to work out arrangements for the Vietnamese to "return to their homeland," if they desired. They were certainly welcomed as returning countrymen and -women by the Vietnamese authorities, though their integration amounted to a further burden on the beleaguered nation. According to Vietnam, their numbers reached 170,000

52

within three years. That would indicate that very few of the 600,000 ethnic Vietnamese of 1970 remained in Kampuchea by late 1978.

All other departures were opposed violently. The Khmer Rouge conducted raids against Thai border villages similar to those they mounted against the Vietnamese, and they clashed with Laotians on the Lao border as well. The Thai frontier became a sort of no-man's-land, mined and heavily patrolled by the Khmer Rouge.

A few Kampucheans took advantage of their location or work to slip undetected into Thailand. A handful made the crossing along the coast by rowboat or fishing launch.

> For most, however, the voyage was long and perilous. First, they had to escape the vigilance of their guards, which was no easy matter in a system as thoroughly policed as that of the new Khmer society. Then they had to walk for weeks through forest and over mountain, living on roots and leaves. They were eaten alive by mosquitoes and bloodsuckers, and they also had to reckon with panthers and wild elephants.[9]

The Khmer Rouge publicly executed recaptured escapees as a warning to others who might be tempted to try. They were also known to have pursued Kampucheans across the border and to have slain them on Thai soil. Those who reached safety in Thailand were often totally exhausted and near death. "Sary, whom I met immediately after his arrival on June 15, 1976, was a hunted man with haggard eyes, his face and limbs swollen with beri-beri," said one account. "He could only speak in monosyllables. The impression he gave me was of a man who had escaped from a mental hospital."[10]

By the end of 1976, counting a pre–April 17 cross-border rush, an estimated 35,000 Kampucheans had gone to Thailand, though only about two-thirds of them had registered with UNHCR as refugees. Others were living in or near Thai villages, or unregistered on the fringes of refugee camps. The registered tally rose to 33,651 by the end of 1978, as survivors limped in at the rate of about 50 a month.

They were mainly younger men. Few women and children

53

made it, and practically no families; they just couldn't get out alive. The flow increased perceptibly in mid-1978 as Kampuchean troops were deployed away from the Thai border to the eastern front, facing Vietnam.

Although it was not known at the time, Kampucheans took refuge in Laos as well. When a UNHCR team visited remote Attopeu province in 1980, it found about 10,400 of them up to 30 miles inside Laos. Dispersed through three districts, they were living quite agreeably with the local population, though it was learned that others had been sent back in 1975–76.

Vietnam, however, continued to be a much better prospect than Thailand or Laos for Kampucheans terrified out of their wits or dying of disease and malnutrition. Vietnam was especially favored by Khmer Rouge defectors and the intended victims of Pol Pot's purges, who were almost exclusively Khmer; they knew Vietnam was not only geographically close but sympathetic to Pol Pot's opponents. The opportunities to seek sanctuary in Vietnam increased as Vietnamese forces pushed into Kampuchea in late 1977 and 1978, apparently trying to trigger a coup in Phnom Penh. Vietnam ended up occupying a slab of eastern Kampuchea.

It is true that in order to appease the Pol Pot government, Hanoi in the first year returned about 2,000 Kampucheans who had sought asylum in Vietnam. They were immediately executed, according to unconfirmed reports, as were the returnees from Laos. Since these tactics obviously did not succeed in mollifying Phnom Penh, Vietnam began accepting all refugees from Kampuchea without discrimination.

This policy was implemented at considerable cost to Vietnam. Apart from taxing limited resources and services, the refugees represented something of a security threat, since the authorities, otherwise preoccupied, carried out little screening. Some of the refugees are known to have been formerly employed by the fiercely anti-Communist Lon Nol and his American backers. On the other hand, the exiled Kampucheans later served Hanoi's purpose when it became more serious about replacing the Pol Pot government.

A survey by Vietnam in mid-1978 showed 150,000 refugees from Kampuchea, almost 90 percent of them Khmer, most of the others ethnic Chinese. According to UNHCR, a "substantial

54

proportion" of the refugees were children, with women and the elderly accounting for most others. The majority, from rural backgrounds, settled in eight southern provinces, while several thousand urban dwellers moved to Ho Chi Minh City. Those Khmer who remained in the countryside often joined friends and relatives among the Khmer Krom, ethnic Khmer who have their roots in the Mekong Delta of Vietnam.

For a while it seemed that Laos, a landlocked kingdom with a tradition of patience, moderation and gentleness, would escape the human hemorrhage of its Indochina neighbors. A cease-fire in 1973 paved the way for a coalition government, set up in April 1974, between the right-wing Vientiane regime and the Communist Pathet Lao guerrillas. But following the stunning developments in Vietnam and Kampuchea in April 1975, the Laotian Communists began to flex their muscles.

Armed forces of the two sides clashed, and rumors of a Pathet Lao takeover caused panic in Vientiane. Ethnic Chinese, ethnic Vietnamese and ethnic Thai merchants began to withdraw from the capital, along with some ethnic Lao, making their way to Thailand across the Mekong River. They took their families, autos and other possessions with them.

Among the refugees were several thousand Tai Dam, an ethnic minority whose traditional home is in northern Vietnam. They had migrated to Laos and Thailand after the French defeat in North Vietnam in 1954. Most settled south of Vientiane, abandoning their farming role to become domestics, drivers, artisans and the like. With another Communist takeover in prospect, they were uprooted once more.

A wave of anti-American sentiment swept Laos in May, and demonstrators forced the resignation of rightist ministers and generals, who were accused of being U.S. lackeys. Most of them promptly joined the lines seeking exile abroad, in Thailand and elsewhere.

With de facto control, the Pathet Lao did not bother to maintain the coalition. Supporters and members moved into government departments and agencies and provincial and municipal authorities, after mass meetings demanded the removal of allegedly corrupt and inefficient officials. The monarchy was abolished and the Lao People's Democratic Republic proclaimed on December 2, 1975.

The new Communist government led by Prime Minister Kaysone Phomvihane ordered many people on the Vientiane side to attend "seminars," the equivalent of Vietnamese *hoc tap.* Held on the spot at first, reeducation for most people was fairly brief. But members of the administration, army and police were sent to upcountry camps.

Among the generals to leave Laos in May was Vang Pao, aged 45, who had led a clandestine army of Hmong hill tribesmen financed by the American CIA for fifteen years. He flew to Udon Thani province in Thailand, accompanied by an aide, one of his 6 wives and one of his 28 children. He was followed immediately by some of his tough little troops and their families, in all numbering about 11,000. Some went by air, but most traveled overland. By the end of 1975, about 55,000 Laotians had departed for Thailand. Some 30,000 of them were hill tribesmen, predominantly Hmong, who are sometimes known as Meo.*

The Hmong had every reason to feel endangered. Since the late 1950s the CIA had organized some 40,000 of them to blunt the drive of the Pathet Lao and its North Vietnamese sponsors, whose regular army was penetrating northeastern Laos. The Americans saw the hill tribesmen as a ready-made *maquis* that could do the job the Royal Lao armed forces were incapable of doing. If the Hmong had not been available, Washington would have faced a difficult choice. It would have had to decide either to commit American forces to Laos or to risk losing a government in Vientiane that allowed the United States to bomb the significant section of the Ho Chi Minh Trail that passed through eastern Laos. Communist troops, weapons and supplies were moving down the trail from North to South Vietnam.

Not all the Hmong in Laos, roughly estimated at 300,000, joined the anti-Communist cause. A smaller group was recruited by the Pathet Lao, while others kept their distance from both sides.

The CIA had also organized other groups called Lao Teung, as well as significant numbers of lowland Lao, into Special Guerrilla Units. They were to hold the line against the Communists elsewhere in the country.

* There is an academic discussion about the meaning of *meo,* which is derived from the Chinese *miao.* Increasingly, Hmong regard the term as pejorative. Hmong translate the word *hmong* as "free men."

The irregulars shouldered the main burden of the war effort. The number of Hmong in action at any time fluctuated; some dropped out and returned home to resume rice and corn farming—and perhaps opium growing as well—once their villages had been retaken. They might sign up again, the sons joining the army if the father was dead, as the fighting seesawed back and forth across the Plain of Jars and beyond.

From late 1968, Vang Pao's forces were generally in retreat, migrating with their families, under Communist pressure, south across Laos. U.S. aircraft bombed heavily in the region, helping create a nation of refugees: about 700,000 of Laos's 3 million people were displaced by 1973. By the time the cease-fire was signed in February that year, the Hmong army was hanging on by its teeth, its ranks depleted by the loss of a whole generation of men, its soldiers pitifully young.

Vang Pao's decision to quit Laos while the country was nominally still governed by a coalition was timely and wise. When the rightists and other opponents of the Pathet Lao were being flushed out of the government structure, the door to Thailand, across the Mekong, was open. Once the Communists took control, they moved to tighten security on the border. As early as June 1975, Pathet Lao troops started ambushing Hmong as they left their homes on the summits and flanks of mountains in central and northern Laos. The Hmong, who were joined by other hill tribesmen, descended from several centers. The main one was Phou Bia, northeast of Vientiane on the southern edge of the Plain of Jars, which had been Vang Pao's base at the end of the war.

There were only a few practical points of exit. Traveling without food and water, even the hardy Hmong did not have the stamina to trudge straight up and down rugged mountains for weeks on end. They had to choose the five or six easier routes to have any chance of making it. The Pathet Lao and Vietnamese forces mined those routes and sat in wait astride them. When the Hmong came into range, they opened fire on them.

In the peak of fitness, a man might be able to walk from Phou Bia to the Mekong River, which acts as the boundary with Thailand, in one week or more. From other Hmong areas, it might take six weeks of steady hiking. But it was impossible for the Hmong to maintain a steady pace. They abandoned their country in groups, as small as 15 or 20, as large as 1,200. Sometimes it was an extended family; or perhaps two of the four clans in a village; even the entire village on occasion.

It could take six months for a group to cover the distance, weakened by exhaustion, scratching around for food—bark, berries, roots and insects—and forever detouring over steep hills and through rain forests to avoid security patrols. If a few members fell sick and the whole group camped and waited for them to recover, they all became easier targets for prowling troops. In many cases, the painful decision was made to abandon the debilitated.

The government was not content merely to stop the hill tribesmen from escaping. It went after them in their mountain strongholds. Obviously regarding the Hmong in particular as a threat, Pathet Lao and Vietnamese forces unleashed aerial and artillery bombardments to drive them down to the plains. Where necessary, they tried to starve them out.

The Communists also used gas or powder against the Hmong. Both Laos and Vietnam denied they were employing toxic chemical agents. Others speculated on the possibility of its being herbicides or the riot-control gases, CS and CN, used by the Americans and others in Vietnam. To the Hmong, the type was academic. That gas or powder was being used was beyond dispute. That it was killing and injuring them was a fact of life.

The Communist objective, to judge from the harsh methods of suppression and the results, seemed to be to exterminate the Hmong. The Vietnamese and Laotian leaders feared that if the Hmong reached Thailand, they might be rearmed by the Chinese, the Americans or the Thai and sent back to undermine the government of Laos. Nevertheless, the government insisted that it practiced a lenient policy, given the Hmong's past, and wanted only to resettle them on the plains and bring them under local control.

Some Hmong ran the gantlet successfully, only to be shot down by Laotian border police as they attempted to swim the last few hundred yards to freedom. The Mekong River presented special problems for the Hmong, who cross their swift mountain streams on vines and log bridges and generally do not know how to swim. To negotiate the Mekong, they scoured for pieces of bamboo, or anything else that could be used as a float, such as plastic water and fuel containers. Drownings were commonplace. Survivors emerged from their unnerving experience in the water clutching their floats as a child clings to a security blanket. Some refused to let go of them for weeks.

Among those who made it to Thailand, malnutrition took a heavy toll. Children, as always, were the saddest of all. Youngsters with marasmus, a condition in which the body feeds on itself and wastes away, often failed to recover and died in refugee camps. Kwashiorkor, a protein-deficiency disease, revealed itself by turning the dark hair of the Hmong an unnatural reddish shade.

Jack Reynolds, a National Broadcasting Company correspondent, interviewed an 11-year-old boy named Bee Xiong, the sole survivor of a group of 54 Hmong who had come under Communist fire as they entered the Mekong. Bee, who was suffering from malnutrition and dysentery, saw his father, mother and younger sister die in the river, becoming, as Reynolds reported, "an orphan and a refugee at the same time."

As the Communists tightened their control, it was not only the smaller minorities that wanted to get out of the Lao People's Democratic Republic. They were joined—and outnumbered—by Lao, the largest of some 68 ethnic groups in the country. The Lao are no strangers to northeast Thailand. Long before the Mekong was a political barrier, they used it as a highway, sliding back and forth across its quarter-mile width, following the dictates of weather and commerce. Even before the Pathet Lao took over in Vientiane, it was estimated that eight times as many ethnic Lao lived in Thailand as in Laos. The Thai and the Lao are closely related by language and race, though the Thai consider themselves socially superior.

Even so, urban Lao who left Vientiane and its environs and the towns of Thakhet, Savannakhet and Pakse were scarcely enthusiastic emigrants. They went because they found the newly unveiled Lao People's Revolutionary Party, as the ruling Communist organization called itself, determined to institute Marxist reforms without delay—and without much regard for the consequences.

The wives of rightist generals and civil servants who had been sent for six months' reeducation were informed that their husbands would need two or three years of thought reform. The bureaucracy stagnated as key posts were filled with those of the correct persuasion, who happened in many cases to be the least competent. Red tape became a nightmare. At one stage a peasant needed up to seven signatures to cross a provincial line, three to move his pig to the next village and just one to kill a chicken.[11]

Mass organizations stretched their tentacles to embrace most people, to mold them along the desired lines and to keep them from straying back to the old ways. Particular attention was paid to the young. Investigative groups were set up in every village to search for signs of wealth and to report any antigovernment activity.

Despite resistance, the government pressed ahead with plans to bring the former rightist zone into line with the Pathet Lao areas. The free market in Vientiane was curbed. The liberation kip became the sole national currency in June 1976. Some farms were collectivized by coercion, contrary to declared policy, which was that joining cooperatives should be voluntary. Scattered Lao farming families joined the refugee throng. Although most farmers stayed on the land, they refused to grow any more than they needed to feed their families.

The lowlanders found it easier to escape than the hill tribes. Many bribed border patrols and police. Some paid clandestine organizations to take care of these details and arrived on the western bank of the Mekong in the safety and comfort of a hired boat. Border patrols had orders to shoot refugees, but enforcement was sporadic, depending on government control at a particular point of exit.

After the Pathet Lao stopped people from carrying their possessions across the Mekong in July 1975, many used other ways to escape. Some crossed legally on a border pass and did not return. Ethnic Chinese and others who were not nationals would obtain an exit visa to avoid being shot. Once they were through the checkpoints and before they reached Thailand, they would discard their papers in the river, to become instant refugees who had fled their "homeland."

Although witnesses saw Pathet Lao forces shoot and kill Lao refugees in November 1975, controls remained fairly lax through most of 1976. Lao were still smuggling themselves out, using one ruse or another. In late 1976 and the first half of 1977, however, more had to resort to swimming.

In one of the most daring exploits, John Everingham, an Australian journalist deported from Laos in 1977, swam the Mekong from Thailand the following year and rescued his Lao fiancée, whose name was Keo. She waited for him by arrangement on a sandbank stretching into the river from Vientiane. To avoid detection by armed soldiers manning an island garrison, Everingham outfitted Keo, who could not swim, with diving mask and regulator to breathe from an air tank he wore. He towed her underwater back to the Thai side, swimming normally, while she traveled on her back with her face almost breaking the surface.

In the first two years under Communism, more than 100,-000 Laotians departed for Thailand, including a substantial slice of the country's professional and commercial elite. At least 10,-000 others evaded Thai authorities and lived illegally with relatives and friends.

If all these flows of refugees in the first years of Communist domination of Indochina had the makings of a disaster, disaster surely followed.

The scene was set for a further outpouring by a Vietnamese government decision in March 1978 to abolish "all trade and business operations of bourgeois tradesmen" in the southern half of the country.[12] The measure, abruptly closing more than 30,-000 of the large private businesses, struck a serious blow to Sino-Vietnamese who for generations had dominated the commercial and industrial enterprises in and around Saigon and Cholon. Stocks were purchased by the state, and businessmen and their families were asked to return to their native villages or transfer to New Economic Zones. Some wealthy entrepreneurs were allowed to switch their capital to joint industrial ventures with the government, or to "productive activities"—handicrafts and agricultural and fishing projects. But others were packed off to the countryside at once.

The closure order, enforced by thousands of youth volunteers, soldiers and security personnel who visited every shop and businessman's house to make an inventory of assets and goods, was preceded by the removal of incompetent and corrupt Communist cadres. Unlike haphazard earlier socialist regulations, it was conceived and executed in secrecy to prevent any organized attempt to circumvent it. The raid caused anxiety in the Chinese community and for several days brought most business activity to a standstill. Few Sino-Vietnamese took comfort from the fact that thousands of small merchants were allowed to continue retailing goods not controlled by the state.

Their apprehension was well founded. The following month the government again fielded its youth brigades to clean up open-air markets, and in May it introduced a single new currency for the whole country. The second currency reform since 1975, it effectively wiped out savings, again hitting hardest the middle class and wealthy strata of society.

These follow-up moves to crush capitalist activity were carried out with the same determination as the closure order. Without doubt Hanoi had abandoned its soft-pedal approach to socialist transformation.

The change in strategy followed worsening economic conditions, including soaring inflation, which were increasingly attributed to private businessmen who cornered markets for food items, forced up prices, speculated and hoarded consumer goods and cash. Spreading corruption was also causing concern. Along with the sweeping new measures in the South, controls were stepped up against the ethnic-Chinese traders and shopkeepers who dominated the North's small private sector.

Although the crackdown on capitalism was supposed to apply to all traders "regardless of nationality or religion," it became one more irritant in the rapidly cooling relations between Vietnam and China. The countries had boasted during the years of the anti-American war of being "as close as lips and teeth," but long-standing differences became public, and border tension rose in 1978, linked in part to Peking's support for Kampuchea. With large numbers of Sino-Vietnamese from northern border districts—almost exclusively those who had lived nearly twenty-five years under socialism—crossing into China, Peking went to the defense of Vietnam's 1.5 million ethnic Chinese.[13]

Exercising what it called its consistent policy of "protecting the interests of overseas Chinese," Peking accused Hanoi of "ostracism, persecution and expulsion" of Sino-Vietnamese at the instigation of the Soviet Union. Hanoi rejected the accusation and in turn charged Peking with "campaigns which almost amount to coercion" to get Sino-Vietnamese to leave the country.

The plight of Sino-Vietnamese, whatever its cause, did not appear to be anything like the main reason for the falling-out between the two countries. Rather, it was symptomatic of deeper conflict, including historical antagonism, ideological divergence, territorial disputes and a battle for influence in Southeast Asia.

As the vitriolic duel sharpened, border skirmishing increased. When Hanoi announced that all Sino-Vietnamese who wanted to leave the country need only apply, the rush to China from both ends of the country became a stampede. Peking called a halt four months later after more than 130,000 refugees deluged towns in Guangxi and Yunnan, the two provinces bordering Vietnam. They stretched facilities to the breaking point, and Peking alleged that Vietnam was sending "spies and other bad elements" with the refugees into China. A joint announcement by the two provincial authorities said that Sino-Vietnamese returning to China would be required to produce official repatriation certificates issued by the Chinese Embassy in Hanoi, together with an exit visa granted by Vietnam.

The falling-out with China also had an immediate, dramatic impact on departures of boat people. In April 1978, 5,012 Vietnamese landed in neighboring countries—more than double March's total, and almost eight times that of a year earlier. The number edged up to 5,569 in May, dipped marginally to 4,924 in June, then hit a record 6,232 in July.

No longer were most of the refugees ethnic Vietnamese. Before long, ethnic Chinese became a majority, although they constituted only 3 percent of the total population of 50 million. And they ventured in larger boats, each carrying between 150 and 600 passengers, crammed into slots little bigger than their bodies.

A report by UNHCR showed that by October 31, 1978, some 195,000 refugees had arrived overland in Thailand since April 1975, about 150,000 had journeyed overland to Vietnam and 85,000 had taken to the high seas. In addition, 160,000 refugees had gone overland to China from Vietnam.

It was against this canvas that those on the ground in Asia greeted the *Hai Hong*. And with every new detail of the vessel's mysterious voyage, the alarm mounted. For there were reports that more large foreign ships were already in Vietnamese waters preparing for refugee-running operations. Others, also controlled by syndicates, were waiting in Singapore, Hong Kong and Taiwan for word that would send them to sea on similar missions. The consequences of any effort by Vietnam to organize refugee departures, against the backdrop of upheaval in Indochina, could only be immense. "We are facing the prospect," warned one Western refugee official, "of tens of thousands more leaving Vietnam."

His numbers would prove to be low.

WAYNE GIBBONS

Voyage to Nowhere: In October 1978 the *Hai Hong,* crammed with 2,500 persons who had paid for their passage in gold, became the second of the large refugee freighters to sail from Vietnam and the first to be detected by neighboring countries. When the vessel was turned away by Indonesia, it headed for Malaysia, while a high-level diplomatic war of nerves was waged over the fate of the passengers.

WAYNE GIBBONS

WAYNE GIBBONS

Island of Exiles: Bidong, a normally uninhabited Malaysian island that became a major haven for refugees fleeing by small boat from southern Vietnam, looked almost idyllic from a distance. But a closer view shows beaches littered with the rotting hulks of the flimsy craft that had carried the escapees across the open sea. The camp itself was crowded, hot, smelly and without adequate sanitation. Wells became contaminated and water had to be brought in by tanker as the population of the island rose from zero to 40,000 within a year.

Callous Hearts: Prime Minister Lee Kuan Yew of Singapore took a hard line throughout the crisis, saying that where Vietnamese refugees were concerned it was necessary to grow calluses on the heart or bleed to death. Neighboring Malaysia was more welcoming, at least at first. But it soon was overwhelmed and, in 1979, started closing its coast. Here a vessel of the Malaysian Navy prepares to tow a foundering refugee boat back to sea. Malaysia's toughening stance helped awaken the international community to the urgency of events in Southeast Asia and spurred leaders of the key industrial nations to put the refugees on the agenda at the summit meeting in Tokyo.

Crowded Haven: Refugees sailed into Hong Kong in large craft and small. Below, the freighter *Skyluck* lies at anchor with 2,651 Vietnamese still aboard. In the foreground is the smaller vessel *Ha Long*, whose 571 passengers included 240 children. All endured almost unimaginable crowding on their trip across the South China Sea, as Hong Kong officials saw when they glanced into the hold. Some escapees made the voyage squatting on open decks or lashed to the sides of tiny fishing boats.

GOVERNMENT INFORMATION SERVICES, HONG KONG

GOVERNMENT INFORMATION SERVICES, HONG KONG

Unlikely Envoy: Hong Kong's Governor, Sir Murray MacLehose, traveled abroad in 1979 to help impress upon the Western world the seriousness of the crisis. The U.N. invited the Governor to address its second refugee conference, partly in recognition of the fact that the British colony maintained a liberal asylum policy despite one of the highest population densities in the world.

UNHCR PHOTO BY D. HAN

Man in the Middle: The U.N. High Commissioner for Refugees, Poul Hartling, called the refugee crisis "an appalling human tragedy." It had aspects not widely appreciated—the fact, for example, that hundreds of thousands fled from one Communist country to another, such as these Kampucheans who found haven in Ho Chi Minh City.

Kampuchean Exodus: Hundreds of thousands of men, women and children, fleeing war and famine, surged out of Kampuchea in late 1979 and 1980. They took refuge along the border with Thailand, where the scenes were of terrible misery. Above, temporary shelter erected at Sa Kaeo, Thailand, by followers of the Khmer Rouge; below, a first-aid station for them at Khlong Kai Thuan, Kampuchea.

Human Flotsam: In the first half of 1979 refugees washed up daily on the shores of Thailand, Malaysia and Indonesia. It was a common but dangerous practice for them to hole their boats so they would be allowed to land—if they could flounder through the last few desperate yards.

THREE

The first thing Nguyen Dinh Thuy did when the Communists entered Saigon was hide the family savings, which were held in gold. He and his mother had about 30 taels between them. They buried it in the backyard of her home and stashed it in the ceiling and behind light fittings. Thuy did not keep any at his home because he occupied a company house, which he thought he might have to relinquish.

Although Thuy prepared for the worst, it was only ranking army officers such as his uncle who were sent away for years to reeducation camps. Considered a specialist, Thuy was allowed to keep his job at the government-owned Industrial Development Bank of Vietnam, where he was an assistant loan officer. He also was allowed to keep his house. But he never considered staying in the country. "Call me chicken if you like," he said. He hoped the Americans would return and help restore an anti-Communist government.

Eighteen months later, Thuy realized that the Ameri-

cans were gone forever. The economy was sliding fast, and he concluded that life was going to get a lot tougher before it got any better.

At the bank, he and his fellow employees played Scrabble, Chinese checkers and chess to kill the time. Communist cadres told them they ought to be more serious, but they saw little point. The bank had become in effect the industry branch of the Vietnam State Bank, and their main function was to supervise loans extended to companies by town and district branches. Since all large companies had been nationalized and were government-owned, the staff had no authority and served little purpose. . . .

THE HUMAN DELUGE hit Southeast Asia in the second half of 1978 along with a freakish series of tropical storms. Both caused havoc. Indochina refugees, in the numbers that had been feared after the *Hai Hong's* voyage, inundated countries of the region, while floodwaters swirled across much of the same territory. Behind the departure of tens of thousands of Vietnamese was an unannounced but officially sponsored program to facilitate the exit of ethnic Chinese and others considered undesirable.

Precisely when the Vietnamese government decided to reverse its policy of stopping refugees is not known. For several years Hanoi had spoken of detaining "reactionary elements" fleeing abroad; accused foreign powers, including the United States, of instigating people to run and demanded the return of ships, boats and planes used by refugees. As late as December 1977 the government was threatening anyone caught escaping with a stiff prison term.

In April 1978, however, Vietnam did not make its usual shrill demand for the return of a freighter and the men who had hijacked it in Vietnam and sailed it to Singapore. The following month, Robert Oakley, U.S. Deputy Assistant Secretary of State for East Asian and Pacific Affairs, told a congressional subcommittee: "We have a number of well-documented reports of refugees who have been arrested trying to escape . . . of refugees being shot at by Vietnamese patrol boats. But at the present time the increase in the flow of refugees out of Vietnam seems to indicate some slackening of efforts to keep them there."

In August, Oakley testified that "it is clear that the Vietnamese government continues to make strong efforts to stop the flow of refugees out of its territory." Nevertheless, the 50,000 boat people who had left Vietnam at that stage had done it the hard way. Those days were over. The slackening efforts noted earlier by Oakley gave way to what might be called a half-open-door policy.

It had its origins in concern among the Vietnamese leaders about the security risk allegedly posed by the ethnic-Chinese minority as relations with China deteriorated. Their eagerness to return to China, some repudiating Vietnamese nationality, disturbed Hanoi. As far as can be determined, the Central Committee of the Vietnamese Communist Party decided that the best way to deal with the matter was to allow ethnic Chinese to leave Vietnam, at the same time deriving maximum economic advantage from the process by impounding their assets. Some sources reported a secret government edict, promulgated in May or June, explicitly stating that Sino-Vietnamese were to be permitted to go in return for payment in gold. Although the policy was authorized at the highest level, it was implemented indirectly in southern Vietnam so that it would not be associated with the government.

As the message spread and the program took shape, more and more ethnic Chinese were plugged into the system. Significant numbers of ethnic Vietnamese joined them, in most cases carrying false papers identifying themselves as Sino-Vietnamese. The organization was well enough oiled by November 1978 for Vietnamese with the requisite amount of gold to feel confident that they could escape at any time. One Western official interviewing prospective emigrants in Vietnam under a family-reunion program was told bluntly by an applicant: "If I'm not accepted in three weeks, I'm going to Malaysia; I've already booked."

Conditions in Vietnam, the basic reason for the outflow, did not improve; rather, they worsened. As the quarrel between Vietnam and China reached fever pitch, Peking stopped all foreign aid to its onetime ally, suspended work on all its technical-assistance projects in the country and withdrew its specialists. Vietnam also failed to attract significant amounts of aid and investment from the West, particularly the United States, which initially vetoed Hanoi's application for U.N. membership, with-

67

held diplomatic recognition and widened its trade boycott of North Vietnam to include the entire country. Vietnam countered by joining COMECON, the Soviet-bloc economic grouping. Moscow and its East European allies, a few of them grudgingly, took over some of the seventy-two abandoned Chinese projects, but their help was no substitute for previous Chinese assistance.

The violent storms and flooding, described by Vietnamese officials as the worst for decades, hit all three countries of Indochina. For the third successive year Vietnam had its crops damaged by natural disaster.

The Vietnamese economy was also severely hamstrung by inefficiency and mismanagement, acknowledged in the official press, and by corruption that flourished in new forms as fast as the old ones were eliminated. Thousands of more trusted cadres were sent south from northern areas. Although the government explained that it was necessary because many of its experienced revolutionaries in the South had been killed by the Phoenix program, southern Vietnamese were left with the impression that the northerners were acting more like conquerors than liberators. This goes some way toward explaining the defection of southern Communists who were sprinkled among the refugees.

People assigned to New Economic Zones sought to avoid going. Those who fled the zones and returned to the cities had illegal status, could not accept a job and received no rations. Visitors could see thousands of them living on the pavements of Ho Chi Minh City. Official policies discriminated against some groups because of their wartime links, including Vietnamese women who were married to foreigners or had children by them. The women were, in some cases at least, deprived of jobs and rations, the children locked out of government schools.

In addition, reeducation for many drifted on beyond the three-year limit set originally by the government. The authorities disclosed no numbers beyond the 50,000 they claimed to be holding in February 1977. Amnesty International, the London-based human-rights organization, said it believed the number of political prisoners in prisons and camps was "far higher." From other sources it was known that they included people who had not been involved in politics previously and had not worked for the Thieu regime.

All these developments were reflected in statistics maintained by UNHCR. From 2,829 refugees who arrived by boat from Vietnam in August 1978, the lowest total for five months, the number leaped to 8,558 in September, 12,540 in October and 21,505 in November, setting a record every month. These figures were startling. The 21,505 refugees registered in the single month of November far and away exceeded the 15,690 total for the entire previous year, which in turn was up threefold from the 5,247 who left in 1976.

While the boat traffic previously had been considered seasonal, influenced strongly by the weather, the rush to leave Vietnam now had reached such proportions that conditions at sea meant little. The northeast monsoon, treated warily by sailors and professional fishermen, was all but ignored by the refugees from Vietnam. December 1978 saw the flow of boat people decline, but still 13,730 landed safely, while January 1979 recorded 9,931 and February 8,568.

Most of them continued to favor Malaysia as a destination. East-coast Malay villagers, rising each morning and rubbing the sleep from their eyes to begin a centuries-old daily fishing routine, stared wide-eyed and fascinated as a flotilla of refugee boats tracked the coastline south. At the Pantai Motel in Kuala Trengganu, foreign correspondents sipped drinks at the bar and, staring out the window, watched refugees drown. Drinks still in hand, they would wander across the motel lawn, past the swimming pool, and interview survivors over the fence.

The numbers were boosted tremendously by more *Hai Hong*–style freighters. The *Huey Fong* arrived in Hong Kong in December carrying 3,318 Vietnamese, the *Tung An* turned up in the Philippines three days later with 2,300 and the *Skyluck* slipped into Hong Kong harbor in February with 2,651 after dumping 600 on the Philippine island of Palawan. Refugee receiving points in the region resisted the open trafficking in human lives, which, it was confirmed, was organized by syndicates of overseas-Chinese businessmen with the cooperation of the Vietnamese government. Using a variety of methods and tactics, the first-asylum countries were able to curb the wholesale trade, but they were not able to stem the flow from Vietnam. It continued as before, in smaller boats.

Nor were the boat people deterred by pirates, who made

increasingly bold forays into the main shipping lanes between Vietnam and Malaysia in active pursuit of the refugees. Most of the attacks were carried out by fishermen from southern Thailand, who have turned to piracy in the past to supplement their incomes whenever the opportunity arose.

Refugees by definition have no leverage of their own. They are vulnerable to exploitation and abuse, and they have little recourse when the inevitable occurs. The Indochinese were no different, as was painfully apparent to them on many occasions. Nowhere was it more obvious than in the piracy against the boat people. There was no practical source of protection for them. Not until 1980 did UNHCR get around to providing Thailand with a single, unarmed antipiracy patrol craft. For the Thai and Malaysian navies, the priority was to deter refugees, not pirates.

The suspicion was that the pirates were allowed to do their worst because their depredations could only help dissuade Vietnamese from taking to the water. And yet it must be remembered that piracy is endemic in the waters and islands on both sides of the peninsula in southern Thailand, just as it is elsewhere in Southeast Asia. Amid the lawlessness that prevails both on- and offshore, pirates regularly kill, sometimes for no other reason than to steal a fisherman's catch. Suppressing them would be a difficult, costly exercise should it ever be elevated to a serious consideration.

The boat people were aware of the danger, having heard about the pirates on foreign radio broadcasts and read about them in letters from friends and relatives who had escaped earlier. But there was little they could do about it. By late 1978, at least 2 of every 3 boats leaving Vietnam and heading south and west were being hit by pirates, many of them several times. Swooping on a boat within twenty-four hours of its departure from southern Vietnam and willing to pursue it to within hours of landfall in Malaysia, the pirates often attacked in groups of 6 or so vessels, keeping in touch by radio and surrounding their victims.

If it was the first time the refugees had been intercepted, the pirates usually robbed them of valuables—personal jewelry and gold pieces and leaf. Refugees took to hiding these items in fuel tanks, batteries and their boat's structure. In second and subsequent attacks, pirates grabbed food and any possessions still on board, leaving their victims nothing but the clothes they were wearing. And in more than one case refugees were stripped to their underclothing.

Although pirates were sometimes armed with rifles and pistols, more often than not they carried knives, iron bars, hammers and clubs. While they were content mainly to rob, in many instances they killed refugees and raped mothers in front of their terrified children. In one case, a youth was shot by pirates out of pique because his boat, which had been looted by others earlier, contained no valuables. In another incident, a boy crippled by poliomyelitis drowned when thrown overboard after going to the defense of his sister who was being assaulted.

Young women were sometimes abducted. What became of them can only be surmised. Most were never seen again. The evidence, admittedly slim, supported the popular belief that they were sold into prostitution in some of the wild frontier towns along the Thai–Malaysian border.

Some kidnap victims were taken to Kra Island off the eastern coast of southern Thailand, where they were hunted and assaulted by pirates who returned day after day. Kra, usually uninhabited, became notorious. According to a UNHCR report, 160 refugees died on the tiny island in one stretch of just over 12 months while 1,250 others were rescued from it in the same period. Said the report: "One woman was severely burned when pirates set fire to the hillside where she was hiding in an attempt to flush her out. Another cowed for days in a cave, waist-deep in water, until crabs had torn the skin and much of the flesh away from her legs. A young girl who died after being gang raped is buried under a simple slab at the edge of a clearing."

Despite the danger and the availability of weapons in Vietnam, most of the refugee boats chose not to carry arms. Nor did the refugees generally put up a struggle, even though they often had numerical superiority. They took the passive view that it was better to escape with their lives than defend their property.

The most vulnerable boat people were the small groups who left clandestinely and hugged the coast. They were often ethnic Vietnamese, the same sort of people who had been trickling out of Vietnam since 1975. Pirates attacked them with the idea of leaving no evidence: when they had taken what they wanted, they set about killing everyone and sinking the boat.

71

Where there were survivors to recount such ordeals, the details bespoke a savagery and inhumanity that staggered the civilized mind.

The small lighter *KG-0729* was just another refugee boat when it left Vietnam with three other vessels in October 1978. No more than 30 feet in length, it separated at night from the others off the coast of Thailand when the water pump of its single engine failed. While repairs were being made, the refugees hailed a large, steel-hulled Thai fishing boat painted green and red that approached in the moonlight.

When it was alongside, the 30-odd-member Thai crew invited the Vietnamese men aboard. About 30 refugees, including a couple of boys and women, scrambled onto the fishing vessel. Among them were Luong Bot Chau and her husband. "When the fishing boat moved away, we thought they were going ashore for help," she said. But the Thai produced iron bars, knives and boat hooks, tied up the Vietnamese men and robbed them before throwing them into the ship's refrigerated hold.

Luong Bot Chau watched as the pirates tried to steal the wedding band her husband was wearing. "He had become fat," she related, smiling faintly through her tears. "They could not remove the ring. His head was bleeding from the beating with an iron bar. He fainted. I also fainted. When I recovered, they were cursing and laughing and trying to pull off the ring. But it was too tight. So they led him to the side of the ship. They held his hand down on the wooden rail and chopped off his finger. They chopped away his ring finger. Once again I fainted."

The pirates then tried to slit her husband's throat. "But the knife they had was too blunt." Instead, they clubbed him to death and threw him overboard.

One refugee who was advising his people to remain calm and surrender all their valuables was misunderstood by the pirates: they bore down on him with iron bars, beat him to a pulp and threw him to the sharks. Refugees were running wildly, and children were screaming. Truong Hue Anh, aged 66, saw 4 of her sons killed and their bodies heaved into the ocean.

The women were ordered belowdecks, into the hold of the *KG-0729*, stripped and searched. Truong Hue Anh was beaten all over because her gold necklace would not come off easily.

The rest of the men were also searched, some tossed into the sea at the whim and fancy of the pirates. The younger girls were dragged up to the deck and systematically raped. "We heard them scream and scream," Luong Bot Chau said. "We could not get out, because they had nailed down the hatch."

The attack lasted about three hours. When it was almost over, the pirates shoved the Vietnamese male survivors back onto the *KG-0729*. Some were so stiff after being in the cold room that they had difficulty moving. So the pirates kicked them into the sea, their hands bound behind their backs. All food and water was also flung overboard. Almost as an afterthought, the pirates went below and battered the refugee boat's engine with hammers.

The nightmare was not quite finished. The pirates left about 1 A.M., but turned back after a few minutes and rammed the fragile wooden boat at high speed. Their second and third charges tore holes in the side of the *KG-0729*.

None of the refugees thought they would live. But the few surviving men took off their clothes and stuffed them into the gashes in the boat. The children undressed next, then the women. They kept the boat afloat, bailing out the bilges by hand. The children slept in the blood and wreckage as the men set to work on the shattered engine. Using knives, string and bits of timber and metal, they got it working again as the sun rose.

Two days later, the *KG-0729* arrived at the Pulau Bidong refugee camp in Malaysia, its hungry, thirsty occupants too shocked and stunned to ask for food and water.[1]

Meanwhile, Sino-Vietnamese were still trekking overland to China, despite the directive in July 1978 from Chinese provincial authorities attempting to almost close the border. At home, they were encountering more and more official hostility. Hanoi suspected Peking of trying to use them to destabilize Vietnam.

When some Sino-Vietnamese found their way to China blocked, they followed the lead of their brethren in the South and took to boats. But instead of heading south, they pushed northeast through the Gulf of Tonkin to China and Hong Kong, opening up a new escape route—one without predatory pirates.

73

They found the Vietnamese authorities in the North just as willing to see them go as in the South, and just as eager to charge exorbitantly for the privilege.

The main difference was in the method of transport. Many vessels leaving northern Vietnam were junks and other sailboats, while those in the South were motorized. The difference reflected the degree of modernization in the two parts of the country. Subject more to the vagaries of the weather, wooden junks often took six weeks or more to reach Hong Kong. They would put in for repairs and take shelter along the coast of China.

Northern Vietnamese refugees began to trickle into Hong Kong in September 1978, heralding a flood tide. Previously, only a handful of boat people had made their own way to the tiny British colony—191 in 1976, 1,007 in 1977. Arrivals rose sharply toward the end of 1978, giving a count for the year of 8,938, more than 25 percent of them in December.

It was amid this trend that, in the closing days of 1978, the Vietnamese invasion of Kampuchea brought a new and tragic phase in the Indochina refugee story. Bolstered by a recently signed friendship-and-cooperation treaty with the Soviet Union, Hanoi on Christmas Day dispatched 120,000 troops across the border and quickly crushed the main units of the Kampuchean Army. Within two weeks, the Vietnamese had taken Phnom Penh and installed Heng Samrin at the head of a hastily formed National United Front for the Salvation of Kampuchea. The fighting created new waves of refugees—peasants fleeing in all directions to escape the danger, like ripples from stones dropped into a pool.

As Pol Pot's Khmer Rouge retreated to mountain hideouts stocked with food and ammunition and reverted to their former guerrilla tactics, they were pursued across the country by Vietnamese forces determined to wipe them out. Few areas escaped the turmoil. For months, battles were fought for control of sizable towns and villages in western provinces near the Thai border and in the south. At the heart of the armed struggle was a vicious attempt by both sides to control the population, a contest that had dire consequences for civilians.

Food was already in short supply in Kampuchea early in 1979. A reasonably good crop was standing in the fields, but much of it was left untended, in some places after being cut and stacked but not threshed, when the Vietnamese invaded. Where retreating Khmer Rouge forces had time, they burned rice fields and mills and destroyed food stores, as well as blowing up bridges and digging trenches across highways to slow the advance of Vietnamese armor. In the first flush of freedom, ordinary Kampucheans looted granaries and ate without restraint, often with the approval of Vietnamese troops intent on fulfilling the role of liberators. Food stocks were depleted dangerously.

Late in April the rump of the Khmer Rouge passed through Thailand, the Vietnamese not far behind. There were about 80,-000 in all, of whom perhaps 10,000 were regular troops, and not all were enthusiastic and willing parties. They won Bangkok's permission to transit 10 to 15 miles of Thai territory south of the border town of Aranyaprathet, to escape entrapment. It was the first chance the outside world had had to see Pol Pot's bloody warriors at close range. The spectacle they presented was eye-opening in many ways. Among other things, observers saw the seeds of further refugee tragedy in their ranks.

The Khmer Rouge caravan actually consisted of three different groups, each totaling about 25,000 to 30,000 persons, who appeared on successive days. The first was a mixture of soldiers and their families and civilian followers. Some were in poor shape, obviously short of food; others not so bad.

The second lot were no less than the elite of Democratic Kampuchea, those chosen by Angka to build a new Khmer society in purified form. They were well fed, strong and fit—men and women, boys and girls, and robust little children, all clad in distinctive black. About 5,000 young soldiers, disciplined and impressive, trekked single file, marshals on horseback keeping the line in order. Some of them talked and joked among themselves; there was no dissension, no sign of unhappiness. The colorful sight inspired awe. "I could do nothing but hold my mouth open," recalled Neil Davis, a National Broadcasting Company correspondent and sixteen-year veteran of Indochina. "I thought, 'Jesus, it's Hitler Youth. It's the master race.'"

There was a chilling aspect as well. The elite had no elderly or sick people with them. What had happened to them? The answer was provided the following day by the third group: tens of thousands of what can only be described as slaves—peasants forced to accompany the Khmer Rouge at gunpoint. They trudged wearily beside some 2,000 oxcarts carrying supplies of rice, ammunition and an odd assortment of things. They were sick, really sick, from exhaustion, disease and lack of food. The aged hobbled along with the children whose stomachs were distended by the effects of malnutrition.

"Save us—please save us," some of them begged Western onlookers, encouraged by the presence of Thai soldiers. But there was to be no respite. Snarling Khmer Rouge soldiers policed the column to ensure that no one moved off the road. Hostile and nasty, they threatened to shoot anyone who demurred.

The Thai were not about to rescue anyone. They had permitted the incursion on the clear understanding that it would be temporary. However, some Kampucheans managed to cross the frontier at other parts of the border. About 85,000 of them— mostly women and children; their menfolk were all too often dead—found sanctuary in Thailand, at least temporarily.

Vietnamese policies were also responsible in part for the rising stream of refugees from Laos. With about 40,000 Vietnamese troops assisting the Pathet Lao, Hanoi's big-brother role was indisputable. The flow of Laotians from the country reached a peak of 6,000 a month in early 1979, double the rate of a year earlier.

There was no letup in the drive against the Laotian hill tribes, a fresh offensive being launched against the Hmong in late 1978. Lao and ethnic Chinese continued to leave for a variety of other reasons. High among them were poor economic prospects, Hanoi's stifling influence and continuing repressive government practices. As in Vietnam, reeducation dragged on.

Many Lao nationalists who had stayed on in hopes of building a brave new independent country felt betrayed by the revolution as Laos marched to Vietnam's beat. Purges were carried out in the government's own ranks. Senior cadres were dispatched to seminars for reindoctrination, often to Hanoi. This drained the meager pool of technically trained personnel and lowered further the standard of administration. Fear of meeting the same fate spurred large numbers of officials and long-standing Communists to escape to Thailand.

In short, by early 1979, Indochina was gripped in turmoil every bit as traumatic as that which the world had sanguinely supposed might end with the April 1975 conquest of South Vietnam. But that was not to be all. For in one of the most dramatic moves in decades of war in the region, China made a play that was to suddenly, and perhaps irreversibly, alter the stakes in the game.

On February 17, 1979, after a period of increasingly bitter verbal spats and border tussles during which Peking vowed to teach Hanoi a "lesson," China launched a major punitive attack. For almost a month, its forces waged a destructive battle with Vietnamese troops in six northern provinces of Vietnam. All along, China had stressed the limited nature of the invasion, and its troops were withdrawn by March 16. But if Peking's campaign was aimed partly at forcing the Vietnamese to pull out of Kampuchea, it failed. And the backlash from the attack had terrible consequences for hundreds of thousands: it sealed the fate of residents of northern Vietnam of Chinese extraction.

Privately justifying its policy by arguing that some Sino-Vietnamese in the northern frontier areas had collaborated with the invading Chinese troops, Hanoi decided to get rid of them. Vietnamese policy moved into a distinct new phase: from not stopping Sino-Vietnamese from leaving, to actively pressuring them.

Although once again no decision was announced, security officials began calling on Sino-Vietnamese and explaining that they had two choices: leave the country or be regrouped at "concentration points," away from economic centers, that would become in effect New Economic Zones exclusively for ethnic Chinese.

The tactics employed in the North were crude. First, Sino-Vietnamese cadres in responsible positions in the party, armed forces and other branches of the state were dumped. Ordinary ethnic Chinese were dismissed from government posts, and employers were told not to hire them. Their children were barred from schools. Their food rations were stopped, or they were threatened with such a fate if they did not meet a specified deadline to leave. A curfew was imposed on them in some areas, preventing them from leaving their homes during the hours of darkness. Their mail was censored, their homes looted in some cases, and a few were jailed without cause. Security officials who went knocking on doors to spell out the choices followed up with warnings over loudspeakers that if Sino-Vietnamese did not leave, their protection could not be guaranteed. The pressure was maintained by regular house meetings in streets where ethnic Chinese lived. They were asked to explain why they were taking so long to depart.

These harassing and discriminatory tactics were necessary to dislodge the remnants of several hundred thousand Sino-Vietnamese who had adjusted fairly comfortably to socialism since 1954. After Ho Chi Minh's victory over the French, they had had the chance of moving to South Vietnam; they had stayed. Ethnic Chinese living in provinces near the Chinese border had remained farmers and fishermen or continued to work in mines, factories and ports. Some had operated in the small, officially tolerated private sector. Others had come to occupy substantial managerial and technical positions in Hanoi's major industrial enterprises as well as in the government bureaucracy. Those who had not panicked when rumors of war between Vietnam and China spread in late 1977 and 1978 were unlikely to leave voluntarily now.

Hanoi's extreme measures, however, brought rapid results. When a group of 77 Sino-Vietnamese arrived by motorized junk in Hong Kong in May 1979, they reported that they were the last of 7,000 inhabitants of Co To Island, about 40 miles southeast of Hon Gay City, to pull out. All the islanders were ethnic Chinese, most of them poor fishermen with little education. The island was now deserted. About the same time, the British Ambassador to Vietnam, J. W. D. Margetson, privately estimated that only 20,000 to 30,000 ethnic Chinese were left in the North.[2] By early July, the arithmetic showed the exercise almost complete: 240,-000 had crossed to China, though not all from the North, and between 30,000 and 40,000 had arrived in Hong Kong.

Little specific anti-Chinese pressure was applied to make Sino-Vietnamese leave southern Vietnam. Little was needed. Life was becoming less and less tolerable for them there too; but as noted earlier, it was as a result of policies directed along lines of class more than race. The closure of most large businesses in Ho Chi Minh City and the curbs on private trading, though later relaxed, had effectively deprived many Sino-Vietnamese of their livelihood. They were happy to leave Vietnam in much the same way as were middle-class ethnic Vietnamese. Both saw the Communist system equalizing the poverty rather than redistributing the wealth. Since enforced movement to New Economic Zones, with departure from Vietnam an alternative, was being widely implemented in the South, the result in both halves of the country was much the same.

Vietnam's general mobilization, begun during the Chinese invasion but maintained after Peking's withdrawal, suggested to the entire Vietnamese population that peace, not to mention prosperity, was as distant as ever and that sacrifice was an indefinite standing order.

In March 1979, refugee-boat arrivals at Asian ports totaled 13,423—enough to put first-asylum countries in a near panic and cause distress to overworked resettlement officials. Then the floodgates opened. With Hanoi vigorously applying the boot, almost 135,000 Vietnamese descended on neighboring countries in the next three months: 26,602 in April, 51,139 in May and 56,941 in June. Naturally enough, a large majority of them were ethnic Chinese.

In May, for the first time, most of them headed for Hong Kong, reflecting the exodus from northern Vietnam and the British colony's liberal asylum policy. But tens of thousands still followed the more familiar route to Malaysia, despite the pirates. The overall result was what Poul Hartling, the U.N. High Commissioner for Refugees, called "an appalling human tragedy."

An international conference in Geneva called by U.N. Secretary General Kurt Waldheim at midyear brought a halt to some of the madness. Under considerable diplomatic pressure, Vietnam, while not admitting complicity in the refugee traffic, gave private assurances that it would undertake to turn off the tap for a while and to help organize safe and orderly departures.

It was time to pause and take stock. The record was not good, nor was it promising. By the end of July 1979, in just over four years, nearly 1.7 million Indochinese had sought refuge in another country: 320,000 Khmer and ethnic Chinese* and an es-

---

* The figure 320,000, which was given UNHCR by Hanoi, appears to be too high. It is probably a reasonably accurate count of Kampucheans under Hanoi's control, rather than refugees in Vietnam, late in 1978, when Vietnamese forces occupied parts of eastern Kampuchea. UNHCR preferred to use 150,000, which it said was Vietnam's estimate of the refugees who had arrived from Kampuchea "by mid-1978."

timated 200,000 ethnic Vietnamese from Kampuchea to Vietnam; 293,000 boat people from Vietnam to scattered points; 250,000 residents of Vietnam—230,000 of them ethnic Chinese, 30,000 ethnic Vietnamese—to China, mostly overland but some by boat; 250,000 assorted hill tribesmen, Lao, Khmer, ethnic Thai, ethnic Vietnamese and ethnic Chinese overland to Thailand from Laos, Kampuchea and Vietnam, in addition to 85,000 so-called "new" Kampucheans, mainly Khmer and ethnic Chinese, who crossed into Thailand after the Vietnamese capture of Phnom Penh. Perhaps another 60,000 had entered Thailand quietly and filtered undetected into the community—20,000 from Kampuchea, 40,000 from Laos. On top of that, 134,000 had gone to the United States at the time of the Communist victories in 1975, as well as 15,000 to other countries. To the total must also be added 110,000, the author's estimate of the refugees who died fleeing all these countries.

All but 30,000 of the Khmer and ethnic Chinese from Kampuchea who went to Vietnam returned to their homeland once the Khmer Rouge had been routed. But the vast majority of the refugees, maybe a million, were permanent and thus required resettlement. Voluntary repatriation seemed out of the question for all but a few. Local settlement would account for some— notably the 200,000 ethnic Vietnamese from Kampuchea and about 230,000 of the overlanders who had gone to China from Vietnam. But most would have to be resettled in third countries. All in all, it was one of the great population shifts in history. And it was continuing.

There was much more to it, of course, than mere statistics. Figures did not start to come to grips with the callousness of a government prepared to export its own people for profit while knowing that some of each human consignment would die in transit. Nor did they reveal the depth of ancient hatreds and racial antagonisms behind policies being practiced by Vietnam and Kampuchea and, to a lesser extent, Laos and China.

In Kampuchea, Vietnamese occupation forces let their anti-Chinese paranoia get the better of them. They set about expelling longtime Sino-Khmer residents who had suffered along with other Kampucheans at the hands of Pol Pot. Many were trucked to the Thai border and compelled to pay transportation fees, leading to conjecture that Vietnam was determined to eject as many ethnic Chinese as possible from all of Indochina.

Anti-Chinese sentiment began to surface in Laos as well, as Vientiane moved closer to Hanoi. But most of the ethnic Chinese of Laos—the Pathet Lao government said they totaled 100,-000 in 1975, but independent estimates put the number at about 60,000—were destined to leave the country after nationalization of private business and industry anyway. Many went legally by agreement, though thousands also crossed the Mekong with the Hmong, Lao and other Laotians.[3]

Numbers also tended to obscure some facts that compounded the tragedy.

Fact No. 1: Refugees were arriving faster than they were being resettled. In four years, more than 575,000 Indochinese had turned up outside their own countries requiring resettlement, but only 203,000 had been moved out to permanent homes.

Fact No. 2: The so-called land cases were being overlooked as the glare of publicity focused on the plight of the boat people. Of the 250,000 Laotians, Vietnamese and early Kampucheans who had crossed to Thailand and been accepted as refugees by July 1979, permanent homes had been found for only 85,000. And some had been in Thai camps for three or four years.

Fact No. 3: The non-Communist countries of Southeast Asia were fed up with the unending influx and what they saw as the reluctance of developed nations to share the refugee burden. Thailand had denied refugee status to the "new" Kampucheans, had forcibly repatriated 42,000 of them and was threatening to send more home. Malaysia had cordoned off its east coast and was pushing boats back to sea, and others were espousing a similar tough line.

One frightening figure was missing from the plethora of statistics: the death toll. How many had run but had not made it was unknown. And there seemed no way that anyone would be able to produce an accurate assessment, even with the passage of time. In the absence of anything firm, numbers were tossed around and caught by politicians like balls put into the air by a juggler.

Vang Pao, the former hill-tribe warlord in Laos, said in

1980 that he believed that 40,000 to 50,000 Hmong had died since 1975. The number seemed exaggerated. But anyway, who could establish if they had perished leaving Laos, or had been bombed in their mountain villages, or had been killed in combat with government troops? Casualties were obviously lighter among the Lao and other lowlanders, though they also had drowned and been shot escaping. Those best placed to offer an informed guess were Western refugee officials specifically handling Laotians. They spoke the languages and followed the situation closely. Generally, they agreed on about 20,000 refugee deaths in Laos. The estimate consisted of several thousand lowlanders and 15,000 or more hill tribesmen.

Kampuchea presented just as much difficulty. Trying to separate those who had died as refugees was an exercise as frustrating as it was grim, given the wholesale executions and massacres, widespread famine and rampant disease while the country was sealed off. John Barron and Anthony Paul, who systematically interviewed refugees for their book on the Pol Pot regime, said it was clear that of all who attempted to escape, fewer than half succeeded.[4] Thus, they estimated that at least 20,000 had died trying to flee to Thailand between April 1975 and the end of 1976. To that total must be added those who died trying to get out in 1977 and 1978, two more full years of Khmer Rouge tyranny.

Others believed that the death rate was much higher than one in two. The Citizens Commission on Indochinese Refugees, the American panel cochaired by Leo Cherne that investigated the matter in early 1978, concluded that one in five was a more realistic escape ratio.

All these estimates, rough as they might be, related only to Kampucheans seeking sanctuary in Thailand. No casualty figures at all were available for Kampucheans escaping to Laos and Vietnam. It is presumed that the easterly route was much less dangerous, judged by the numbers negotiating it safely. But it was undoubtedly fatal for some: for a start, the 2,000 refugees that Vietnam initially returned to the Khmer Rouge who reportedly were executed.

An estimated 53,000 Kampucheans had reached Thailand alive by the end of 1978 when the Vietnamese invaded, though only just over 60 percent of them were registered with UNHCR.

Using a one-in-two attrition rate for them and tacking on some thousands for Laos and Vietnam, it can be said, conservatively, that at least 60,000 died as they fled the pogroms of the Khmer Rouge. But the actual number could be two or three times that.

No statistics were more abused, though at times for the best of motives, than Vietnamese boat losses. Leaders and public officials throughout the Western world pounced on "the grim subtraction," as Hong Kong's Governor, Sir Murray MacLehose, once called it. Everyone said at least 40 percent. Some went as high as 70 percent. None provided data or computations on which their figures were based, though some attributed them rather perfunctorily to refugee interviews and intelligence sources. Those who tried to translate their chosen percentages into human lives came up with 100,000 to 250,000.

In fact, 50 percent was wide of the mark. Western resettlement officials with years of experience interviewing refugees are convinced the death toll was much, much lower—probably no more than 10 percent of departures. They arrived at this figure by routine questioning of arrivals, which led to the accumulation of considerable information. By tracing relatives and friends, in the course of their work, who had set out on different boats, they built up a fairly comprehensive picture of what conditions were like in various parts of Vietnam, how the escape systems worked, how many were being caught, who was being raided by pirates and when conditions changed. Some of the information was shared, often informally, as every effort was made to press ahead with the bureaucratic and tedious process of resettlement.

In these circumstances, it was impossible for entire shiploads to vanish without a trace, as was frequently rumored or speculated. Individual boats with 20 or 30 passengers, yes. Freighters carrying 1,500, no. If there were any doubts about this assessment, those doubts were dispelled by a variety of small, daily events. For instance, when a boat capsized in Malaysia with fewer than 200 deaths resulting, word flashed through the Malaysian refugee camps as a hot item of news— hardly likely if every second boat were overturning with the loss of all lives, day in and day out. The inescapable conclusion is that the death toll was highly exaggerated.

Anyway, 10 percent is no mean figure: in four years, more than 30,000 human beings died unnecessarily at sea.

FOUR

His nerve restored after an initial period of uncertainty, Nguyen Dinh Thuy investigated the possibility of escape from Vietnam by boat. There were two standard methods: slip out at night and risk being apprehended and jailed, or cultivate and bribe Communist cadres, police and officials. In late 1976, he tried sneaking out.

With a group of relatives, he contacted a boat owner and made a down payment of 2 taels of gold. The boat owner prepared for the voyage, buying gas, rice and water. They were to go by truck to the point of embarkation, the port of Ham Tan, east of Ho Chi Minh City. But the arrangements fell through, and he lost his gold.

In early 1978, they investigated the business of bribery. An approach was made to a former Communist guerrilla officer. At the same time, a deal was worked out with a boat owner in My Tho, in the Mekong Delta. Thuy delivered 15 taels of gold to him, as part payment for passage for 9 persons: himself and his wife and 2 children, his mother, his stepfather, 2 stepbrothers and a distant cousin. An extra 30 taels of gold, to be raised in part by the sale of his mother's diamond ring, was to be paid on departure.

A day before the group prepared to board trucks in Ho Chi Minh City, a cable from the boat owner aborted the plan. His explanation was that some of the sailors on the boat had been caught playing cards by security officers. But Thuy and his fellow conspirators knew they had been swindled. Despite earlier promises, the boat owner refused to return their gold.

Poorer but wiser, Thuy became less trusting. He opened negotiations half a dozen times but refused to hand over any gold until he was aboard the departing vessel. Only close friends and members of the family were aware of what was going on. They had to be wary of government agents and informers. However, the talks came to nothing. . . .

VIETNAM MIGHT HAVE been in the economic doldrums, but Rach Gia, capital of Kien Giang province, was bustling. The main activity: exporting boat people. While a limited number of persons were directly involved in the trade, the relative prosperity it generated percolated through the community. Boatbuilders were busy patching up wrecks for the hazardous trip across the sea, and the influx of budding refugees from the Ho Chi Minh City metropolis, awaiting embarkation, offered an opportunity for the sale of rice, vegetables and other services. Refugees seemed one of the few worthwhile ways left to make a free-enterprising dollar in Communist Vietnam.[1]

In fact, the same thing was happening throughout the South and in parts of central and northern Vietnam. It seemed as if the whole country had gone into the refugee business.

The principal southern centers, apart from Rach Gia, were Long Thanh, Vung Tau, My Tho, Vinh Long, Tra Vinh, Can Tho, Bac Lieu and Ca Mau, as well as smaller towns and ports in between. All were approved outlets for disgruntled residents of Vietnam who were prepared to pay for the risk of crossing the ocean in search of a better life. The operation, dubbed by some

Western diplomats Rust Bucket Tours, Inc., began in about the middle of 1978.

Although efforts were made to keep Hanoi's role in it secret, it was soon obvious that approval had come from the highest levels. Transit camps catering to those preparing for departure sprang up all along the southern coast. The Rach Gia camp, located on a river island about 8 miles from the city's marketplace, was one of the largest. It consisted of about fifty buildings that could hold several thousand persons.

A section of the Cong An, or Public Security Bureau, was entrusted with the task of handling sponsored refugees. Main PSB offices were organized into functional divisions, each headed by a deputy chief of police. The political-security division of the PSB, known as B-2, was given responsibility for refugees.

Little was known about the PSB, which came under the control of the Interior Ministry. B-2 officers wore plain clothes and were responsible for both internal and external aspects of security. They relied on networks of informers and agents to keep tabs on anyone who might threaten the government or deviate from its political line.

For the refugee trade, PSB officers sometimes recruited passengers directly. But in the South they relied heavily on intermediaries to do their legwork: contacting would-be refugees and arranging for them to pay their fares, often by installment. A single voyage, subject to much negotiation, took up to twelve months to package. The price was always flexible, the PSB charging as much as the market would bear. In one case the haggling with middlemen lasted seven months, with PSB officers halving the price eventually when they became convinced that the passengers could not afford more.

Refugees paid the intermediary in gold after he had settled the matter with the PSB. They often had to hand over what was called an application or registration fee—about 2 taels of gold for an adult—when their names were first submitted to the PSB.* The rest of the payment, looked upon as an exit fee, was

---

* A tael, valued at about $220 on the world gold market at mid-1978, rose quickly to $250 in the second half of the year. The price soared throughout 1979, closing at over $600.

usually made near embarkation. The final terms tended to average between 5 and 8 taels of gold per adult, half price for children, variously defined as under 12, 14, 15 or 17 years of age. Kids under 5 or 6 were not charged at all. The intermediary received about 2 taels of gold per adult as his fee for organizing the exercise and linking up with a boat owner, or alternatively, purchasing a boat himself. A typical split: 50 percent of the proceeds for the government, 40 percent for the boat, fuel and provisions, with 10 percent left over for the boat owner and organizer.

It was common practice for PSB officers to solicit and receive bribes in addition to the negotiated payment. This was what they took on the side for their services; it did not have to be declared and passed on to the government. The bribes were paid in gold, jewelry, furniture and anything else of value. Rolex watches were especially coveted.

Although it was cheaper for prospective refugees to sign up directly with the PSB, most did not. The obvious attraction was a lower fare, usually 3 to 5 taels of gold for an adult. Another advantage was that compensation for the transfer to the government of refugees' fixed assets such as houses and land, though nominal, was deducted from their overall fees. Otherwise, they might simply have to abandon them. It was not uncommon for intended refugees to be required to sign forms donating their possessions to the state. The declaration of one ethnic Chinese, who walked out and left a house, among other things, read: "I am very happy to give all this property to the Vietnamese government; this government is very good to give me the opportunity [to go abroad] to see my family."

Apart from a general penchant for using middlemen, Vietnamese wanting to leave the country were wary of dealing directly with the police. Police were regarded as corrupt and not to be trusted. People also suspected a trap. Security forces had shot and jailed escapees for the past couple of years. Although it was widely known that the government was now assisting the exit of ethnic Chinese, nothing had been announced, and the public's knowledge of the scheme was hazy. Information about it was passed by word of mouth. There was no public assurance in radio broadcasts, wall posters or any other medium that today's refugees would be treated with more consideration.

Sometimes an intermediary who was a boat owner, or had become one during the organizing process, left with the refugees he had helped recruit and consign. Sometimes he stayed to put together a few more deals and acquire a substantial stake before pulling out himself to settle in the United States, Australia or Canada—even France if worst came to worst: France had a reputation among some refugees for a high-cost low standard of living.

At first the middlemen played a substantial role in determining the location and time of departure. But as the system was tightened up, the PSB took firm control of these arrangements. As the numbers increased, the processing time shortened to as little as a month.

Passengers had to provide in advance an old South Vietnamese government identity card, or a voter's registration card issued by the Communist administration for the 1976 elections, birth certificates for children and photographs of everyone. The names were checked off at the time of boarding. The documents were then destroyed, sometimes on the spot.

The mode of operation was for the passengers to gather near the place of embarkation several days in advance, sometimes as early as a week. This was the trickiest part of the exercise. Only in a few known cases, one in Song Be province, did the government provide transport. The passengers, assisted by their middlemen, had to take care of it themselves, usually using false travel documents. They were then held in transit camps, most of them smaller than the one at Rach Gia, until they boarded. In some areas refugees were billeted in private homes. At one stage, near Vung Tau, they were put up in a hotel.

PSB officers were known to sell boats to intermediaries, but for the most part the organizer had to find one himself. Where the PSB did get involved, it was usually in a middleman role. Officers would convince some private boat owner, particularly if he had several vessels, that he ought to part with one. Further, they sometimes persuaded the boat owner to donate up to 40 percent of the price to the state as a "civic duty."

The boats being pressed into service were wooden coastal and river fishing craft, or other workhorses. Most were between 40 and 80 feet in length and had seen better days. Some seemed beyond repair and required a lot of work to get them floating again. The sides had to be boarded up to stop waves from washing in through windows and other openings. Narrow racks looking like church pews without headroom were hammered into place to hold passengers during the one-way voyage, and numerous wide-mouthed funnels were fitted to force air to refugees slotted into the shelves belowdecks.

Rach Gia was the major center for sponsored departures because of the large number of boats around the city. In Rach Gia harbor in the middle of April 1979 there were more than 50 boats specially built or rebuilt for the refugee trade. They had certain features that distinguished them from ordinary fishing vessels: a tentlike lean-to on the foredeck; two toilets, separated by a small cooking area, built over the stern; and the ventilation pipes on deck.

At that time on both sides of the short canal between Rach Gia and Rach Soi, 80 to 100 more boats were being converted along the same lines, all with PSB authorization. A sawmill in Rach Gia was supplying the timber. The construction of new boats was limited by a shortage of marine engines and materials. Small ones, up to 39 feet, could be built privately without permission, provided they were designed as river craft. Small engines normally used for irrigation were often installed in them.

In Cuu Long province, an estimated 40 boats were being outfitted under PSB sponsorship in March 1979. More than 20 of them were in Tra Vinh, the rest in Vinh Long, the provincial capital. The same thing was happening throughout southern Vietnam. Hundreds of scattered boatyards were doing repairs. Each yard could usually handle only 1 or 2 boats at a time, taking several months to refurbish them. It was a relative boom time, leading Charles P. Freeman, Deputy U.S. Coordinator for Refugee Affairs, to observe that a new boatbuilding industry had been established in Vietnam specifically for refugees.

Although the program officially covered only ethnic Chinese, little or no attempt was made to stop ethnic Vietnamese from joining the boats, provided they had identity papers showing they were ethnic Chinese, and provided they could pay—generously. There was no trouble with the false papers; they were supplied by the middlemen and even, on occasion, by the PSB itself. Ethnic Vietnamese were charged a loading premium, which, like everything else associated with the refugee traffic, varied from time to time and from one province to another. Generally, though, the surcharge amounted to 50 percent of the going rate for Sino-Vietnamese.

Since false papers were always required, it was assumed for a long time that ethnic Vietnamese were being smuggled out through bribery at the local level, without the government's knowledge or approval. But the practice persisted, and on a few boats as many as half the passengers were ethnic Vietnamese. While there is no evidence that the government deviated from its original policy of allowing only ethnic Chinese to go, it is impossible that Hanoi was not aware of what was happening. Ethnic Vietnamese were surfacing all over Asia.

Furthermore, middlemen, assisted by PSB officers, could sometimes arrange for a person to be released from a reeducation camp, if he or she was not being detained for serious political reasons, and put aboard a boat. This service cost, for each individual, between 5 and 25 taels of gold.

Some residents, particularly small groups of ethnic Vietnamese, continued trying to escape clandestinely. Although they often had to take the precaution of bribing local officials, it was still a much cheaper way to go. But once the approved system was introduced, those trying to bypass it were exposed to harsh treatment if caught. Accused of departing illegally, they could be jailed arbitrarily as before, more than likely being stripped of all their possessions as well. It was open season on them.

PSB officers as well as border-defense security forces were charged with the detection and prevention of clandestine departures. In Rach Gia they used a variety of small craft to patrol the harbor and coastal waters. Farther offshore, state-owned fishing boats, sometimes fitted with machine guns and crewed by armed border-defense forces, kept watch. Through the use of agents, the security forces blocked many escapes. Officers preferred to wait until the last minute before swooping so that they could net all the passengers. As an incentive, they were given a share of the money and valuables taken from these escapees.

Refugee boats all along had been ill-equipped, overcrowded and unsafe, but the situation became more acute when Rust Bucket Tours, Inc., went into business. Although departure was more assured, the boats were still often commanded by inexperienced sailors. PSB officials themselves injected a potentially lethal element by invariably putting additional groups of refugees on board at the last minute. These were persons they had recruited themselves, and they were over and above the load planned by the intermediary. The intermediary might object on the ground that it made the boat unsafe, but the PSB officers always insisted. They had good reason: they made more out of these direct recruits, because they did not have to split the payment, discounted rate though it was, with a middleman, and they cut the government out too.

Still, the only way to be certain of leaving from mid-1978, it was said, was to go through the PSB. One ethnic-Chinese resident of Ho Chi Minh City made inquiries and was put in touch with Ba Thanh, who was Deputy Chief of the Rach Gia City PSB and ran the B-2 office. For a time Ba Thanh, alias Bay Sung, had operated from Rach Gia police headquarters. But he and some others handling refugee affairs in various parts of southern Vietnam moved to less official premises, probably in an attempt to conceal the government's involvement. By the time the ethnic-Chinese organizer caught up with him, Ba Thanh had shifted to a private house in a back lane in Rach Gia. Later, the office was reported to be in a sawmill that had shut down.

The organizer frequently visited Ba Thanh in the private dwelling to negotiate details of the trip. The B-2 office was fully staffed, one Ba Cao acting as secretary. Several other PSB officers worked there, one called Chinh, another Thanh. Ba Thanh was businesslike, generally confining himself to the negotiations. He referred in passing to "the state policy" of allowing ethnic Chinese to leave.

Ba Thanh's first piece of advice was to get a boat. The organizer found an old river transport in Long Xuyen, the capital of An Giang province, paid 80 taels of gold for it, and arranged to have it repaired in a small private yard on the Rach Gia–Rach Soi canal. The refitting cost 220 taels.

Six days before departure, the organizer submitted a list of more than 350 passengers he had recruited, together with the usual documentation. In the case of more than 100 ethnic Vietnamese on the list, copies of voter registration cards and birth certificates belonging to ethnic Chinese were provided. The PSB asked no questions about the ethnic origins of the passengers.

The organizer and Ba Thanh agreed on a payment of 850 taels of gold for the voyage. In addition, Ba Thanh sought and was given some watches and 20 taels of gold for his services. The organizer in turn charged adult passengers 8 taels of gold, children under the age of 17 years half price, with those under 6 exempt. Relatives of the organizer did not have to pay either.

Ba Thanh fixed the date, time and place of departure, informing the organizer three days beforehand. The boat left from Vinh Hiep ward in Rach Gia City. As the passengers boarded, Ba Thanh and several other B-2 officers checked off their names and photographs. One of the officers, Chinh, boarded the boat and accompanied it for about six hours, until it reached Son Gai Island. There they met 3 other refugee boats and a vessel manned by PSB personnel. After waiting fourteen hours at the island, all 4 boats set out, escorted by the PSB vessel until they reached Chuoi Island, off the tip of Ca Mau Peninsula. The PSB craft turned for home, leaving them to choose Thailand or Malaysia as a destination.

The contact for other ethnic-Chinese organizers from Cholon was Ngoc Minh, an officer of the Dong Nai provincial PSB. When the boat set out from Ben Ngo Gia village, about 14 miles south of Long Thanh in Dong Nai province, 20 to 30 provincial and district PSB officers were present. It was a popular point of embarkation. Two other refugee boats had left in the previous five days, and another was making preparations to go. About 20 others designed specifically for refugees were observed in the area.

Ngoc Minh told the organizers that when they arrived overseas they should say, if asked, that they had left clandestinely. He had ordered them to paint the white vessel blue for better camouflage on the water in order to make it look more like one that had left secretly.

More than 500 refugees on a 65-foot boat that left Dong Nai province under PSB sponsorship had to assemble on Highway 15 just southeast of Long Thanh, which is halfway between Ho Chi Minh City and Vung Tau. They were led on foot along a track on the western side of the highway to a camp 3 miles away in a cleared area on the bank of a river.

The camp consisted of two large barracks with thatched roofs. The refugees occupied one, while passengers for another boat were housed in the other. A well provided water for drinking and cooking. Two PSB vessels were moored at the end of a short jetty that ran out over the river. PSB personnel patrolled the perimeter of the camp, and no one was allowed to leave.

The boat was one of 4 to depart the area within two days, carrying an estimated total of 2,000 refugees. During the same period, 2 or 3 others returned to the camp with engine trouble. As soon as repairs had been completed, they set out again. Some more boats, old fishing vessels, were anchored in the stream, apparently awaiting passengers.

The major flaw in the overall program was that there was no coordination between authorities in different provinces and between different organs of the government. Because it was carried out covertly to a certain extent, most of the refugees had at least some fear of arrest until they had actually departed. Since land transport was rarely provided, the threat was most real when they were traveling to their rendezvous point. Groups from Ho Chi Minh City were often stopped by PSB officers who were not connected with the organizer of their departure. And the navy might intercept others being sponsored out of the country by a particular provincial PSB office. Those with fewer provincial boundaries to cross obviously were less likely to run afoul of the vagaries of Vietnamese government bureaucracy.

When they did, they were apprehended temporarily. Officials who bumped into the results of someone else's handiwork sometimes took advantage of the situation and helped themselves to refugees' possessions and valuables. If the refugees objected, they were threatened with stiff jail sentences for trying to sneak out of the country. A representative of the organizer or the particular PSB office often had to secure the refugees' release.

Orders occasionally arrived from higher authority, presumed to be Hanoi, to suspend operations. Major refugee-exporting centers received such a directive in late January and early February 1979. One businessman who was organizing a boat for 500 persons through Rach Gia submitted his passenger manifest to the PSB in January along with 1,050 taels of gold in fees. He also passed on four cassette players, one used Toyota sedan and 100 taels of gold to smooth the way. But the ban was observed, and he had to submit the list again in April.

February recorded the lowest count of boat people landing in East and Southeast Asia for five months. When the green light was given to resume, 10 boats were flagged away from Rach Gia within five days, between March 22 and 26, each packed with more than 200 refugees. As they set out for the uncertain sea crossing, about 70 boats, recently repaired and ready to go, were still anchored.

One result of all this refugee activity was a shortage of black-market gold in Vietnam. It was illegal to possess gold anyway, and police and security officials confiscated it upon discovery. They went searching for it by digging in private yards and ripping up floors. By April 1979, gold was becoming so hot and scarce in Ho Chi Minh City that it was being sold in pieces no bigger than 3 to 20 taels; dealing in larger amounts was considered too risky. The price rose from 1,200 dong to 1,500 dong per tael in the second half of 1978. Over the first four months of 1979, it ranged from 1,850 dong to 2,150 dong: $841 to $977 a tael at the official exchange rate, but about $185 to $210 at black-market prices.*

The apparent contradiction between expecting refugees to pay in gold and not allowing them to hoard the metal could be explained by the government's various objectives. Apart from purifying the population, Hanoi was also attempting to tighten the state's grip on the southern economy. And that meant draining the community of extensive private wealth in the form of gold, currency, commodities and other assets.

The dazzle of gold and the expensive fares led many foreign observers to conclude that only wealthy Vietnamese became refugees. It provided ammunition of a sort for opponents of resettlement, who called the refugees drug traffickers, vice kings and other exploiters from Thieu's days. Vietnamese government propaganda encouraged this line of thinking.

The reality was different. Many southern Vietnamese—middle-class, petty traders, professionals and workers—held their savings in gold, a common hedge against inflation and upheaval in the country. When the Communists came, they had buried it in backyards, cemented it under floors, hidden it be-

* The official exchange rate hovered around 2.2 dong: $1. Visitors to Vietnam with hard currency received a 50 percent premium that raised it to about 3.3 dong. The black-market rate fluctuated from 10 to 15 dong to the dollar.

hind walls—as searching police well knew. Mostly it was in modest amounts, though merchants and businessmen who had prospered during the war years held, all together, tons of gold, doubtless a lot of it ill-gotten.

Countless Vietnamese lost their gold as they tried to buy their way out between 1975 and 1978. Racketeers and confidence men, claiming the right connections but without any intention of arranging escapes, fleeced them mercilessly. The victims could scarcely complain to the police. Many dared not even cry on the shoulders of friends, so fearful were they of informers.

Supplies of personal gold dwindled further as Vietnamese thrown out of work by the change in government bought food and other necessities at high prices on the free market. The result was that when many were thinking of leaving, they had to make a conscious decision to split families. By pooling their resources, they could afford to send 2 or 3 members out while the others, perhaps 10 to 15 of them, stayed behind. Husbands separated from wives, brothers from sisters. There was no guarantee that they would see each other again. Many did not.

In the best tradition of Chinese business, however, methods were devised to assist those who did not have the price of a passage. Hanoi not only acquiesced in such schemes, it actively promoted some of them.

The government's desire to cleanse Vietnamese society found common ground with the aims of another group who could help it: ironically, the fat cats of Cholon who had made millions out of the war, a class Hanoi professed to despise. The government's cleansing exercise involved getting rid of Sino-Vietnamese, dissidents and other elements judged to be of doubtful loyalty or difficult to assimilate. The fat cats wanted to get their gold caches out of the country. Together they conspired literally to sell hundreds of thousands of ordinary Vietnamese, predominantly ethnic Chinese, down the river—and into the sea.

The solution was as simple as it was ingenious. Potential refugees without the means to purchase a passage arranged for friends in Hong Kong, Singapore or California—anywhere overseas—to pay the U.S.-dollar equivalent into the bank account of a wealthy merchant still in Vietnam. The relatives then posted copies of the deposit slips to the potential refugee, who exchanged them with the merchant for gold. The refugee won his place in the queue of boat people which he could not otherwise afford, the merchant in the process transferred part of his assets abroad—he would follow later—and the government, for no modest fee, got rid of yet another undesirable.

Another method was for a wealthy Cholon businessman to ask that funds be deposited in a dollar bank account in the name of a relative of his in Hong Kong, or elsewhere. When the relative cabled the businessman in code that the money had been received, the businessman contacted the would-be refugee and paid him in dong. The businessman was trying to unload dong before leaving, since it was worthless outside Vietnam. In return for hard currency, he was usually willing to pay about 10 dong to the dollar—almost five times the official exchange rate.

Although the Vietnamese government offered a special rate for hard-currency remittances from abroad, the rate was still so poor as to discourage many people from sending funds legally to help friends and relatives in Vietnam buy a ticket out. All sorts of ruses were devised to circumvent the system and get dollars directly to recipients in Ho Chi Minh City. It was unofficially estimated that by 1980 as much as $100 million a year were being channeled into Vietnam by one illegal means or another, much of it simply to help people stay alive.

Bank notes mailed into Vietnam inside the folds of a letter—not registered and not sent express, because this would draw unwelcome attention from the authorities—sometimes got through. But in many cases they were confiscated. When it became known that the Vietnamese government was making use of an X-ray machine left behind by the Americans to detect bills, savvy hands began inserting them between sheets of metal-based carbon paper inside the letters: the carbon thwarted the machine. Light-fingered officials had the last laugh, however. They steamed open letters, removed the bills—which they no doubt pocketed—resealed the envelopes and dutifully delivered them.

Opportunities to exploit the "Chinese connection," as it was called, declined when Sino-Vietnamese started leaving in large numbers in 1978. The only reliable substitute, short of using the bank, was to send gift parcels by mail or on the weekly Air France flight. Every Thursday, Flight AF 198, originating in Paris and the only Western air link to southern Vietnam, carried tons of goods for residents of Ho Chi Minh City, after a stopover in Bangkok.

The items sent by freight or mailed were carefully chosen for their yield on the black market. A carton of 555 brand cigarettes, manufactured in London rather than Singapore and costing $6 at a duty-free shop in Thailand, brought $15 to $20 in hard cash on the streets of Ho Chi Minh City. Other hot lines included jeans, black satin material for women's trousers, needles, thread, zippers and clothing. There was always a demand for all sorts of medicines, especially vitamin, ulcer, malaria and diarrhea pills. And—most important—seasick tablets, the French brand Nautamine preferred.

With skillful packaging by the sender, three 42-pound parcels—Air France imposed the same minimum rate charge for all parcels up to 42 pounds from Bangkok to Ho Chi Minh City—could turn over 10 taels of gold in Vietnam. And with 10 taels, a potential refugee could do business with a middleman.

In central Vietnam, the government tended to play a more direct role in the refugee service, apparently in an effort to hasten the exit of ethnic Chinese. Pressures brought to bear on them were not nearly so intense as in northern Vietnam, but nevertheless there was a strong element of coercion. It manifested itself in fewer middlemen, lower boat fares, organized land transport and few ethnic Vietnamese in the boats.

Fifteen refugee boats were registered to leave Nha Trang, the capital of Phu Khanh province, in July 1979. They were fairly typical. Huynh Quang Hinh, the Deputy Chief of the Phu Khanh provincial PSB, called the shots. He approved applications and kept things moving.

In June, he prepared letters of introduction for 255 ethnic Chinese from the coastal town of Tuy Hoa to facilitate their purchase of a boat. The PSB told representatives of each family registered in the group to pay their departure tax directly to the Tuy Hoa City Bank, a branch of the government's Vietnam State Bank. In early July, the refugees were moved to the departure area in buses hired by the PSB.

Another group of 259 Sino-Vietnamese made preparations to leave after PSB officers informed them that if they did not they would be sent to a New Economic Zone. Before boarding their 55-foot boat 2 miles from Nha Trang, they were warned not to make any adverse comments about Vietnam once they reached their destination, which was Hong Kong. The warning was hardened into a threat by PSB officers who dispatched 217 ethnic Chinese on another 55-foot boat around the same time. They said that if anyone told of the Vietnamese government's involvement in the refugee outflow, the remaining Sino-Vietnamese would all be sent to New Economic Zones and no more would be allowed to leave the country.

In neighboring Nghia Binh province, the familiar pattern was repeated, though prices were higher and officials were more lenient in allowing refugees to retain personal belongings and valuables. All approved departures were channeled through Qui Nhon, the provincial capital, and the large coastal city at the other end of the province, Quang Ngai. After ethnic Chinese were screened and approved for exit by security police, they each paid 8 to 12 taels of gold to the organizer, who in turn passed on 6 taels per adult to the provincial PSB office.

Farther north, in Quang Nam–Danang province, the authorities preferred to work through the Chinese community. The operation, once again controlled by the deputy chief of the provincial PSB, required community leaders to provide lists of names for screening. These leaders became the organizers, with responsibility for purchasing boats and supplies for the voyage. Once cleared for exit, refugees had to sign declarations of intent to leave the country and waivers of future claims against the Vietnamese government.

All sanctioned departures from the province were staged through Danang City. On the day, passengers assembled in various abandoned houses in groups of between 30 and 50. They were collected at about 2 A.M. by trucks driven by border-defense security forces and taken to Danang harbor, where they were put aboard small boats.

They were transferred not directly to their boat, but to an uninhabited part of the offshore island of Cu Lao Cham. There, in the predawn gloom, heads of households and males had to furnish biographical details and submit to being photographed and fingerprinted. They also declared—or were supposed to declare—all gold and jewelry in their possession. It was then confiscated, except for 2 taels of gold per person. As a parting shot,

98

Communist cadres offered an hour-long lecture in which they explained the government's policy to give ethnic Chinese the choice of leaving Vietnam.

Ethnic Chinese in northern Vietnam had to make their own arrangements to leave the country where, by Hanoi's word, some of their families had lived for centuries. They were encouraged forcefully to buy boats, though it involved bribing Communist cadres to permit freedom to move around the country and facilitate arrangements. The two approved departure points were Haiphong, the main port for northern Vietnam, and Hon Gay, another port a little farther along the coast, in Quang Ninh province. Again, it was the PSB that took charge of the evacuation. In the North, however, neither the government nor the police bothered to conceal their role in the operation.

The cost of a passage proved a heavy burden for many Sino-Vietnamese, who were ordinary workers in a Communist society, earning as little as $25 a month as primary-school teachers in the provinces, or $36 as drivers in the city.* Dong were used to pay bribes and purchase boats. Whether motorized or not, boats were extremely expensive. The choice was between state- and commune-owned vessels, which were registered, and private ones that were not. A 60-ton wooden vessel with an engine, which eventually carried 329 persons to Hong Kong, cost $59,000, and a 35-ton sailing junk in need of repair went for $22,700.

Some Sino-Vietnamese with limited means had to wait weeks and months for an opportunity to get a berth on a boat they could afford. While fares of $600 or $700 were common, some of the poorest ended up paying only $45. One couple had to dispose of all they owned—a few sticks of furniture, a bicycle and clothes—to raise this paltry amount.

One device employed by the authorities was to debit the purchase of a boat against the contributions of ethnic Chinese in a commune's compulsory savings scheme. Savings amounting to $8,636 were withheld in payment for a 46-foot fishing junk

* Converted at the official exchange rate of 2.2 dong: $1. Monthly salaries ranged from 40 to 150 dong, averaging about 70 dong for the whole country.

equipped with a 23-horsepower engine to carry 77 persons from Co To Island in May 1979.

In a typical operation, the 60-tonner mentioned earlier was purchased by a China-born restaurant proprietor, aged 60, and a 51-year-old cook earning $43 a month in a state-run restaurant. The proprietor, who went to live in Hanoi in 1946 from Guangdong province, started making plans to leave when the government in February 1979 forced him to close the restaurant he had run for ten years. He got together to make arrangements with the cook, who decided his time was up when he was summoned to a meeting of ethnic Chinese in March by PSB officers and had the standard choices explained to him: departure or concentration.

After organizing a group in Hanoi, including 18 members of the restaurateur's family and 10 of the cook's, they paid a $2,045 bribe at the Hanoi PSB office for permission to travel by car to Hon Gay to buy the boat from a cadre in charge of a cooperative. The cooperative obtained clearance for the sale from local PSB officers. They spent $4,545 repairing the boat, which came with 6 tons of fuel oil, and were given a time and date for their departure by the Hon Gay PSB. The restaurateur returned to Hanoi to get the 327 others in the party, leaving the cook to ready the boat and buy food, which cost a further $1,818.

When the refugees traveled to Hon Gay in buses, they were checked on board by PSB officers against a prepared list. They were allowed to take with them only their clothes. Their final payment was $455 for the service of a motorized junk, manned by 5 ethnic-Vietnamese shipbuilders, which towed them about 60 miles out of Vietnamese waters.

Some discontented ethnic Vietnamese took the opportunity to leave as well. About one in every 20 boat refugees from the North was ethnic Vietnamese. Where they were married to ethnic Chinese, they also suffered official harassment by association. In numerous documented cases they were told to separate from their spouse or be treated as Chinese.

Other departing ethnic Vietnamese had general grievances about the country, its system and its living standards. As in the South, they had to pay a premium. Adults among the 138 passengers on a 66-foot sailing junk that left Hon Gay in April 1979 had to pay $682 each. But an ethnic-Vietnamese couple found themselves having to shell out an extra $2,727 to an ethnic-Chinese family to join the vessel. The bribe was to enter them in the family's "notebook" which, together with photographs, had to be supplied to the Hanoi PSB office. The 26-year-old woman, a veterinary surgeon earning $27 a month, and her husband, aged 30, who was paid $30 as a national table-tennis instructor, assumed Chinese names.

Although long-distance internal travel was not permitted without good reason, some Vietnamese from the South chose to leave by boat from the North because it was cheaper. One was a 51-year-old well-connected and confident ethnic-Chinese businessman, who owned a small factory in Ho Chi Minh City that manufactured soya sauce. He wanted to take 24 people with him: his wife, 6 nephews, 3 old servants over 80 years of age and 14 other family members. From his extensive contact with government officials, he estimated it would cost 100 taels of gold for only 10 of them to leave from their home, whereas all 25 of them could go from the North for that price.

The businessman paid his 100 taels to the main PSB office in Ho Chi Minh City, where his relations with officials were obviously good. This amount covered the trip to Haiphong and passage on a boat leaving Vietnam for his entire group, with food and water for the voyage. Officials arrived from Haiphong to escort them north, and when they set out in April 1979, they traveled on a ferry named *Unity* that was usually reserved for cadres. They joined 261 others on a motorized vessel that departed Haiphong for Hong Kong.

Refugees who managed to avoid being fleeced completely on boarding still risked being worked over again by officials before they left Vietnamese territorial waters. One sailing junk carrying 140 Sino-Vietnamese that left Haiphong in April 1979 was intercepted three times by PSB vessels. Officers snatched all valuables, including rings, tape recorders and so on. One young couple saved the husband's wedding ring and the wife's other rings only by secreting them in their mouths.

An underground organization set up to spirit people to China after Peking all but closed the border in July 1978 did limited business. Run by ethnic Chinese, it was similar to the operations that sent others across the sea, though the weight of evidence tended to suggest that the Vietnamese government was not directly involved in it. According to refugees, the organization could arrange travel by train from Ho Chi Minh City to Hanoi, and it provided documentation, guides, lodging and food along the route leading north from the capital to the border. Fees ranged from $455 to $1,136. However, interest in going to China dwindled, especially among people from southern Vietnam, when they found they would have to remain there permanently.

The use of large foreign freighters to ship out refugees in bulk was conceived by the Vietnamese authorities as a logical extension of the operation in the South, where up to 1.2 million ethnic Chinese lived in 1975, mostly in Cholon. It was a sign of official impatience. No matter how many refugees were jammed into fishing boats—some made the ocean crossing lashed to the open sides of vessels, or squatting on crammed decks, unable to move but just as assuredly unlikely to fall over—hundreds of thousands more remained in the country. And for external political reasons, the operation could not be allowed to drag on for years.

The organization of the freighters was left to state-approved ethnic-Chinese business groups such as the Rice Exporters Association of Vietnam, which had links throughout the region. According to intelligence sources, there were 54 such groups. Some of them had former members already living and working as businessmen in Singapore, Hong Kong and Taiwan. Tay Kheng Hong, who put together the *Southern Cross* and *Hai Hong* deals, was one of these outside links in an overseas-Chinese network.

Inside, one of the shadowy go-betweens used by the Vietnamese government was a certain "Mr. Lee," who became a kingpin, if not the "Mr. Big" of the entire freighter operation. A Sino-Vietnamese who was believed to have amassed a fortune in the war years, Mr. Lee nevertheless enjoyed a position of privilege with the Communist government. He usually arrived with an armed militia escort to negotiate with the captain and others on foreign freighters.

As part of an emerging routine, freighters interested in getting into the racket would make a dry run to Vietnam to check out prospects. Many of their operators were introduced to Mr.

102

Lee, who spoke Vietnamese, Mandarin, Fukien and a little Cantonese. Investigators in Hong Kong obtained photographs of Mr. Lee. They showed a typical Chinese, about 5 feet 5 inches tall, 35 to 40 years of age, of medium build and dark complexion, with a sparse mustache and wearing spectacles with plain lenses and brown plastic frames.

Indonesian naval intelligence got a glimpse of what was involved in the freighter operations when the *Southern Cross* crew were interrogated. Singaporean authorities threw more light on the matter when they detained Allan Ross, the local businessman who had traveled to Vietnam on the *Southern Cross,* and persuaded him to make a full confession. Tay Kheng Hong, in custody in Malaysia, made a statement admitting he had organized the voyages of both the *Southern Cross* and the *Hai Hong* to trade in refugees. But it was the *Huey Fong* trial in Hong Kong that revealed the racketeering in all its fascinating and incriminating detail.

In the dock were 11 men: the captain of the *Huey Fong,* 6 of his officers and 3 ethnic-Chinese businessmen, together with the son of one of them. One of the businessmen was from Vietnam. The 2 others lived in Hong Kong, but like Tay Kheng Hong, they had spent time in Vietnam. As events unfolded in court, the government of the Socialist Republic of Vietnam became, morally if not legally, an unindicted co-conspirator.

Prosecuting counsel Peter Duncan, opening his case on June 7, 1979, said the 1,700 adults among the *Huey Fong*'s 3,318 passengers had paid an average of 12 taels of gold each for the voyage from Vietnam; children under 16, 1 tael. Ten of the 12 taels for each adult had gone to the Vietnamese authorities, he said, the rest of the gold to a business syndicate for arranging the transport. With a tael of gold worth about $250 in late 1978, it could be calculated that Hanoi's share amounted to more than $4 million, over and above confiscation of property and other exactions. Police found 3,273 taels of gold valued at $800,000 hidden in the *Huey Fong*'s engine room when it reached Hong Kong.

Evidence given in the early stages of the trial pointed to an organized traffic that made use of vessels supplied by international racketeers, with the Vietnamese government shown to be a pacesetter and coordinator, displaying distinct impatience when its overseas-Chinese contacts appeared to be dragging their feet. Tiet Quoc Lien, the accused businessman from Vietnam, confirmed that the government had vigorously spurred the refugee outflow in 1978 and profited from it. When government security officials opened contact with overseas-Chinese entrepreneurs to speed up the rate of departures and put the trade on a more systematic and profitable basis, he said, Hanoi had coined the saying "You Chinese should rescue your own Chinese people."

One of the most revealing scenes was set on the second floor of a private building in Ho Chi Minh City. A witness, Kwok Wah-leung, aged 48, who was escorted from the *Huey Fong* to the room, believed to be a PSB office, vividly described the sight: Vietnamese officials sat around a table piled high with gold leaf, watches, rings, brooches, necklaces and pendants taken from the *Huey Fong*'s passengers—counting, examining, weighing and evaluating, in complete silence.

Kwok, standing about 4 feet 8 inches and known to his friends as "Kwok the Dwarf," was driven late at night to a camp by a river outside Ho Chi Minh City that was surrounded by a high barbed-wire fence and patrolled by armed guards. Every twenty minutes a truckload of miserable, pathetic persons arrived. On production of a receipt, they were allowed to board wooden junks, which took them in silent procession downstream for four hours to the 4,200-ton *Huey Fong*.

Kwok, who had traveled on what was supposed to be the last junk, said that more refugees had arrived later as junk after junk came down the river. Informed that there were more than 1,000 refugees yet to board, the captain had protested. But armed security guards had offered him 300 taels of gold, backed up with threats, to take the lot. Before the ship set sail, the captain had remarked, "There is not enough room, not even if they all stand."

Kwok testified that it was he, in liaison with Vietnamese authorities or their representatives, who had arranged with a Taiwan shipping company for the *Huey Fong* to be made available for the operation. The details were hammered out in a long series of meetings in sleazy hotels and tea shops in downtown Hong Kong, Bangkok and Taipei. Like Tay Kheng Hong before him on the *Southern Cross*, Kwok had gone to Vietnam on the

Huey Fong to rescue family members. He had succeeded in bringing out a second wife, a son and 2 younger brothers. He agreed to testify for the prosecution at the trial in return for immunity.

Kwok said that when the Panamanian-registered *Huey Fong* arrived off the coast of southern Vietnam in December 1978, it had been met by a Vietnamese government liaison group, including an unidentified "high-ranking" official and plainclothes police, aboard a gunboat, said to be a PSB vessel. Another man involved in the Vietnam end of the operation was Kwong Shuk, described as a powerful figure in western Vietnam with a record of having acted as a Viet Cong paymaster in "pre-liberation" days.

In conspiring that the *Huey Fong* would pick up the passengers and pretend they were refugees in distress, the Vietnamese authorities and the syndicate members worked out a code for use in telephone and cable communications. Passengers were referred to as "frozen ducks," the ship was "the bride" and the proposed date of the ship's arrival in Vietnam was "the wedding date." The ship purported to be on a run from Bangkok to Taiwan, and the code was part of the camouflage needed to justify its diversion to Hong Kong.

Kwok told the court of anxious telephone calls and cables received in Hong Kong from Kwong Shuk in Vietnam when the *Huey Fong* preparations had seemed to be getting bogged down. What was the use of having all the "frozen ducks" ready, Kwong had complained, if "the bride" could not get to "the wedding" on time?

So lucrative did the refugee trade become that in June 1979 Hong Kong's Information Secretary, David Ford, said it was known that the Vietnamese regarded it as a major source of foreign exchange. "Indeed, it is now said to have overtaken their largest export earner, their coal industry," he said. And if Hanoi carried through "this terrible program" until the last ethnic Chinese had been expelled, its foreign-exchange earnings would amount to a staggering $3 billion from refugees alone.

Just who was looking after the business on behalf of the Vietnamese leadership was not known for certain, though reliable information said it was an official with Politburo rank who was answerable directly to Premier Pham Van Dong. One Western intelligence report named the official as Nguyen Van Linh, who was removed early in 1978 as chairman of the committee for the transformation of private industry and trade in southern Vietnam, allegedly for incompetence. But Linh took over the Vietnam Confederation of Trade Unions, and he seemed much too busy attending overseas conferences and establishing international contacts to be devoting much time to coordinating refugee traffic at home.

A more likely name was provided by Tran Ngoc Chau, one of the best-known dissidents from the days of the Thieu regime and a former national assemblyman. Chau, who had fought with the Viet Minh against the French but later had broken with the Communists, had been imprisoned by Thieu because of contacts with his brother, who had sided with Hanoi. After escaping from Vietnam with his wife and 5 of their 7 children in mid-1979, Chau said he had received information from former comrades who were currently ranking cadres with access to policymaking in Hanoi. They had told him that the overall refugee operation was the responsibility of Interior Minister Tran Quoc Hoan.[2]

FIVE

Nguyen Dinh Thuy searched for alternative escape routes. One surfaced in the form of the Vietnamese government's unannounced decision in mid-1978 to permit ethnic Chinese to leave by boat. It was no secret that Sino-Vietnamese were welcome to go, if they could afford the fee. There was hope for ethnic Vietnamese such as Thuy as well, though they would have to go through the farce of pretending to be ethnic Chinese.

Middlemen took care of everything. In February 1979, Thuy handed an ethnic-Chinese organizer a first installment of 32.5 taels of gold, which was valued at more than $9,500 on the world market: 13 taels for himself, 13 for his wife and 6.5 taels for their daughter, Nguyen Dinh Phi Phuong, aged 14. Their 6-year-old son, Nguyen Dinh Long, did not have to pay. The price covered false identity papers to show they were Sino-Vietnamese, as well as their passage to Malaysia. Thuy became Ngo Bao Thoai and, fearful that something

107

would go wrong, took the trouble to learn how to write his new name in Chinese characters.

Nguyen Thi Phi Yen's decision to accompany her husband and family was the subject of emotional torment. The night before departure, they talked it over again. On balance she was inclined to go, but at times she wavered. Thuy decided to take no chances. On the morning of the escape, he drove her to his mother's house so that his mother could keep watch on her. Although their marriage was far from perfect, he remembered that his father had died when he was very young, and he did not want his children to grow up motherless. . . .

ON THE HONG KONG waterfront near the end of the central commercial district stands an unlikely building known by various names. The confusion over its identity is understandable. The first floor is a police station, above that is a multistory car park, and the top levels serve as headquarters for the Hong Kong government's Marine Department. But the building had an additional function that was less obvious. It housed, within the Marine Department, one of the most secret, and most effective, commercial spy operations ever put together in Asia.

This was the Refugee Ship Unit. Under the command of a sturdy Irishman named Tim Frawley, the aggressive little unit had one of the key assignments in the vast refugee drama unfolding in Asia: stopping the big boats. To do this it employed traditional cloak-and-dagger tactics supported by a battery of modern electronic equipment.

The story of the Refugee Ship Unit was never fully told. Yet it waged all-out war on the refugee syndicates and their Vietnamese collaborators from one end of the world to the other. It was an unorthodox response to an unusual problem that probably could have come only from Hong Kong, itself rather unique as a prospering colony in an anticolonial era.

Concern voiced by Australia, at the time of the *Hai Hong*'s voyage, about organized trafficking in refugees was shared not only by Hong Kong but by nations throughout Asia: A succession of packed freighters, as Canberra had noted, threatened to swamp countries of first asylum and upset existing resettlement programs. If this happened, Vietnam's neighbors, which had to pick up that country's human rejects, would be the chief victims in terms of lost opportunities—housing, jobs and social services—for their own residents.

True, it might be safer for Vietnamese to leave their country in a large ship rather than a leaking fishing boat. But the freighters already were encouraging other nations in the invidious course of differentiating between genuine refugees and illegal immigrants—those apparently poor who traveled in small boats as opposed to those who could afford to bribe corrupt cadres and purchase their passage. Such a division was bureaucratic nonsense, since wealthy persons also arrived on small boats, and many of the so-called genuine refugees paid just as much to leave as freighter passengers. If the first-asylum nations nevertheless insisted on making the distinction and refused to accept Vietnamese, as had Indonesia and Malaysia with the *Hai Hong*, it would be the refugees themselves who became the ultimate losers.

To allow the freighters to continue thus seemed in the interest of no party, except perhaps Hanoi and the organizing syndicates. First-asylum countries could do little about Hanoi, for the time being at least, but they came down hard on the syndicates. They found it intolerable that "those who traffic in human misery," as Hong Kong's Chief Secretary Sir Jack Cater put it, should be allowed to profit while distorting the tradition of the sea that victims of shipwrecks be rescued. Boat people were floundering all over the South China Sea, but only those loaded at pickup points in Vietnam after paying were being offered space on the syndicate freighters. Those in distress at sea could drown—as many did—as far as the syndicates were concerned.

Independently but no doubt influencing each other, first-asylum countries for boat people adopted a double-barreled approach to discourage the successors to the *Hai Hong* and *Southern Cross*. The first barrel was aimed at the refugees: they had to be taught, so that the word would filter back to Vietnam, that a passage on an organized freighter was a ticket to nowhere but the end of the queue. The second was directed at the operators: they stood to make fortunes from the trade in human cargo, but in the future they also must risk spending years behind bars and losing the lot.

In handling the *Huey Fong*, which dropped anchor outside Hong Kong on December 23, 1978, the government insisted on the principle that shipwreck survivors rescued by oceangoing vessels should be landed at the first scheduled port of call. For the *Huey Fong*, en route from Bangkok to Taiwan, this was Kaohsiung, but the ship refused to move. For almost a month the authorities resupplied the vessel and airlifted out the sick and pregnant for medical attention. Then, on January 19, 1979, the captain entered the harbor on two clear conditions: the ship's entry would not be opposed, but he would be charged in court.

By this time, the government had rushed through legislation to deal with the *Huey Fong* and to deter others. The Merchant Shipping (Amendment) Bill of 1979 increased prison sentences, from six months to four years, for masters and owners carrying excess passengers. It put the burden of proof on them to show that excess passengers were shipwreck survivors. It also added provisions for the forfeiture of ships carrying excess passengers. The package included two other bills, one providing for a fine of up to $40,000 and four years' imprisonment for disabling, abandoning, scuttling or beaching a vessel in Hong Kong waters "without reasonable excuse."

Making use of the new laws, police charged Captain Hsu Wen-hsin, aged 52, 6 of his officers, 3 businessmen and the son of one of them over the *Huey Fong*'s voyage. After a protracted trial and appeals, Hsu, the 6 officers and 1 businessman stood convicted.

Hong Kong gave a similarly hostile reception to the 3,506-ton Panamanian-registered *Skyluck*, which slipped into the harbor just after midnight on February 7, 1979, carrying 2,651 Vietnamese. It was towed to an outlying island, where it remained for almost five months, despite a mass protest swim and a hunger strike by its passengers. When the anchor chains were deliberately cut and it drifted ashore, Captain Hsiao Hung-ping, aged 42, and 4 of his officers were charged with conspiracy, though they beat the charges on a technicality.

As Hong Kong law-enforcement agencies continued to prosecute others involved in the organized transport of Vietnamese, the government backed them up by considerably stiffening penalties for refugee racketeers. Under the Immigration (Amendment) (No. 3) Bill of 1979, the owner, agent, captain and crew of a ship carrying illegal immigrants to Hong Kong, and anyone helping make arrangements for the voyage, were liable to a fine of $1 million and imprisonment for life. It put the refugee trade on a par with drug trafficking.

The Philippines likewise resisted when the 1,235-ton Panamanian-registered *Tung An* appeared on December 27, 1978, with 2,300 Vietnamese aboard and the usual tattered tale about rescue on the high seas. While providing a landing ship to give the passengers more room, the government refused to allow them ashore except for emergency medical treatment. The dilapidated *Tung An* remained anchored in Manila Bay for more than seven months, under constant threat of expulsion. The United States and other major resettlement countries were reluctant to take the refugees because they did not want to encourage queue-jumping from large ships, as had happened with the *Hai Hong*. Priority in resettlement was given to those already in camps. By the time the *Tung An* was authorized to discharge its passengers, 905 were still aboard. Although a criminal court ruled that the ship's captain, Sheu Dah-shing, aged 36, and his 17 crew members were not guilty of importing refugees into the Philippines, the government fined the *Tung An* for immigration-law violations.

Malaysia did its bit with the *Hai Hong* by holding for six months on board the vessel at Port Klang Captain Serigar; his 15 crew members; Tay Kheng Hong, the organizer of the trip to Vietnam, and his employee Lee Sam. The crew were then allowed to return home to Indonesia, but Captain Serigar, Tay and Lee were taken ashore and locked up under the Internal Security Act of 1960, which provides for detention without trial.

Malaysian authorities hesitated to take the 3 men to court because they were likely to beat the only charge that could be brought against them. The possible loophole was the claim that the Vietnamese passengers had forced them to go to Port Klang. In mid 1981 Tay alone was still detained, still not charged. The ship itself was confiscated and, little more than a rusting hulk at that stage, was put up for sale as scrap.*

However, all of this action was essentially defensive, designed to punish those who hauled fare-paying refugees from

---

* Sold in May 1981, the *Hai Hong* sank as it attempted to leave Malaysia.

Vietnam as an example to others who might be tempted to try it. But with potential returns so high, there was obviously no guarantee that more would not join the racket. It was almost certain that they would. Hong Kong, which was becoming the prime goal for boat people, wanted the odds against the criminals narrowed further. It wanted an offensive to dissuade them. It wanted them stopped.

Hong Kong's answer was the formation of the innocuous-sounding Refugee Ship Unit, which was known to the few who had any dealings with it as the RSU. Its sole task was to identify suspect vessels and to take preemptive action to stop them from trafficking in refugees. In keeping with its undercover nature and low profile, no formal announcement was made when it was put together in February 1979. It subsequently received little publicity.

Tim Frawley had the right temperament and training to head the RSU. For some years he had been, in civil-service terminology, "senior marine officer, ocean shipping control," which translates as Hong Kong's harbor master, responsible for the movement of ships into and out of the colony. But Frawley also had once been employed by the U.K. Home Office, where his function had involved security. Three other men, with similar specialties, were recruited in Britain for the RSU. Others were seconded from other duties in the Marine Department.

The RSU was able to remain almost invisible because its members continued to perform some of their ordinary departmental functions. Frawley, for example, remained in his office, Room 1032, as harbor master. All correspondence from the RSU, like other letters from the department, went out in the name of the "Director of Marine." All telegraphic traffic from the RSU bore the Marine Department's cable address and call sign, "MARDEP HONG KONG."

Who gave the RSU its authority, and precisely what were its instructions and budget, were never disclosed. But approval almost certainly came from the very top. And its orders clearly were to stop the big ships—at just about all costs. The one qualification, presumably: Don't slip up and don't get caught.

It was quite a challenge. Ships in Asia regularly disappear—some scuttled for the insurance money, others just dropping out of sight to run a little dope, collect a little contraband.

112

Such vessels change ownership with bewildering speed, names even faster. Today's *Fairweather* becomes tomorrow's *Lucky Lion* for no other reason than to bring a change in joss, or fortune. And they fly flags of convenience, registered in Panama, Liberia, Honduras, when their owners live in Hong Kong, Taiwan, Japan.

The changes are sometimes made on paper only, and are designed to confuse as well as to conceal the identity of the owners. Vessels are frequently spun through a web of interlocking companies. Where it is possible to trace these concerns, the trail often ends in a tiny office, no more than a cubicle, where a junior clerk sits with a note pad taking phone messages.

With a free hand, often operating outside the law, RSU agents roamed Asia trying to penetrate the seamier side of regional shipping. A network was established that provided both information and supporting photographs. Word arrived from many points, including Vietnam. Frawley's ability to read Chinese and speak the Cantonese dialect helped, since the syndicates were almost exclusively overseas Chinese. The emphasis was on results rather than the niceties of diplomacy and protocol. The RSU took no one to court.

As part of their undercover work, RSU operatives tapped phones, raided premises at night and confiscated documents, and hassled otherwise legitimate businessmen who were being tempted to enter the refugee trade. Ship owners and agents on the verge of becoming racketeers were invited in for a chat. The tactic was to let them sit for half an hour or more in an empty room with photos of the *Huey Fong, Skyluck* and other well-known syndicate ships plastered on the walls—perhaps with a shot of their own vessel completing the lineup. If they did not acknowledge that the game was up, the extent of the RSU's knowledge of their involvement in planning refugee operations was made known to them—a little at a time. If they still did not seem convinced that they ought to pull out, they might be presented with tape recordings of all their phone calls for the previous month.

The RSU's capabilities were considerably enhanced by a dazzling array of sophisticated equipment, much of it acquired by the government for search-and-rescue purposes but with some added just for Frawley's team. It included a powerful radio

113

receiver with a range of 8,000 miles that could effortlessly sweep Asia. It was possible to listen in to cabdrivers chatting in downtown Tokyo, to overhear Citizens Band radio operators in Taiwan, kids chatting on walkie-talkies in Singapore and aircraft receiving landing instructions in Indonesia—all with hi-fi sensitivity and in the comfort of an office in the Marine Department headquarters in Hong Kong.

More to the point, the receiver could pick up the regular Morse Code broadcasts by Ho Chi Minh City port authorities allocating wharf space and pilots to ships anchored off Vung Tau waiting to enter the old southern capital. It could also monitor radiotelephone calls from any merchant ship in Asia to its owner's or agent's offices ashore. So sensitive was the equipment that a telephone ringing in a Tokyo apartment, from a call placed from a ship in Hong Kong harbor, sounded as if it were emanating from a phone in the same room as its eavesdroppers in Hong Kong. It made it possible to hear someone breathing thousands of miles away.

The RSU used other gear as well. Its equally powerful radio transmitter had impressive jamming ability, should it ever be needed. For telephone tapping, the RSU had a portable box of tricks, looking like an innocent heavy-duty luggage trunk, which could be thrown into the back of a car. The box could intercept both parties to a call with crystal clarity up to half a mile away. Some of the office phones used by the RSU for business were permanently bugged. Gadgetry was available to recall phone conversations for instant replay.

The entire results of the electronic-surveillance program mounted by the RSU, including round-the-clock monitoring of frequencies of special interest as well as phone calls, were fed into a master tape-recording unit kept under lock and key. This machine, recording simultaneously on 29 tracks—28 of them for information, the other noting the time down to one-tenth of a second—consumed one complete spool of tape in twenty-four hours. Then another one took over—automatically.

The RSU operated with the knowledge of other Western intelligence services but independently of them. Information was sometimes passed on, but it was felt in Hong Kong that the RSU, to be effective, had to maintain complete control over its

114

own operations. The others, with a multitude of other interests, could not afford to be so specialized.

Although not much was known of the RSU's operations, it obtained many of its leads from dogged legwork, painstakingly tracking rogue vessels from one port to the next, watching for signs of odd behavior which might signal that a consignment of refugees was next on the manifest. With the better-run harbors of the region, such as Singapore's, the movement of ships in and out was published daily by the port authority. At, say, a port in Burma, the RSU would simply tune in to the port authorities calling or clearing a particular vessel. Tip-offs were occasionally received by the Marine Department. But a recurring clue for the RSU was a ship listing an intended destination and failing to show up there.

The paperwork for the RSU's operations was considerable. At one stage the Port of Singapore Authority protested—by letter—that it was blowing its budget answering so many routine inquiries by telex from Hong Kong. The compromise was for port-authority officials to place the information in a sealed envelope and pass it to the RSU's Singapore representative. For confidential messages, the RSU used a code. Digits, for instance, might refer to ships, while letters of the alphabet designated locations, depending on their frequency and sequence. A different code was used for every operation.

Within eight months the RSU had fingered 90 to 100 dodgy vessels and compiled files on maritime companies, owners, agents and other outfits and individuals likely to get mixed up in refugee trafficking. Although some of the ships had been engaged previously in other illegal activities such as drug running and smuggling, most were in the hands of opportunistic businessmen lured by gold.

The results were published weekly in a confidential "RSU Suspect Vessel Report," which circulated to everyone who counted in the Hong Kong government, and to British embassies and high commissions, especially in Southeast Asia. If the circumstances were judged appropriate, the results were leaked through diplomatic channels to host governments. Such was the case with Singapore and the *Tonan Maru*.

Alerted by the inclusion of the 3,500-ton Japanese-registered *Tonan Maru* in the "RSU Suspect Vessel Report," Singaporean authorities smashed a local syndicate planning to get into the refugee racket. It consisted of 4 Singaporeans and 2 businessmen from Taiwan, who were conspiring with an Indonesian Chinese contact in Vietnam to transport 15,000 refugees out of the country in three batches. The takings were being calculated at $6.9 million, with the syndicate due to collect $2.8 million of it.

A bonus for the Singaporean government was that the *Tonan Maru* case, through Allan Ross, led back to the *Southern Cross.* They detained and held without trial both Ross and Chong Chai Kok, the managing director of Seng Bee Shipping, who had lined up the *Southern Cross* for its Vietnam excursion and had been involved in the *Hai Hong*'s voyage. Sven Olof Ahlqvist, the Finnish sea captain who had also played an active part in the *Southern Cross* venture, was pulled in and had his employment pass cancelled.

The episode also yielded valuable propaganda for Singapore. Armed with a detailed statement by Allan Ross about his trip to Ho Chi Minh City on the *Southern Cross* and other evidence, it was able to proclaim the "complicity of Vietnamese authorities" in both cases.

In most instances, however, Hong Kong's RSU opted to be self-reliant, to handle the situation itself. Not all countries could be counted on to act with the same determined, if not ruthless, dispatch and efficiency as Singapore. And even in the case of Singapore, the RSU preferred to see to it personally that syndicates abandoned their nefarious schemes.

A typical operation for the RSU involved a combination oceangoing tug, the *Tomi Maru 11,* and huge barge, designated Y.C. 3001, which was designed to transport heavy earth-moving equipment. Registered in Japan, the powerful 144-ton tug, manned by a crew of 10, was not capable of carrying many refugees. But it was estimated that the 3,000-ton barge in tandem with it could hold as many as 5,000.

A regional syndicate, which had lines out on seven vessels that might be used to trade in refugees at any time, was suspected of planning to load the barge with Vietnamese and cast it adrift in waters to the south of Hong Kong. This would have been a clever ploy, a way around the growing opposition to large freighters in Hong Kong, because Hong Kong authorities would have been obligated to coordinate the rescue of anyone in distress, refugees or otherwise. Hong Kong's designated rescue area extends some 380 miles northeast from the colony to the coast of Taiwan, and 430 miles south and east to the Philippine island of Luzon.

Later, the Hong Kong government would close the loop-hole with the Immigration (Amendment) (No. 3) Bill, which made it a serious offense for anyone assisting illegal immigrants to reach waters outside Hong Kong from which they were likely to enter the colony. But when the RSU was tipped off in March 1979 by a seaman, the proposed ploy was alarming, providing further evidence that the syndicates had not slackened at all in their quest for the pots of gold at the end of the Vietnamese rainbow.

In a hastily scrawled letter in Chinese, the seaman said that he and others had been hired on an emergency basis by a Hong Kong agent and flown to Singapore. But they had resigned when they were informed by a company representative that they were bound for Vietnam to collect refugees. Even before the tip-off, the RSU had the tug/barge combination tagged: when it cleared Hong Kong it had listed Kota Kinabalu, in Sabah, as its next destination; it surfaced instead in Singapore.

The author of the letter, who listed his seaman's registration number, was checked out and interviewed. The trail led to Bangkok, where a newly established company run by a Sino-Thai had recently acquired control of the tug. Then the scent faded. The tug/barge sat for months in Singapore harbor, where it was photographed for the RSU. Nothing happened until late in June when the RSU, in its mysterious way, acquired possession of documents showing the links between seven suspect vessels and two companies, one of them the Hong Kong–based concern that had hired the seamen for the tug/barge. After a chat with a local representative of the company, the RSU became convinced that the syndicate would not go through with its plan. Frawley's faith in the instinct for survival, if not in human nature, was well founded.

Despite its undoubted successes, the RSU did not win every round. The refugee runners, for example, scored an initial victory when they managed to get 1,433 Vietnamese into Hong

Kong aboard the *Seng Cheong*, which was little more than floating scrap.

The 387-ton *Seng Cheong*, which had started life in the early 1960s with a Japanese name and had become successively the *Flying Dragon*, the *Tai Sang* and the *Tyler*, had a record of suspected smuggling, especially around Vietnam during the war years. In recent times it had engaged in legitimate trading between Hong Kong and Macao, the Portuguese territory on the Chinese coast 40 miles to the southwest. According to a tip-off, it had left Macao under tow for repairs in Hong Kong on March 18, 1979. But once at sea it had separated from its tug and set out under its own power. It had never arrived in Hong Kong.

RSU intelligence indicated that the *Seng Cheong* was in Vietnam: a vessel of its dimensions was reported loading refugees. Nothing further had been heard of it. Suspecting that it had embarked fully laden, Hong Kong authorities used aerial surveillance in an effort to detect it. The Marine Department sent out precautionary radio messages pointing out that the *Seng Cheong* had not received permission to enter Hong Kong. But there was no acknowledgment of the messages, no sign of the vessel.

On May 26, the *Seng Cheong*, several letters of its name on the stern crudely blacked out so that it read *"Sen On,"* was spotted by marine police cutting into Hong Kong territory through Chinese waters across the Pearl River estuary. Challenged, it abruptly changed course and rammed full speed ashore on an outlying island. The refugees leaped joyfully onto the beach. Dismayed police discovered that the captain and 11 crew members had disappeared the night before on a fishing vessel at the mouth of the Pearl River, no doubt heading for the sanctuary of Macao.

The *Seng Cheong* was in abominable shape. So badly rusted that refugees could see through the hull in places, it was ankle-deep in human excrement and filth. A single-hold vessel, it had makeshift tween decks crudely welded below, using wooden props, reminiscent of a coal mine of the last century. The organizers had planned to pack 600 to 700 passengers into the 160-foot freighter, but under Vietnamese pressure, somehow or other, 1,433 human beings were crushed and squeezed aboard. Little wonder that one observer in Hong Kong was reported by a

U.S. House of Representatives fact-finding mission comparing Vietnamese refugee boats to the slave ships from Africa depicted in the television epic *Roots*.

It turned out that when the *Seng Cheong* had dropped out of sight during the aerial search, it was aground in China, where it had remained for weeks while the hull and propeller were repaired.

A year after the *Seng Cheong* burst into Hong Kong, marine police brought charges against 9 persons in connection with its trip to Vietnam. A court freed them after finding discrepancies in the evidence of 2 witnesses who testified in return for immunity. However, an appeals court reversed the ruling, and 4 were convicted, in a retrial, of conspiring to aid and abet illegal immigrants to enter Hong Kong.

The RSU usually notched up more clear-cut victories. One ship called the *Lucky Dragon* and another named the *Sea View* did nothing but go to Vietnam empty and return empty. But their experience showed that Hanoi was vulnerable to pressure—not the outcry of a morally enraged international community, but quiet diplomatic representation backed up with a touch of the strong-arm stuff in which the RSU specialized.

The 7,488-ton *Lucky Dragon*, registered in Panama, was giving the newly formed RSU heartburn. After a dry run to Vietnam, it returned to Singapore before setting out empty once more, listing Hong Kong as its destination. A check showed that it had loaded 424 tons of fresh water for the trip.

When a request for details of the voyage and its crew strength brought no response from the *Lucky Dragon* at sea, the Hong Kong Marine Department sought information from the Singaporean authorities. It also employed the tactic of issuing a standard overdue-vessel cable that goes out to all shipping. The vessel had departed Singapore on February 26, 1979, the cable noted, and its whereabouts was causing concern. "ANY VESSELS SIGHTING THE LUCKY DRAGON ARE REQUESTED TO ADVISE MARDEP HONG KONG AT THE EARLIEST OPPORTUNITY."

With nothing to show for its efforts, the Hong Kong government began aerial surveillance and, through Britain, raised the matter with the Vietnamese government. The press was informed, and the movements of the *Lucky Dragon* became the subject of public speculation. On March 2, the *South China*

119

Morning Post, a Hong Kong daily, quoted John Slimming, the government's Director of Information Services, as saying that the *Lucky Dragon* had been seen off the central Vietnamese port of Danang before returning to Singapore for its voyage to Hong Kong. "There are reasons to suspect that this ship may be planning a rendezvous in Vietnamese waters to pick up fare-paying passengers," he said.

Although the *Lucky Dragon* was not known to have done anything illegal, its Hong Kong agent, an active and apparently successful company, did not enjoy being quizzed by the RSU about the vessel. The company resigned as agent "in view of the adverse publicity," informing the Marine Department of its decision, as it was required to do by law.

Meanwhile, the RSU's cables brought results. An Indian ship, the *Jalayayini,* reported the *Lucky Dragon* off the northern Philippines in the early afternoon of March 6. It was heading north at about 10 knots, and though it did not reply to a visual signal or answer a radio call, it appeared to be sailing normally.

A northerly course would take the *Lucky Dragon* to Taiwan, but if its destination was still Hong Kong, it could cut northwesterly along a freighter channel without difficulty. Hong Kong decided to take no chances. Apart from requesting information from other ships in the area, it sent a cable to the *Lucky Dragon* warning that it had been refused permission to enter Hong Kong waters.

The RSU also wanted to get in touch with the owner of the *Lucky Dragon.* But the only name it had on record was that of a Panamanian-registered company, Hong Choon Hing Enterprises S.A., which was of little use. Investigators noticed, however, that the former agent's telex of resignation had been sent to the owner at an address in Singapore, not Panama. A check showed that the telex number was registered in the name of Thunderbird Pte., Ltd.

On March 7 the Marine Department sent a telex to Thunderbird containing a single sentence asking the company to advise immediately the name of its Hong Kong agents for "YOUR VESSEL LUCKY DRAGON." This simple inquiry elicited an extraordinary, 217-word reply by telex the following day, in which Thunderbird claimed the loss of $5 million of business because the vessel had been linked in the press to refugee trafficking and threatened to sue for defamation anyone spreading such "FALSE INFORMATION."

The following day, however, the *Lucky Dragon* arrived at Kaohsiung, and within two weeks it was broken up for scrap.

The tracking of the 2,152-ton *Sea View* started with a small Hong Kong shipping broker and sometime agent, whose activities caught the attention of the RSU. Registered as usual in Panama and owned by Taiwan interests, the eighteen-year-old general-cargo vessel had been cleared by the agent from Hong Kong on May 7, 1979. Its stated destination was Bangkok, but inquiries showed that it had never turned up there.

Further investigations suggested that the *Sea View*, with a Hong Kong captain and a crew of 20 from Taiwan, was already in southern Vietnam. On June 15, the RSU sent a radio message to the ship, asking that it give its position, course and speed. No answer was received. Soon after, however, the RSU confirmed that the ship was anchored about 16 miles up the main channel of the Saigon River, halfway between the sea and Ho Chi Minh City. Later the vessel moved closer to the river mouth, where the RSU managed to obtain a photograph of it. According to separate information, 5,000 refugees were preparing to board the vessel.

Adopting its usual tactics, the RSU began pressuring the agent, warning of nasty consequences if refugees appeared in Hong Kong on the *Sea View*. To turn up the heat, it cabled the master of the *Sea View* that he had been refused permission to enter Hong Kong waters. At the same time it cabled the owner of the vessel in Taipei with the same message and demanded to know "IMMEDIATELY" the *Sea View*'s whereabouts.

Although nothing was heard from the ship or the owner, within days the Marine Department's Port Control received a letter from the agent in Hong Kong. The company was giving up the agency for the *Sea View*, which it had taken on less than seven weeks earlier. In the letter, dated June 19, it said the owner's instructions were that the vessel proceed to Bangkok to collect a full shipment of maize for Taiwan. "To our surprise," the company said, it had learned that the ship might be contemplating picking up refugees near Ho Chi Minh City. "Apparently, the owner had given us false instruction when asking us to clear the vessel for Bangkok," the letter added.

121

Still no word from the owner; still nothing from the ship. Weeks passed. Hong Kong decided to switch to the open-confrontation tactics it had tested with the *Lucky Dragon*. In London, the Foreign Office summoned Le Ky Giai, Vietnam's chargé d'affaires, laid the facts on him and expressed serious concern. Giai fulminated, refused to accept the case and accused Britain of inflammatory conduct in its relations with Vietnam.

But within days, on July 13, the master of the *Sea View* broke his two-month silence to cable the former Hong Kong agent: "NO CARGO, FORCED SAILING. WE ARE AWAITING THE ORDER FOR NEXT PORT."

The protest to the Vietnamese had brought quick results, but the key question was whether the *Sea View* was carrying 5,000 refugees, its disclaimer about cargo to the agent notwithstanding. The Hong Kong Marine Department asked the ship to report immediately its last port of call, present position, course and speed. Back came the answer the same day, July 14: "POSITION 112 DEGREES, 12 MINUTES EAST, 10 DEGREES, 56 MINUTES NORTH. LAST PORT MUI VUNG TAU, VIETNAM. COURSE 013, SPEED 6.5 KNOTS."

The 013 course meant almost north, toward Hong Kong. But were there refugees aboard, in bigger numbers than the world had ever seen on one ship from Vietnam?

On July 16 the department again asked the *Sea View* for its position, course and speed. This time, though, it pointedly requested the ship's "NEXT PORT OF CALL AND TOTAL NUMBER OF PERSONS ON BOARD."

The reply, in the name of the ship's master, on July 17, raised a wry smile or two at the RSU: "COURSE TO TAIWAN. TWENTY CREWS [*sic*]. NOTHING ON BOARD. DON'T WORRY TOO MUCH. HAVE A GOOD TIME."

SIX

WHATEVER THEIR MOTIVATION for fleeing, in whichever direction they ran, however they chose to escape, the refugees of Indochina with few exceptions came to rest in neighboring countries. In theory it was first, or temporary, asylum they sought while they waited for conditions to settle before returning home, or prepared for a new life abroad. With Vietnam, Laos and Kampuchea spewing out people in all directions, refugee camps became a feature of the landscape in East and Southeast Asia. But the theory started to go awry as arrivals overwhelmed departures and the camps assumed a permanence that few had anticipated, none desired.

The influx created such serious problems that it threatened the stability of Southeast Asia. At different stages the flows, particularly to Thailand and Malaysia, took on massive proportions. With Kampucheans and Laotians arriving at the rate of 17,000 a month in 1979, Thailand's Prime Minister, Kriangsak

123

Chomanand, complained to a U.S. House of Representatives delegation that the country was being not only flooded but "drowned."

It was not just a matter of numbers. The mass movement of people disturbed highly complex ethnic balances. Southeast Asia is a kaleidoscope of different groups. They are distinguished by racial characteristics, as with overseas Indians and Chinese. But they are also separated by subtler differences in language, religion and social organization, sometimes combined with various political affiliations, economic livelihood and status, and ties across national borders and even abroad.[1]

With events of 1975 splitting the region into Communist and non-Communist blocs, ideology was also a factor, though the disputes among the practicing Marxists of Asia confused that too. The fighting—initially between Vietnam and Kampuchea, then Vietnamese troops and their Kampuchean allies against other Kampucheans, followed by the China–Vietnam clash—added a military and strategic aspect. And behind the immediate causes loomed the larger issue of Sino–Soviet rivalry. The whole drama was played out against a background of ongoing Communist insurgency in each of the countries sheltering refugees, providing a security element that also could not be ignored.

ASEAN member countries ruled out providing permanent homes for the refugees on any significant scale. Although local settlement is often the ideal solution for refugees, harsh realities prohibited it in Southeast Asia. The possibility never existed except in the dreams of some international relief officials and others. The developing states of ASEAN had limited resources and were in a fairly fragile stage of nation building that accompanies the first generation of independence, Singapore's relatively high per capita income notwithstanding.

Singapore was at one extreme: a city-state and small island with a population of only 2.3 million and in need of imported labor to keep its factories producing at capacity. But with a total land area of a mere 227 square miles, it was hardly an ideal dumping ground for tens of thousands of people. The government allowed the first wave of refugee boats into Singapore harbor in 1975, even accepting a symbolic 200 fishermen for residency, but that was the limit. At the other extreme was

124

Indonesia, the world's fifth-most-populous nation with 135 million people of its own that it had difficulty feeding and housing, combined with severe overcrowding on the key island of Java that a transmigration program had failed to correct.

The Philippines, with a population of 43 million, and Thailand, with 44 million, were certainly not short of people either. Manila accepted about 600 refugees from Vietnam with Philippine family ties, but drew the line at that token gesture.

Malaysia, relatively rich in resources and with a population of 12 million and some open spaces, might have been a possibility but for other factors that were not so tangible but just as real. In a country where Islam is the state religion and all Malay are Moslems under the constitution, the government accepted several thousand Cham, the Kampuchean Moslems, as residents. It said no Vietnamese would be allowed to stay permanently, because the additional numbers would upset finely tuned calculations on which poverty eradication and economic and social restructuring exercises rested. Government leaders specifically denied it, but there was little doubt they feared a backlash from Malay if non-Moslems, especially ethnic Chinese, were permitted to settle. It did not go unnoticed that the government allowed 70,000 to 130,000 Filipino Moslems to take refuge semipermanently in Sabah from 1972.

Much as one might lament anti-Chinese sentiment in Malaysia, Indonesia and to a lesser extent the Philippines and Thailand, it was a potent force nevertheless and had to be acknowledged. Anti-Vietnamese and anti–hill-tribe feeling in Thailand was a similar fact of life. To enforce a program of accommodation in support of a principle, no matter how noble, could be an act of gross irresponsibility, given the potential for racial conflict.

Despite these sensitivities, Thailand was a possible exception to the blanket ban on permanent settlement. The right combination of refugees, location, goodwill and extensive foreign aid might just produce results. Unofficially, it had already happened to a limited extent. As noted earlier, an estimated 60,000 refugees—40,000 from Laos, 20,000 from Kampuchea—had evaded authorities over four years and gone to live with friends and relatives in Thailand. The ones who counted on staying permanently were predominantly lowland Lao, and they usually put down roots in the more remote border areas. Some managed to obtain identification papers and were effectively integrating. But others could not get papers, and they found themselves and their children shut out. Some of them began drifting, reluctantly, to refugee camps in early 1980.

When U.S. Vice President Walter Mondale visited Thailand in 1978, he offered $2 million for a formal study of local settlement opportunities. Many senior Thai officials privately accepted that considerable numbers of refugees eventually would remain in the country. But they refused to entertain the idea as policy until the influx abated, or the overall problem had been brought under control. Among other things, they were worried that they might attract more refugees and that developed nations might slacken their resettlement efforts.

Historical animosity between the Thai and the Vietnamese seemed to preclude the possibility of either the overland ethnic Vietnamese or those who arrived in Thailand by boat being able to remain. Thai officials suggested that when local resettlement eventuated, it was likely to be considered only in the underdeveloped north and northeast. But even in these politically sensitive regions there were formidable obstacles, including a limited number of suitable sites where settlers could become economically self-sustaining. Thai peasant resentment of any aid for refugees also had to be taken into account.

For the hill tribes such as the Hmong, resettlement in the north, which had similar terrain and climate to that in their home areas of Laos, might have appeared logical. But there were objections on two specific grounds. Their resettlement in large numbers would aggravate serious deforestation caused by the traditional slash-and-burn cultivation of hill tribes already in the area. And the powerful Thai military viewed the refugees as an increased security threat in a region troubled by armed Communist insurgency that had its base in disaffected hill tribes. Insurgency was even more serious in the northeast, where it was open to support from Laos and indirectly from Vietnam.

An American government study tentatively concluded that initial Thai resettlement activity would be in the northeast. "The vast majority—perhaps 75%—of refugees who might eventually be permanently resettled will likely be lowland Lao and Khmer, who share a common linguistic and cultural heri-

tage with [the] local population in the Northeast," it said.*
". . . Most of the Hmong will probably be settled in the mountainous North, or in remote districts of Loei and Nong Khai provinces."[2]

Temporary asylum was a different matter. Most refugees managed to find shelter, though they were scarcely welcome in Southeast Asia. Only Singapore turned them away from the start. But as the impact of their presence was felt over time, and as the influx showed no signs of slowing while more distant and affluent nations demonstrated a marked reluctance to share the burden, they were greeted with hostility elsewhere as well.

Since UNHCR picked up the tab for feeding and sheltering the refugees, theoretically it did not cost first-asylum countries anything to look after them. Indeed, millions of dollars poured in from refugee-related spending. UNHCR's funds covered the construction of camps and the daily purchase of tons of rice, vegetables, fish and meat, all from local suppliers. In 1979, the agency disbursed about $35 million in Malaysia, $23 million in Thailand, $13 million in Indonesia and $1.7 million in the Philippines. It budgeted for increases in 1980 in all countries except Malaysia.

UNHCR spending was boosted by what resettlement countries committed, for land and air transport for the refugees and numerous other items. Then there was the spending by the refugees themselves. The boat people quickly converted to local currency any gold that had survived robbery attempts as they fled. Some refugees, particularly the Vietnamese, also received remittances from relatives and friends abroad. Remittances to Thailand's Nong Khai camp alone were estimated at $50,000 a month in 1979 and early 1980. Malaysia, however, did not permit remittances, and it attempted to limit refugee spending by temporarily confiscating their savings.

Apparent gains by host economies, however, were more than offset by costs elsewhere. Black-marketeering and corruption flourished; wages for local labor were undercut, at least in Thailand, and the social dislocation generated political pressures. Some camps were increasingly occupied by uprooted people with little or no future. This was especially true in Thai-

* Khmer and Thai are in fact separate language families.

127

land, where tens of thousands of overland refugees languished for several years without any prospect of resettlement. The danger was that this sort of misery, squalor and hopelessness would turn the camps into breeding grounds of discontent.

A report prepared by the U.S. Embassy in Bangkok concluded that the refugees reaching Thailand—148,000 by the end of 1977, 215,000 by 1978 and 410,000 by 1979—had imposed strains on the country and set it back. "In trying to cope with the problems forced upon it from outside its borders, the government has been unable to devote adequate attention and resources to some of its long-standing internal problems," it said.

Part of the problem was that the refugees concentrated in some of the most vulnerable locations. In Thailand, the large majority of Laotians crossed the border into the chronically depressed north and northeast. While the spending on refugees in these localities enabled some Thai to prosper, it also brought widespread resentment. Feeling the backlash, the government turned down millions of dollars of aid offered by UNHCR because it was unwilling to see the standard of living in refugee camps improved beyond that of its own rural poor. The point was driven home when it was discovered that local Thai were admitting themselves to camps as refugees, some even being resettled abroad. Consequently, UNHCR was spending only about 25 cents a day to support each refugee in the 16 camps it sponsored in Thailand in 1979, compared with $1 a day for each refugee in Malaysia.

The situation in the north and northeast was exacerbated by long-felt tensions noted earlier between Thai and other ethnic groups that became refugees, principally the Vietnamese and the hill tribes. Thai resentment of the Vietnamese was not only historical but the result of a previous experience with Vietnamese refugees that had left bitter feelings and was still unresolved.

This had come about when tens of thousands of Vietnamese residents of French-ruled Laos and Cambodia fled to Thailand after World War II. Joined by others from Vietnam and allowed by Thai authorities to stay, they had organized support for the Communist-led Viet Minh cause in Indochina that carried Ho Chi Minh to power in North Vietnam in 1954. Under an agreement signed in 1959 between Bangkok and Hanoi authorities, more than half the 70,000 Vietnamese who had registered for repatriation were returned to North Vietnam. But with the two countries taking opposite sides in the global cold war, the rest remained in Thailand, where the government viewed them as too susceptible to Vietnamese Communist influence to be assimilated.[3]

With Thai–Vietnamese relations back on a fairly even keel in late 1977, Hanoi sent a team to Bangkok to discuss the matter, the Thai insisting that the original agreement apply and the remaining 36,000 be returned, the Vietnamese reluctant and calling for a new arrangement. The talks stalled, but the Thai were resolutely determined to get rid of a hard core of about 3,500 Vietnamese they regarded as a threat to Thai society. The last thing they wanted was a new pool of ethnic-Vietnamese refugees, whether boat people from Vietnam or land cases from Laos and Kampuchea.

Even the presence of displaced lowland Lao and Khmer led to local conflicts and caused ill feeling in Thailand. The refugees imposed a heavy administrative burden, forced up prices and overtaxed local facilities and resources. Along the Kampuchean border, up to 200,000 Thai farmers and their families were disturbed. Some were permanently displaced and had to be moved farther inland, along with their draft animals, houses, schools and shops.

In Malaysia, the Vietnamese boat people landed on the east coast—mainly the states of Kelantan, Trengganu and Pahang, the country's soft underbelly—where the population is overwhelmingly rural Malay, including some of the poorest and most conservative. The Japanese had landed in the same area when they took Malaya in World War II, and the refugee armada was viewed as another kind of invasion force. The initial reaction of the villagers, who live in thatched-roof houses on high stilts among coconut palms near the water's edge, was muted. Some helped distressed refugees ashore and provided food; others were not sure what to make of it all. But attitudes soon hardened, encouraged by threatening noises from politicians.

Malaysian leaders encountered the same attitudes among their constituents as did their counterparts in Thailand. Villagers griped that the refugees in UNHCR camps, receiving three meals a day, were living better than locals. Politicians found it difficult to explain that the international community, not the

Malaysian government, was paying for the upkeep of the refugees. Villagers also claimed that the Vietnamese sometimes stole food and animals. Devout Moslems, the Malay even objected to Vietnamese women wearing shorts and exposing their legs.

In an effort to ease tension, the government decided to transfer the camps to offshore islands, the largest of them on Pulau Bidong, which was eventually to house 40,000 refugees. That worked for a while. But the rapid buildup in camp populations—7,000 boat people had been admitted by the end of 1977, 70,000 by 1978 and 123,000 by 1979—swamped the whole program. Some permanent camps had to remain on the mainland, while groups of refugees also were held under guard at dozens of temporary sites along the coast.

However, when some government officials held the refugees responsible for a substantial rise in the cost of living, particularly on the east coast, observers were left with the impression that natural resentment was being deliberately fanned. UNHCR and its operational partner in Malaysia, the Red Crescent, had resorted to buying food in bulk in Kuala Lumpur and elsewhere to minimize the impact on the east coast. But many a shopkeeper used the refugees as a convenient excuse to plead shortages in order to charge higher prices.

Asked in a *Newsweek* interview in December 1978 if there was an immediate danger of the east coast population becoming violent, the Home Affairs Minister, Ghazali Shafie, said: "If they find out we are ineffective, that possibility cannot be ruled out. . . . If they see they are getting poorer because of the refugees, they may say, 'All right, let us solve the problem in our way.' " Soon after, a police officer supervising the rescue of refugees whose boat had sunk was injured by stone-throwing villagers. In another incident, angry locals pushed away a leaking boat trying to land at Kuala Trengganu, the state capital; it capsized, drowning more than half of its 250 occupants. Ghazali counseled restraint. He said he could imagine the seas red with blood from attacks with the parang, as the long, curved Malay knife is called, if matters got out of control.

One Malaysian journalist who visited Trengganu reported "disproportionate fear" in the villages and found that the locals were not in any mood to compromise over the refugees. In one incident, fishermen returning to Kuala Trengganu were unable to unload their catch because sacks of rice bound for Pulau Bidong were on the wharf. "That was enough. The fishermen speared the bags from underneath and watched with grim amusement while the rice trickled into the sea."[4]

Being some distance from the sea-lanes favored by the boat people, Indonesia escaped any real refugee problem for years. Only 923 Vietnamese had arrived by 1977, and 3,855 by the end of 1978. But when Malaysia began denying asylum in early 1979, Indonesia's refugee population rose dramatically. UNHCR counted 48,440 arrivals in 1979, raising the total to 53,218. Of those who landed that year, 46,604 disembarked in the first seven months, 22,743 of them in June alone. Again, though, it was not just sheer numbers but their distribution across 16 of Indonesia's 13,000 scattered islands.

About 33,000 of the Vietnamese took refuge in the remote Anambas, a group of islands 160 miles northeast of Singapore, where they outnumbered the Indonesian population by up to 6 to 1 and had an adverse impact on the local community. Even within the Anambas the refugees were scattered from north to south, east to west.

Transporting food and medical supplies to the malnourished Vietnamese and arranging for their resettlement proved a major headache. It was logistically difficult and expensive. There were no regular air or shipping services connecting the Anambas to the outside world, nor, indeed, any roads on the islands. Access by boat from Tanjung Pinang, on Bintan Island south of Singapore, took twenty-four to thirty-six hours. Dozens of people, mostly babies and young children, died while the relief operation was organized.

Not surprisingly, Indonesia was miffed at Malaysia for pushing the refugees its way. Most of the boat people who landed in the Anambas had either been towed away from the coast of Peninsular Malaysia by navy vessels, or pushed back to sea after breaching a security cordon and reaching the shore. Malaysian security patrols often advised the Vietnamese that they would be allowed to land in Indonesia and towed them in the direction of the Anambas.

Although differences between the two countries were concealed for the sake of ASEAN solidarity and harmony, relations beneath the surface became frayed over the refugee issue, particularly between Malaysia's Home Minister Ghazali and Indonesia's Foreign Minister, Mochtar Kusumaatmadja. Ghazali rubbed it in by privately telling correspondents that part of Malaysia's strategy was to create a refugee problem for Indonesia. That way, he said, Malaysia hoped to enlist Jakarta's support for a Kuala Lumpur initiative to set up special refugee processing centers.

The presence of a high proportion of ethnic Chinese among the Vietnamese refugees gushing into Southeast Asia—about 60 to 70 percent overall—injected an unpredictable racial factor into the flow. This had to be seen in the context of the delicate racial compositions that obtained in the region. All the ASEAN countries except Singapore, where ethnic Chinese predominated, had ethnic-Chinese minorities. Although they had been around for generations, as in Vietnam, these Chinese communities were not all effectively integrated, and any unplanned or unforeseen development that upset the racial balance could cause alarm.

With the arrival of the boat people, the situation was sensitive enough in Indonesia, where tens of thousands of ethnic Chinese were killed following the abortive pro-Communist coup in 1965, and where anti-Japanese demonstrations during the visit of Premier Kakuei Tanaka in 1974 quickly turned into anti-Chinese riots. But it was acute in Malaysia, which had a particularly tense ethnic balance—47 percent Malay, 34 percent Chinese, the rest of Indian and other origin—and a long-term program called the New Economic Policy to advance Malay in the mainstream of economic activity. The arrival of so many ethnic-Chinese refugees deepened the concern of some Malay, who already suffered from insecurity stemming in part from being a minority in what is considered their homeland. On the east coast, some Malay villagers believed ethnic Chinese were being sent as part of a plot to outnumber them. As racial tension surfaced, concern was all too often expressed in Parliament in Kuala Lumpur about ethnic-Chinese, rather than Vietnamese, refugees.

Prime Minister Lee Kuan Yew of Singapore articulated what until then was one of the great unspoken fears: the possibility, however remote, that another nation in Southeast Asia might be tempted to follow Hanoi's lead in solving the problem of its Chinese minority. Nobody, including Singapore, was suggesting that any of the four other ASEAN members were about to risk becoming international pariahs by emulating Vietnam. But there were extremists in these countries who liked the idea, if only it could be accomplished with a little more subtlety and finesse.

Left unstated was the fact that Singapore saw the greatest potential for trouble in Malaysia, where any flight of ethnic Chinese could bring hundreds of thousands of persons to the causeway that linked the two countries. Malaysia's Chinese community of 4 million had been on the defensive since vicious race riots had shaken the country in May 1969. It was those disturbances which had given birth to the New Economic Policy, a bold attempt to restructure the economy and, indeed, the entire society. Already disadvantaged politically, the ethnic Chinese were bewildered and uncertain as they saw more and more opportunities reserved for Malay and other races judged to be indigenous rather than immigrant.

In this atmosphere, it obviously would not be necessary to employ Vietnam's crude methods to trigger a rush from Malaysia. There was certainly no immediate panic, but a rather sick joke made the rounds among non-Malay. "Got your boat ready?" they liked to ask each other.

The high ethnic-Chinese content of the inflow also contributed in large measure to the Southeast Asian perception of a security threat from the refugees. That they came from a Communist country gave it substance. That most of them were fleeing from what they regarded as Communist repression did not dilute the fear. It was understandable, if not fully justified, that the refugees should raise the specter of Communist infiltration in a part of the world that had been battling Communist insurgents, many of them ethnic Chinese, since World War II. Clandestine Communist parties operated in every country of the region, with the aim of overthrowing the established governments. In Thailand, the Philippines and Malaysia they were engaged in what they called "armed struggle." Providing the Chinese connection in the minds of many: all the parties were ideologically swayed by Peking rather than Moscow.

A widely reported warning by Squadron Leader Prasong Soonsiri, Deputy Secretary General of Thailand's National Security Council, that at least 10 percent of Vietnamese refugees were espionage and subversion agents dispatched by Hanoi did nothing to allay fears in rural areas in the region. Although the claim was not taken seriously in ruling circles, the lack of information about the backgrounds of the refugees caused some unease. Few of them carried identification papers, and it was known that the camps contained some former Communist cadres.

Indonesia, which was under internal pressure from the military to continue viewing Peking as the major long-term threat to regional stability, worried that subversives from China might slip into the country in the unscreened flow of boat people. Even genuine ethnic-Chinese refugees were treated with suspicion by both the military and some Moslems. The attitude of the general community was little better, colored as it was with racial dislike and permeated with the belief that Sino-Vietnamese would attempt to stay and join the local Chinese community, which accounted for only 3 percent of Indonesia's population but controlled much of its economy.

Although the Philippines, like Indonesia, was off the flight path of the boat people, those who arrived provoked the usual security anxieties. The total rose from 1,865 by the end of 1977 to 6,778 by 1978 and 14,599 by 1979. At one stage President Ferdinand Marcos expressed concern over whether "supposedly Vietnamese refugees are actually refugees."

The most undeniable and immediate security threat, however, was always in Thailand. Some refugees in the north and northeast, both Lao and Hmong, were starting to turn their camps into Palestinian-style bases for subversion in Laos. After resting in the Thai camps, they would filter back across the Mekong to continue the armed resistance to the Pathet Lao government. Although the cross-border guerrilla movement was weak and the cause was virtually lost, it carried the danger of importing bloody Laotian feuds into Thailand.

The situation on the Thai–Kampuchean border was much more complex and threatening. While Pol Pot and his associates presided in Phnom Penh, Thai forces were hard-pressed trying to contain savage border raids by his Khmer Rouge, who seemed to delight in slaughtering and disemboweling villagers. The activities of the right-wing Khmer Serei and other Thailand-based

134

groups opposed to the Pol Pot regime, though ineffective, provided an excuse for the Khmer Rouge attacks, if one was needed.

The Khmer Rouge added to the border turmoil by cooperating with the underground Communist Party of Thailand. Together they would kidnap Thai villagers, march them to Kampuchea for Communist indoctrination and training, and return them to their homes just across the border.

If all that was not confusing and dangerous enough, the situation changed for the worse, as far as the Thai were concerned, when Vietnamese forces took Phnom Penh and installed Heng Samrin as president on January 7, 1979. As the retreating Khmer Rouge fought a rearguard action across the country, many of them joined civilian groups flocking across the Thai border as refugees. With Hanoi warning of serious consequences if Bangkok gave refuge to the Khmer Rouge, the Thai feared a Vietnamese incursion into their territory. It was in these circumstances, which the Thai called "sensitive, complex and dangerous," that they pushed 42,000 Kampucheans back to their homeland.

But tens of thousands remained, and many more, including hard-core Khmer Rouge and their supporters, continued to enter Thailand's eastern provinces, inviting hot pursuit by Vietnamese troops deployed along the border.

Malaysia's largest English-language daily, the *New Straits Times*, reflected the feeling of extreme vulnerability throughout non-Communist Southeast Asia when it commented in June 1979: "The crux of the issue is that the flow from Vietnam is no longer just a humanitarian problem. It has become as much a weapon of war as a softening-up raid by waves of bombers."

The strains imposed by the refugees on China and Hong Kong were of a different nature. Although for the most part there was no ethnic clash, that did not mean that Sino-Vietnamese were necessarily welcomed by host Chinese populations. Food, shelter and everyday services, always in short supply, had to be shared with the new arrivals. Violence flared on more than one occasion in Hong Kong.

Before China sharply defined those who could enter from Vietnam in July 1978, more than 130,000 had waded unhindered across border streams. Explaining the need for the restrictions, the official Xinhua news agency said that the refugees created "enormous difficulties" in border towns and villages. It cited the example of Tunghsing, in Guangxi province, which usually had a population of 10,000 but was submerged by 84,000 refugees. Almost all the local government offices and schools were being used as temporary residences, and local people were sharing their homes with the refugees. The work of the township offices was disrupted, and the local primary school had to close. In Yunnan province, a 280-bed hotel in one county had to put up more than 11,000 refugees, and a 60-bed hospital was treating 300 persons a day.

About 202,000 refugees had arrived in China by February 1979, some of them by boat, joining a camp at Beihai, a fishing town on the Gulf of Tonkin. They continued to pour in at the rate of 10,000 a month, reaching 235,000 by June and more than 250,000 by late July.

Unlike Southeast Asian countries, China attempted to absorb most of the refugees. Peking allocated $450 million in addition to sums spent by local authorities to help them engage in "productive work." This usually meant transferring them to state farms. "Exerting great efforts to mobilize its resources, China by mid-1979 had managed to resettle 200,000" preliminarily," leaving 30,000 still without shelter and about 25,000 waiting at border posts. Said Zhang Wenjin, Vice Minister of Foreign Affairs, in July: "China is an economically underdeveloped country with a large population and comparatively scarce arable land. The burden we have borne is already very heavy."

The motives of the escapees leaving Vietnam for China were giving rise to another problem. Many went overland simply because it was cheaper than a boat trip. They also were deterred from crossing the South China Sea by stories of overcrowding and of vessels being lost. Moreover, southern Vietnamese initially believed that after a brief transit period in China they would be able to travel on to Hong Kong and then apply for resettlement as refugees in the West.

As noted earlier, however, this was not to be. As far as Peking, UNHCR and major resettlement countries were concerned, China was their place of settlement. While most Sino-Vietnamese seemed to be adjusting to farm life well enough—it was simply another brand of socialism for those from northern areas—thousands of others felt trapped. They were mainly for-

136

mer city folk and unreconstructed capitalists from southern Vietnam. People such as 38-year-old Lam Sy Sang, who had once owned a banana plantation north of Ho Chi Minh City. "I left Vietnam because I did not like the system," he said. "In China, it's the same system. I can't make the money I want here. I want to go to a Western country, a free country."[5]

To care for the refugees already in China and prepare for a further 10,000 China had offered to accept from camps in Southeast Asia, Peking took the step, unprecedented for it, of calling in UNHCR for assistance. About 19,000 persons applied to the Chinese authorities to be resettled abroad, most of them ethnic Vietnamese. Chinese officials indicated that the number of applicants was likely to exceed 30,000 ethnic Vietnamese alone.

Before Hanoi agreed at the Geneva conference in July 1979 to halt the refugee traffic, people such as Lam Sy Sang often made their way back to northern Vietnam and joined others leaving for the first time by boat from Haiphong or Hon Gay. But with departures from Vietnam officially forbidden, there was almost no chance of getting out. So they opened new escape routes by junk from the coast of China. The destination remained the same: Hong Kong. By whatever route, the two-timers compounded the colony's gigantic refugee headache.

Hong Kong had a people problem long before the first Vietnamese refugee showed up. With a population of 5 million crammed into only 404 square miles, much of it steep, unproductive hillsides and barren islands, Hong Kong has to cope with some of the most crowded urban districts on earth.

Repeated waves of immigration from China have boosted Hong Kong's natural population growth. More than 1 million people crossed the border in the twenty years after the Communist Party took charge in Peking in 1949. The latest wave, which began in January 1978, added about 280,000 inhabitants, legally and illegally, by the end of 1979—more than a 5 percent growth in two years.

Squads of security personnel combed the New Territories bordering China in an attempt to intercept illegal immigrants, commonly known as IIs, and send them back. The IIs were attracted by an anomaly, known as the touch-base policy, that would allow them to stay if they reached the urban areas undetected. The loophole was closed in October 1980, but for the time being Hong Kong deployed four times as many soldiers as usual along the border, three times as many police and twice the number of marine vessels. Even the Governor's launch was pressed into service. Every night dozens of IIs were nabbed, sometimes hundreds.

Coinciding with the new wave of IIs, from the end of 1978 the boat people from Vietnam caused grave disquiet in the community—and literally squeezed everyone and everything just a little bit tighter. In 1979, 72,020 Vietnamese sailed in, 18,718 of them in May and 22,835 in June.

The policy of extending refuge to all, together with the hard line being taken in Southeast Asia, meant that Hong Kong became the primary haven for the boat people. They were supposed to stay only temporarily, until resettlement places were found for them overseas. But "temporarily" was a relative term, since it had taken Hong Kong three years to disperse the 3,743 Vietnamese refugees who had arrived in May 1975 on the Danish containership *Clara Maersk*.

In addition to temporary asylum, Hong Kong accepted some 14,000 refugees and displaced persons from Indochina for permanent settlement after 1975. They consisted of 9,000 illegal immigrants and overstayers from Vietnam, Laos and Kampuchea, 5,021 dependents of Hong Kong residents and 184 boat people.

Not all Vietnamese were allowed to stay, even temporarily, however. The first batch of 25 two-time refugees, who had spent what Hong Kong authorities described as "some time" in China, were returned to the People's Republic in August 1979. Thousands of others would follow, including 142 who were nabbed entering Hong Kong for the second time. In addition, 120 IIs were picked up in 1979 trying to pass themselves off as boat people from Vietnam.

For Hong Kong, finding physical room for the boat people arriving directly from Vietnam was difficult. Some had to stay afloat in the harbor until accommodations were built. In a territory without a minimum wage, manufacturers were pleased to be able to take advantage of cheap refugee labor. But the short-term economic advantage of the boat people had to be weighed against the overall costs to the community. The cost to the tax-

138

payer—a genuine cost in Hong Kong's case, since the government and not UNHCR was paying most of the upkeep—exceeded $14 million in direct spending in 1979.

The Governor, Sir Murray MacLehose, said that Hong Kong had worked its way to the point where the goal of decent housing, medical care and education for everyone could have been achieved by about 1984. "Now, all this is in danger of being diluted—put off," he said in an interview with *Newsweek*. "And more seriously, the living standards of the people will be affected as real wages decline."

SEVEN

*On February 24, 1979, which was a Saturday, Nguyen Dinh
Thuy went to his office and deliberately provoked a quarrel
with the bank's deputy director. He worked himself up to
anger, handed the official a note requesting five days' leave
and stalked out. Nobody would miss him from the office that
afternoon anyway; although he was supposed to work
throughout Saturday, he often called it quits at lunchtime.*

*When Thuy returned to his mother's house at 10 A.M.,
Phi Yen had flown. His wife had changed her mind yet
again: she wanted to remain in Vietnam. He searched all the
obvious places, including her mother's house, but she was
nowhere to be found. At the last minute he was able to get a
cousin, Doan Thi My, to take his wife's place on the boat. In
her late twenties, she had lost a lot of money and had twice
been caught trying to escape. Her substitution saved Thuy
13 taels of gold, but it was no compensation for Phi Yen's
absence. He never did say goodbye to her. . . .*

140

DESPITE THE WEIGHT of evidence against it, the Vietnamese government never admitted publicly to a policy of expelling its people, discriminating against ethnic Chinese or profiting from the refugee outflow. It said that those who left in fishing boats stole them, and the loss harmed the fishing industry at a time when the country was suffering a shortage of food. Moreover, it was impossible to stop the flight, which was instigated by enemies of Vietnam, both within and without. And although some low-level cadres had taken advantage of the situation to line their pockets, such corruption was not tolerated and offenders were prosecuted.

Hanoi obviously suffered a credibility problem over refugees that was just as acute and real as the country's food deficit. At their broadest, Hanoi's denials defied common sense. Did anyone seriously believe that in a totalitarian state 135,000 people in three months could be organized, ticketed, transported to departure points and allocated boats—a major logistical exercise and one that a nationwide travel agency in any Western country would be proud to equal with the assistance of computerized bookings and international airlines—without the government's knowledge? Could anyone seriously accept that people, given a reasonable choice, would opt at the rate of 57,000 a month to risk their lives in vessels that often became floating coffins? As officials from many countries often wondered aloud: if the Hanoi leadership could devise the strategy, enforce the discipline and maintain the morale to defeat the United States, then regarded as the world's greatest military power, how was it that it could not manage to keep tabs on its own people in a time of relative peace?

The question was put to Vu Bach Mai, Vietnam's ambassador to Malaysia, early in 1979. "You don't understand," he told reporters. Mai, like Vietnamese diplomats, officials and leaders everywhere, trotted out the standard line that the authorities were unable to stop the refugees because of Vietnam's long coastline and limited resources, and so on.

Only late in the day, about mid-1979, did Hanoi concede that it had been allowing residents to leave by the back door. It was no confession, emerging only in passing as Vietnam made yet another defense in answer to international criticism. The government said that it had attempted to block escapes for a

141

couple of years after it took over South Vietnam, but that it had allowed them to go freely after 1977.

The Vietnamese made other trite, inconsistent and patently false claims about the refugees, and their willingness to do so should be taken into account. (After they had invaded Kampuchea and ousted Pol Pot, they also denied initially that there were any Vietnamese troops on Kampuchean soil.) But the Vietnamese were not the first to bend the truth in their international relations, nor would they be the last, and they did advance a serious explanation for the massive exodus. Basically, they put the blame on the United States, China and the colonial past. Unlikely as it might seem to critics, this argument was not completely without merit.

Almost a century of colonization followed by decades of war had turned pre-1975 South Vietnam into an artificial zone, first a piece of France in the East, then a little America. The injection of billions of dollars of foreign aid had created an economy that was just as false. It had spawned a Western-style consumer society with all its attendant—and for Vietnam, irrelevant—gadgetry. According to Communist officials, the day Saigon changed hands 300,000 city households were registered as "traders," more than double the number of factory workers, and 1.5 million Vietnamese were living from salaries paid by the American budget.

Hanoi may have exaggerated somewhat when it said it had inherited 3 million unemployed, several hundred thousand prostitutes and drug addicts, thousands of gangsters and criminals, 1 million people with tuberculosis, several hundred thousand with venereal disease and 4 million illiterates. But there was a strong measure of truth in the overall claim: "One had to rebuild not only a country which had been ruined materially, but also a society which had been completely perverted and turned upside down, in which millions of people had forgotten how to perform honest labor and had lost all sense of national and moral values." Some painful adjustment was obviously necessary if the freewheeling South was to be brought into line with the austere North.

The concept of New Economic Zones, emphasizing agriculture and resettling bloated city populations in rural areas, was sound for a developing country such as Vietnam. As the

World Bank noted in its 1977 survey, "New Economic Zones are fundamental to the country's development strategy in that they are intended both to solve the employment problem and increase agricultural output." Even reeducation camps can be viewed as a reasonable trade-off in the circumstances, when the alternative for the "lackeys" of the Thieu regime was likely to be mass murder, the option chosen by Pol Pot's Democratic Kampuchea.

Unified Vietnam was bound to have economic problems. The end of the war ended vast American and other Western aid to the southern half of the country, while the dispute with Peking saw extensive Chinese aid to northern areas discontinued. As Hanoi was not slow to point out, Vietnam embarked on its "immense work of national reconstruction" without three-quarters of the assistance given to North and South Vietnam in the war years. And as it was equally quick to proclaim, Hanoi was not to blame for the "unprecedented" natural calamities that ruined crops in 1976, 1977 and 1978.

A case can be made that Vietnam was never allowed to participate fully in the community of nations. After its humiliating defeat, the United States seemed psychologically incapable of reconciliation with its former battlefield adversary. Apart from maintaining its trade embargo against Hanoi, Washington led a successful campaign to block non-Communist assistance to Vietnam.

The consequences of such a course were spelled out by a U.N. mission that visited Vietnam in March 1976. Members reported that the vast task of repairing war damage far exceeded the human and material resources of the Vietnamese and added: "It is therefore necessary, indeed essential, that the international community should provide assistance to Vietnam. . . . The lack of such outside support will doom the country to great distress for many years to come."

Nothing pointed up more clearly Washington's negative and illogical attitude toward Vietnam than the question of diplomatic relations. After being close to normalization in September 1978, the United States abruptly broke off negotiations with Hanoi and soon after recognized the People's Republic of China, then locked in a fierce struggle with Vietnam. Although American officials denied playing the "China card," the move had the predictable result of pushing Vietnam closer to the Soviet Union. That was something neither the Americans nor the Chinese, nor, presumably, the independent-minded Vietnamese, desired.

On the other hand, Hanoi did not help itself by insisting on a major aid commitment before normalization, displaying preparations for an invasion of Kampuchea and imposing harsh treatment on the boat people. By the time Hanoi dropped its demand for aid, it was too late.

Washington's efforts to isolate Vietnam and pressure it into more responsible behavior toward its own people and its neighbors doubtless made life more difficult for ordinary Vietnamese. The aid boycott certainly did nothing to ameliorate Vietnam's economic malaise. It thus seems reasonable to assume that if it had any effect at all, the withholding of non-Communist aid indirectly stimulated the flow of refugees.

Official Vietnamese statements distinguished between two main groups of refugees: the 1.5 million persons who had once been in South Vietnam's army, police force and bureaucracy, and the ethnic Chinese, whom Hanoi calls Hoa.

Government spokesmen often spoke disparagingly of the first group, because "they have guilty consciences" and "were used to the easy life under American aid." However, a 1979 article in the *Vietnam Courier*, an official monthly publication, was more sympathetic. It said that there had been a regular but limited outflow of these people from 1975 to 1978. Although it was tragic "in certain respects," the flow had posed no problem for Vietnam or countries of first asylum.

The article, reprinted as a forty-page pamphlet titled "Those Who Leave (the 'Problem of Vietnamese Refugees')," identified the categories in the first group:

> —The great majority have left Vietnam for economic reasons, unable to bear the privations and having failed to find occupations to their liking. Among them are not only big traders and rich traffickers but also mere employees—bartenders, for instance—whose trades have dropped out of use and who could not muster the courage to go and reclaim new land.
> —Some are former war criminals, or are now mem-

144

bers of counter-revolutionary networks who feel they are about to be discovered.

—In the case of the intellectuals, there are various factors which combine in varying degrees. All have experienced a serious drop in their standard of living. When a medical doctor who used to travel in a car and live in an air-conditioned villa becomes a cadre in a public hospital, his salary is barely one-tenth of his former income. To this is added the difficulty he feels to adapt himself . . . to the constraints of a revolutionary society. . . .

No matter how reasonable the case might be for leaving, Hanoi nevertheless maintained that the refugees were provoked to go as part of a sinister plot by "imperialist and reactionary forces"—read Washington and Peking—in the same way the mass movements of 1954 and 1975 had been triggered. In 1954, some 800,000 Vietnamese, predominantly Roman Catholics, had transferred from northern Vietnam to south of the 17th Parallel, where the French expeditionary corps was regrouped under the Geneva Agreements. The 1975 reference was to the American evacuation of Saigon. "Those Who Leave" commented: "The aims have remained the same: to stir up and exacerbate serious social and economic difficulties in revolutionary Vietnam, to weaken it from within, thus preparing conditions for renewed armed aggression."

Hanoi argued that Washington did not consider the loss of Saigon to be "definitive" and had set up a counterrevolutionary network of former Thieu army officers. The network was accused by Hanoi of killing civilian and military cadres, setting factories and storehouses afire, ambushing convoys and turning out counterfeit money and propaganda material.

How did the refugees escape? "Those Who Leave" conceded that there was an organized service, but said that it was run by the same subversive network. Ships plying "clandestinely" between Vietnam and neighboring countries—Thailand, Malaysia, Hong Kong, the Philippines and Australia—took out refugees and returned with specially trained agents, weapons and money to finance counterrevolutionary organizations in Vietnam, Laos and Kampuchea, it said.

"This is the way things happen: A rich merchant wants to leave Vietnam. Against payment of a handsome amount of cash—$2,000–$3,000 on an average—a clandestine organization will take him and his family to a coastal port, where they will hide in one of the hundreds of fishing boats that put out to sea every day. At sea, they are picked up by ships which will take them to neighboring countries. For an intellectual, especially a technician with good qualifications, the journey will be free of charge, for the point is to perform a brain drain to the detriment of Vietnam and simultaneously raise a political hullabaloo."

Turning to the second group of refugees, the ethnic Chinese, "Those Who Leave" laid the blame for their plight, which it acknowledged as the new factor accounting for the dramatic upsurge in refugees from early 1978, squarely at China's door. It said Peking had put them on the spot by spreading rumors of war and taking up the cause of ethnic-Chinese traders in Cholon when business was nationalized. Many Sino-Vietnamese who had taken refuge across the frontier had been trained by Peking in special units and used for reconnaissance, commando and sabotage operations when China attacked Vietnam in February 1979, it said, while some ethnic Chinese still in Vietnam engaged in economic sabotage at Peking's instigation.

China's championing of Sino-Vietnamese did indeed seem self-serving and more than a little hypocritical. As Hanoi pointed out, Peking was scarcely consistent in its moral indignation: it had not uttered a squeak of protest in 1975 when 500,000 ethnic Chinese in Kampuchea were violently maltreated and force-marched into the countryside, many to certain death, by China's ally Pol Pot. Peking's defense, that Kampuchea's radical measures affected everybody and not just Sino-Khmers, did not hold water because there was no evidence that Sino-Vietnamese had been singled out when the government shut down capitalist traders in southern Vietnam.

It might be true, as Peking insisted, that the Vietnamese had become "the biggest and most despicable present-day human traffickers," and that, in the words of Chinese Vice Premier Deng Xiaoping, "there is a hooligan in the East." But Peking's intervention in behalf of Sino-Vietnamese did not help them at all. Rather, it contributed immeasurably to their predicament. For example, some ethnic Chinese who registered with the Vietnamese authorities to go to China after Peking announced it was dispatching ships to collect them reportedly were hauled off in the middle of the night to reeducation camps and New Economic Zones. And the ships never arrived, largely because of conditions imposed by China.

Peking's shrill defense of Sino-Vietnamese also raised fears with non-Communist Southeast Asian governments that China was changing its policy toward the overseas Chinese—a concern assiduously fanned for years by Soviet propaganda. It was a double-barreled risk for Peking because it coincided with a fresh interest by China in having overseas Chinese return to contribute to the modernization of the motherland.

Hastily, Peking sought to give an assurance that its policy was still nonintervention. It said Vietnam was a special case because it involved a Soviet plot to encircle China. Another special circumstance was the forced naturalization of ethnic Chinese in South Vietnam by President Ngo Dinh Diem in 1956 and 1957. Peking, under an earlier arrangement, expected Hanoi to reverse what had occurred under duress when it took over the South and give ethnic Chinese the choice of taking Vietnamese or Chinese nationality. But Hanoi's response was to declare "the historical fact that has existed for over twenty years now, that the Hoa in our country have become Vietnamese citizens."

The Chinese government's policy had been consistent, declared an editorial in *People's Daily* in Peking: it supported and encouraged overseas Chinese in Southeast Asia to voluntarily take up the citizenship of their host countries; those who did so automatically forfeited their Chinese citizenship; as for those who kept their Chinese citizenship, Peking expected them to abide by the laws of their country of domicile.

Most China scholars and specialists agreed that there was little cause for alarm, that China was not changing its policy. But to Malaysia and Indonesia especially, the question was of more than academic interest. Both caught a dose of the jitters that did nothing for their relations with China.

On its side, Hanoi could justifiably claim to have accepted more than 26,000 Sino-Khmer refugees from Pol Pot's bizarre policies without discrimination. Peking, Hanoi delighted in pointing out, had refused to allow them to be repatriated to China.

147

As to Hanoi's assertion of divided loyalties among Sino-Vietnamese, it was difficult to evaluate. The most compelling statement that their position had fundamentally altered in 1978 was their panic-stricken flight to China, especially from border areas. Peking agreed with Hanoi that they had become alarmed by rumors of impending war between the two countries, but it accused Vietnam of having spread the rumors.

To support its claim of "ostracism, persecution and expulsion" of Sino-Vietnamese, China produced a fifty-three-page booklet of text and photographs titled "On the Question of Indo-Chinese Refugees," which included graphic personal testimony from alleged victims. One was Vuong Chinh Tai, 29 years of age and a fifth-generation Vietnamese of Chinese descent, who said all 4 members of his family had died through ill treatment by the "reactionary Vietnamese authorities."

Vietnam countered with teach-ins of Sino-Vietnamese "to refute Peking's slanderous allegations." It allowed foreign correspondents to visit Friendship Gate on the border, where they photographed Sino-Vietnamese crossing to China with all their belongings, including television sets and electrical appliances. Hanoi also produced some who had gone to China and then returned to Vietnam, and were willing to blame Peking for misleading them.

Hanoi's most serious allegation, that some of its former ethnic-Chinese residents had cooperated with the invading Chinese army, simply could not be independently tested. Said "Those Who Leave": "Having lived for long years in the border region, they knew every nook and cranny of it. In the course of that aggression, the Chinese command considered them to be a precious trump card."

The wholesale purge of ethnic Chinese in northern Vietnam which followed the invasion is less ambiguous. Although Vietnam denied victimizing Sino-Vietnamese, that it did so was confirmed—if further confirmation was needed—by no less ironic an authority than Wilfred Burchett, who has been perhaps Hanoi's number one propagandist outside Vietnam for more than two decades.

Supporting Hanoi's contention that Sino-Vietnamese had colluded with the Chinese invaders, the Australian journalist asserted that the original Peking accusation in 1978 that ethnic

Chinese in Vietnam were being "persecuted, ostracized, discriminated against and exploited" was false. But it had become a self-fulfilling prophecy after the Chinese invasion, he said. With Peking threatening to teach Vietnam a "second lesson," the Vietnamese leaders, overreacting, believed that the next blow by Peking would be aimed at the most vulnerable economic centers, the port of Haiphong and the coastal coal-mining towns of Hon Gay and Campha. Said Burchett: "They are taking no chances, and this time are really 'discriminating against and expelling' ethnic Chinese from those areas, also from Hanoi only 60 miles west of Haiphong."[1] To sympathetic foreigners visiting Hanoi, Vietnam's government officials made the same admission—that they had overreacted. They blamed the Chinese invasion and the fact that it had taken them completely by surprise.

Weight was added by the testimony of Hoang Van Hoan, aged 74, a ranking member of the Vietnamese Communist Party. Hoan had helped found the party in its original form in 1930 and later had become a member of both its Central Committee and its Politburo. Vice Chairman of the National Assembly, he had defected to China in July 1979 while on his way to Berlin for medical treatment. From Peking, where he had served as Vietnamese ambassador for seven years, he said that while world attention was focused on the boat people, the plight of ethnic Chinese who remained in Vietnam was worse. "They are the most miserable and they suffer the greatest," he said. "They have been expelled from places where they have lived for generations."

The loyalties of ethnic Chinese in Vietnam over the years were not always on open display. By oral agreement between Hanoi and Peking in 1955, Sino-Vietnamese in the North were gradually to become Vietnamese citizens. Scattered interviews with refugees suggested that perhaps fewer took Vietnamese citizenship than outsiders had surmised, though this is an extremely tentative opinion.

The overall record of the Chinese community in Vietnam casts doubt on Hanoi's implied claim that many Sino-Vietnamese had acted as fifth columnists and subverted Vietnam in China's behalf. Although some poorer ethnic Chinese in the South sympathized with the Communists and the really big

149

merchants linked their fortunes to pro-American regimes before 1975, the great bulk of the ethnic Chinese had tried to protect themselves by remaining apolitical and maintaining good relations, where possible, with both sides. In this respect, as in others, they had behaved much as other ethnic-Chinese minorities have come to do elsewhere in Southeast Asia.

The fact that Sino-Vietnamese shared the regional characteristic of playing a disproportionate role in the economic life of the country hardly made them a serious obstacle to Hanoi's socialist aspirations. Some were certainly guilty of opposing economic reforms, hoarding and profiteering—and buying off all-too-willing Communist cadres. But did that mean the vast majority would not fall into line when they realized Hanoi was serious? The example of the North, admittedly with much smaller numbers and less wealth at stake, suggested that most were adaptable enough to find a place in the new order.

Hanoi, in "Those Who Leave," did not face up to the fact that New Economic Zones, without adequate infrastructure and support systems, became in effect punishment camps, with an element of compulsion replacing their original voluntary nature. Official contempt for those resettled Vietnamese who could not hack it was implicit in the reference to refugees who lacked the courage to reclaim land. Similarly, reeducation camps were treated by the publication as if they were no more than recreation centers for wayward youths. And nowhere was it conceded that Vietnam's own actions, including the invasion of Kampuchea, had contributed in large part to the hardship of Vietnamese.

"Those Who Leave" was equally unrealistic and strained credulity when it admitted that there was an organized refugee service from Vietnam but insisted that it was the work of an American counterrevolutionary network, which was supposed to have collaborated with a similar clandestine Peking organization. In addition, a "comprehensive organization" had been set up—by whom Hanoi did not say—to take Sino-Vietnamese "businessmen and traffickers" to neighboring nations in Southeast Asia.

Indeed, diplomats as early as 1976 reported the existence of what was known as an "underground railroad" taking ethnic

Chinese from Vietnam to Thailand for a hefty fee. A Thai fishing vessel was the usual means of transport, and officials were bribed at both ends. To suggest, however, that many refugees left Vietnam this way is plainly ludicrous.

If Vietnam's case was starting to degenerate into absurdity, it was because ultimately it was indefensible and self-convicting.

The clandestine organizations that Hanoi said were operating in Vietnam obviously could not have functioned without some form of official approval. "There may be cadres who have availed themselves of the situation to get their palms greased," "Those Who Leave" conceded, "but this is not government policy." Again, it was the fault of the Americans. "In a country that has been ravaged by war and where Phoenix operations conducted over long years by the American command had literally decimated the ranks of revolutionary militants—in some sectors, 95% of the cadres were murdered—it has been particularly difficult after liberation to set up a state apparatus without opportunistic or degenerate elements worming their way into it." Although a few corrupt officials might besmirch the honor of the whole apparatus, "no senior cadre has ever been involved in such affairs."

To make the point that no government could claim that none of its employees had ever been tempted to pocket a few dollars on the side, "Those Who Leave" and other Vietnamese organs and spokesmen pointed out that the United States had been through the Lockheed and Watergate scandals. The refugee departures, they contended, were "something similar." The analogy with Watergate seems most appropriate. It involved corruption at the highest levels of government and a refusal to the end in the face of incriminating facts to admit any wrongdoing.

Hanoi's awkward position led officials to advance some preposterous arguments at times. Hanoi Radio developed the Chinese-in-disguise line, which was later taken up in Vietnam's behalf by the Soviet Union. It was expanded rather than refined in further comments by Nguyen Co Thach, Vietnam's acting foreign minister for much of 1979 in the absence through illness of Nguyen Duy Trinh. According to this proposition, Peking was dumping its Chinese citizens in Vietnamese waters, later to be produced as Sino-Vietnamese refugees in Southeast Asia. More than 100,000 Chinese had been shipped out by Peking, Thach told American newsmen in mid-1979. "We have arrested some ships from China going to Southeast Asia and we took them as prisoners," he said. China's leaders were very clever, he added, because many people did not realize what was happening—Chinese from China looked the same as ethnic Chinese from Vietnam.

Thach, who formally became Foreign Minister in a reshuffle in February 1980, was Vietnam's principal spokesman on the subject of refugees. Despite a reputation for being sophisticated and adept at handling foreigners, he frequently resorted to verbal sleight-of-hand to explain away the embarrassing boat people. To foreign reporters and visiting VIPs alike, he would say that the theft of 5,000 boats by refugees had cut Vietnam's fishing industry in half. Always it was 5,000 boats that had been stolen from the state, and always their loss had cut the catch by half. However, according to the World Bank's survey of Vietnam in 1977, there were 90,000 fishing boats in the country, though about 20,000 of them were "inoperative because of spare parts and fuel." Not all of them were owned by the government. But the removal of 5,000 of them—if 5,000 was correct—was much more likely to have had about a 7 percent impact on the fleet and on fishing operations.

Thach was also on record as saying, "Peasants don't leave, only urbanites." Even though the majority of boat people were city dwellers, his statement was never true. From the start, some ordinary southern Vietnamese from rural areas fled, while tens of thousands of ethnic Chinese from northern Vietnam who followed were simple fishermen, coolies and other workers from the provinces.

Thach even argued that Sino-Vietnamese preferred to leave as refugees because they could take their valuables with them, whereas if they emigrated legally they would have to surrender much of their assets to the state. "These Chinese, they are very clever," he told a U.S. House of Representatives study mission in August 1979. "They take out their resources and set up firms as soon as they are resettled. If they went legally they could not do this." He ignored the fact that few Sino-Vietnamese had much to take after the PSB was through with them, and what little they escaped with was often taken by pirates. Nor did he explain why they looked forward to going to sea in tiny, unsafe boats when they knew they might drown.

Thach made much of the fact that when China invaded, Vietnam had not incarcerated ethnic Chinese—unlike the United States in World War II, which interned thousands of Japanese in America after the attack on Pearl Harbor. "Here the Chinese are free," he told one group of visitors in Vietnam. "You can see them in the streets." The term "free" hardly seemed appropriate for the "objects of revolution," as one secret Communist Party document reportedly described Sino-Vietnamese.

Thach also liked to point out what he regarded as the inconsistencies and double standards of Vietnam's critics. "Some people say that we have taken money from these refugees, and at the same time they say that they are forced to go," he said. "So it is contradictory: if they are forced to go, why must they pay money? If they must pay money to go, so they are not forced to go."[2] It hardly seemed contradictory to those PSB officials and Communist cadres on the ground doing the fleecing. They had a chance to rip off Sino-Vietnamese only when they were in the process of becoming refugees. And since much of the takings found its way back into government coffers and some went into the pockets of officials, various levels of Vietnamese society benefited financially from policies compelling people to become refugees and making them pay for that doubtful privilege.

Thus, another of Hanoi's answering arguments—that the refugee outflow disorganized the economy and disturbed social order and was not in the country's interest—lost much of its persuasiveness. It undoubtedly caused an upheaval, but Hanoi at the time obviously judged the returns worthwhile.

One of Thach's more subtle rebuttals was to profess confusion. When Vietnam stopped refugees from leaving, he would complain, it was criticized. When it let them go, it was still criticized. It just did not know what to do to please everyone. Apart from admitting that Vietnam had let refugees leave freely, his argument conveniently ignored the central issue, which was Hanoi's primary responsibility for the welfare of its own people. Instead, it turned the issue around to play on the agonizing dilemma of principle and practical behavior that he knew the refugee flow presented to the West. In the case of the United States, the pain was compounded by mixed emotions—war guilt,

153

pique over defeat, the deep desire to forget that Vietnam had ever existed and moral responsibility for at least part of what was still happening in Indochina.

The responsible nations of the world wanted to persuade Hanoi to eliminate the flow of refugees from Indochina, or at least reduce it to modest proportions over the long term. But they had to find a solution so that dissidents and minorities like the ethnic Chinese would not be condemned to an even more brutal fate than being turned into refugees. The issues involved interlocking questions of humanitarianism and human rights—including the right of free emigration proclaimed in the Universal Declaration of Human Rights—on the one hand, and of practical policy toward Vietnam on the other. Hanoi, which had made skillful bargaining use of American prisoners in the prolonged armistice negotiations of 1968–73, fully realized the Western dilemma.

Besides, Thach's reasoning made the refugees a problem for everyone except Hanoi. By allowing them to leave without formal clearance, Vietnam was acting contrary to international law and practice. It was also attempting to dictate the immigration policies of other countries, those which just happened to be in the unfortunate position of being neighbors of Vietnam, and those which assumed a moral responsibility for resettlement. And since when had Hanoi decided to conduct its domestic policies, deciding that dissidents should leave as refugees, according to what would please other sovereign nations, especially critics such as the United States?

A lengthy open letter by a group of Vietnamese intellectuals attempting to explain the refugee outflow as a normal consequence of events and history was excessively defensive and notable for its failure to answer specific allegations of expulsion, bribery and profiteering. Addressed to "Western friends" and published by the official press, it was obviously aimed at members of the old antiwar movement who "might be wondering whether they have in fact contributed to a good cause." The letter described reeducation as harsh but necessary. It conceded "occasional excesses, errors, fumblings," but claimed that "necessary rectifications" had been made. Rather plaintively, it added that "present-day socialist Vietnam is certainly not the hell described by some emigrants."

154

The whole charade reached a fitting, farcical climax at the refugee conference in Geneva in July 1979, when Vietnamese Deputy Foreign Minister Phan Hien issued the usual denials of official knowledge and complicity to a news conference on the eve of the two-day meeting. Within forty-eight hours, in background talks, he authorized U.N. Secretary General Waldheim to announce that Vietnam was halting the exodus over which it allegedly had no control. Most of the boats stopped overnight.

The Vietnamese government was never as coy privately as it was in its public statements. One Vietnamese diplomat readily conceded in December 1978 that Hanoi not only was permitting refugees to leave but was encouraging and facilitating the exodus. The diplomat, who was not identified, made his comments to an official of an Asian country. The record of their conversation was cited in a dossier prepared by the U.S. State Department.[3] There is no reason to doubt its authenticity. Vietnamese envoys in both Asia and Europe were reported to have made similar remarks in private interviews with diplomats and others.

In this instance the diplomat gave three primary reasons for Vietnam's attitude:

1. The ethnic-Chinese population of Vietnam would never support a socialist government and would continue to be a source of problems if they remained in the country, as they had been for years in North Vietnam. It was much preferred that they leave.

2. During the period of the Republic of Vietnam, the people in the southern part of the country had become accustomed to freedom of political expression and to independent economic activity. A whole new entrepreneurial class had matured. That political conditions had changed did not alter the attitudes of these people, and they would be only a source of lingering discontent if they remained. Political and social stability was essential if the Socialist Republic of Vietnam was to develop economically.

3. If there was to be an exodus from Vietnam, it was preferable that it be controlled by the government. In this way, the funds that had been accumulated through exploitation of the people could be recovered by the government and put to work to better the conditions of those who remained.

As to the effects of the outflow on Vietnam's relations with

155

neighboring countries, the diplomat said that of course it was a matter for regret. But in the long run, a politically stable and economically viable Vietnam would be in the interest of the entire region. Hanoi viewed the Sino-Vietnamese, who were a majority of those leaving, as essentially a problem for China.

The *Huey Fong* trial in Hong Kong provided as logical an explanation as any for Vietnam's reluctance to publicly admit its part in the refugee trade. Kwok the Dwarf, the prosecution's star witness, said that while in Ho Chi Minh City he had asked an official why the transaction was not being made in a government building. The official told him that if the international community were alerted, the refugees would not be accepted.

No, clearly the root of the problem was not in Washington or Peking, much as they might have contributed to it. It lay in internal policies instigated by Hanoi that were both rigidly totalitarian and deeply infected with anti-Chinese feeling. As an embattled Hanoi tightened the screws internally in the face of economic difficulties and the burdens of its own expansionary policies in the rest of Indochina, the ethnic Chinese in 1978 and 1979 became a scapegoat target. The elimination of their commercial role became in practice a program of deliberate persecution and eviction, reflecting centuries-old racial antipathy.[4]

So callous and inhumane was Vietnam, so high was the loss of life among the boat people, that two veteran Southeast Asian foreign ministers, Carlos Romulo of the Philippines and Singapore's Sinnathamby Rajaratnam, led the way in comparing Hanoi's answer to its internal troubles to Hitler's final solution for European Jews. "A poor man's alternative to the gas chambers is the open sea," said Rajaratnam. Romulo referred to "another form of inhumanity, equal in scope and similarly heinous" to the holocaust of Auschwitz and Buchenwald. U.S. Vice President Mondale and much of the rest of the civilized world resorted to similar language in an effort to describe their revulsion.

"Those Who Leave" posed a question that no doubt was intended to be rhetorical: "Could the Vietnamese government find any advantage, economic or political, in this question of refugees?" The answer must be a resounding "yes." Apart from expelling unwanted residents, refugee traffic generated hundreds of millions of dollars for a government with extremely meager resources. It also soaked up considerable quantities of hidden

156

gold; while it remained outside the official system, that gold could be used to stoke a black market and build a parallel economy. On the political side, a bonus for Hanoi was the destabilizing effect the refugee flow had on non-Communist Southeast Asia. The ASEAN countries were inclined to bicker among themselves and with their natural allies, the Western resettlement nations, over who was shouldering a fair share of the burden. The West, in turn, was tied up in moral knots on the issue. So all in all, the policy of exporting refugees served Hanoi well. Primarily a domestic measure, it carried a foreign-policy spin-off that amounted to a powerful weapon which Vietnam, war-ravaged and almost destitute, otherwise lacked.

EIGHT

Traveling in small cars, the group set out from Ho Chi Minh City at about 4 P.M., arriving at Vinh Long, the capital of Cuu Long province, southwest of My Tho, three hours later. When he went aboard a fishing boat that night, 37-year-old Nguyen Dinh Thuy became a refugee from Communism for the second time in his life. In 1954, his Buddhist mother had taken Thuy, then aged 12, and the rest of the family that lived in the Red River Delta town of Hung Yen to South Vietnam, as a conscious rejection of President Ho Chi Minh and his associates who had defeated the French in the North.

The boat, TB-41979, was small: about 55 feet long and less than 13 feet wide. The owner, who was leaving along with the organizer, said there would be 160 passengers. But after the vessel had visited Tra Vinh and several other ports downriver over the next few nights, it was crammed with 265 bodies. One of Thuy's stepbrothers, Pham Viet Hung, was accepted, but the other was turned back because he did *not have enough gold. The organizers at first agreed to take him on Thuy's credit, but in the end they rejected him in favor of another with gold in hand.*

The stepbrother was confined to the bilge with other young unmarried men. Thuy squatted belowdecks in the second tier, his knees pressing his chest, his chin on his knees, unable to move. He clutched his son with his right hand, his daughter with his left. Others were packed in just as tightly on the open decks above.

Near dawn on February 27, three days after Thuy had boarded, the boat docked at an island, where Vietnamese security police, bribed in advance, searched all passengers. They confiscated cash and gold beyond the ⅕ of a tael each refugee had been warned was the limit. The inspection lasted four hours, from 8 A.M. until noon. At 2 P.M., the TB-41979 headed out of the river for the open sea. . . .

IN SEPTEMBER 1978, the Premier of Vietnam, Pham Van Dong, packed his bags hastily for an extended trip that was to prove a turning point in Southeast Asian relations. Dong, an ascetic revolutionary in his early seventies, set out to visit Thailand, the Philippines, Indonesia, Malaysia and Singapore, which together form the Association of Southeast Asian Nations. It was not billed as an ASEAN tour, because Vietnam did not recognize the regional organization. But Dong took in all five capitals successively, so that there was no doubt that it was ASEAN, as much as its component countries, at which his diplomacy was aimed. The overture backfired, however, leaving Dong and Vietnam worse off than if he had stayed at home.

The trip was undertaken on short notice by Hanoi for both general and specific reasons. With its war of words with Peking intensifying and Chinese Vice Premier Deng Xiaoping scheduled to visit the ASEAN region, Vietnam wanted to shore up its position. China was warning the non-Communist Southeast Asian countries that Vietnam was Moscow's new Cuba and would try to infiltrate their ranks. Hanoi was countering with accusations that the real danger was Peking, which, after its "volte-face towards Vietnam," might use resident Chinese communities as fifth columnists to subvert the rest of Southeast Asia.

Dong's visit was designed to win over the ASEAN members, or at least ensure that they stayed neutral and did not side with China in the dispute. But unknown to them at the time, Dong was also trying to secure their support, if only tacitly, for a showdown that Soviet-supported Vietnam had planned to end its running verbal and military skirmishing with China-backed Kampuchea.

Although Vietnam's motives were somewhat suspect, Dong was a welcome visitor. The policy of ASEAN since the Communist victories in 1975 had been to build diplomatic bridges to all three Indochina nations. The ASEAN states were anxious to know if Hanoi was sincere in its newfound interest in their welfare. They also wanted to establish whether Vietnam intended to continue supporting Communist insurgencies in the region. Then there was the delicate question of refugees. A growing number of boat people were leaving Vietnam, burdening the countries of first asylum within ASEAN.

The two sides had a great deal of ground to make up. Hanoi did not accept ASEAN as a legitimate regional organization because of its pro-Western, anti-Communist origins. Its reservations were reasonable. At the time of ASEAN's formation in 1967, four of its five members hosted foreign military bases. The Philippines and Thailand were members of the Southeast Asia Treaty Organization, and the U.S. bases on their soil were playing a major role in Washington's prosecution of the Indochina war. Thailand and the Philippines also committed troops in support of the American war effort.

Nor did ASEAN's endorsement in 1971 of a Malaysian proposal for a zone of peace in Southeast Asia mean much of a change in practice. The five foreign ministers called for "joint action to secure the recognition of the region as a zone of peace, freedom and neutrality, free from any form or manner of interference by outside powers." But Thailand and the Philippines made no immediate attempts to end their security links with the United States.

Thus, the attitude of North Vietnam when it conquered the South in 1975 was one of suspicion and even hostility toward ASEAN. It was concerned about the policies the non-Communist countries would pursue, and possible threats posed by the lingering U.S. military presence in Thailand.

160

ASEAN experienced its share of apprehension at the turn of events. While Hanoi had been fighting to reunite Vietnam, its foreign-policy preoccupation was mobilizing international support for its struggle. Now it would have time to devote attention elsewhere. The collapse of the Saigon regime had made unified Vietnam the strongest and most seasoned military power in the region, its capability enhanced by the capture of $5 billion worth of U.S.-made weapons and equipment. Vietnam would want to exert some influence in Southeast Asia, but the extent of its ambitions, both political and military, was not clear.

The Communist victories in both South Vietnam and Kampuchea in April 1975 galvanized ASEAN, spurring its members from eight years of apathy to make a more serious attempt at regional cooperation.

At the same time, ASEAN extended an olive branch to the Communist governments in Hanoi, Phnom Penh and Vientiane. The five foreign ministers, at their annual meeting within a couple of weeks of the takeover of Saigon, welcomed the end of the war and hoped it would lead to peace, progress and stability in Southeast Asia. As part of its conciliatory approach, ASEAN constantly sought to give assurances that it was not a military grouping.

Hanoi's hostility did not abate readily. In radio commentaries and press articles it accused the five countries of adhering to economic policies that would bind them as "subordinates" to the United States and Japan. It also attacked the ASEAN members for "colluding with one another" to suppress the revolutionary movements in their countries.

However, the tone of Vietnam's criticism gradually modified, particularly after the withdrawal of U.S. forces from Thailand in May 1976. In July, Deputy Foreign Minister Phan Hien toured the Philippines, Malaysia, Singapore, Indonesia, Burma and Laos, in line with Hanoi's newly proclaimed four-point policy in foreign relations, which included "respect for each other's independence, sovereignty and territorial integrity." Although he pointedly omitted Thailand, to avoid the impression that Hanoi was affording any recognition to ASEAN, the visit resulted in the establishment of diplomatic relations with the Philippines—despite the continued presence of American bases in that country.

While Vietnam continued to stress bilateral relations with each of the five, its suspicion of ASEAN seemed to decline further in 1977. ASEAN, in turn, was encouraged by Vietnam's concentration on the task of reconstruction, including a declared willingness to accept Western private investment. Hanoi's restraint in supporting Communist insurgents in Malaysia, Thailand, the Philippines and Indonesia—apparently it was not supplying them with arms—also served the cause of détente.

Hanoi's falling-out with Peking, linked with China's support for Pol Pot's Kampuchea, drastically altered the developing relationship between ASEAN and Vietnam. The five ASEAN members were not smug or complacent about the disarray among the Communist nations. They diagnosed it as a threat to the stability of the region, which they feared would become a battleground for destructive Sino–Soviet rivalry.

China, an early critic of ASEAN, had become an enthusiastic supporter of the group and its proposal for a zone of peace. Then, dramatically in June 1978, Vietnam was also squarely on its side, proposing its own version of a zone of peace, "independence" and neutrality. A month after Hanoi floated the idea, Phan Hien again visited Singapore and Malaysia, and included Thailand this time, in what shaped up as a campaign to reassure ASEAN of Vietnam's sincerity.

With Premier Dong inviting himself to visit all five countries less than two months later, the feeling was growing that Vietnam was motivated more by the need to avoid being outflanked by China than by the conviction that ASEAN was not the ogre Hanoi had once branded it. There was concern, too, that Vietnam might be a stalking-horse for the Soviet Union, as Peking propaganda had it. As its quarrel with China became more bitter, Vietnam in June had upgraded its connection with COMECON, the Soviet-led economic grouping, from observer status to full membership. Circumstantially more suspicious was Moscow's own sharp turnaround in its attitude toward ASEAN, coinciding with Hanoi's headlong rush to embrace the group.

All this attention from the Communist world was flattering, nevertheless, implying that ASEAN had held together and become a force to be reckoned with. As one Soviet commentary acknowledged, "ASEAN is a reality which must be taken into

162

consideration by all . . . whether they want it or not." With its steady escorts of the past—the United States, Japan, the European Economic Community and other industrial democracies such as Australia, Canada and New Zealand—being joined by China, Vietnam, the Soviet Union and Kampuchea, ASEAN was finding its almost universal popularity a bit heady. "We're like a young lady being wooed," commented one Indonesian diplomat.

As Dong set out on the first leg of his diplomatic offensive, it became apparent that like all courtships, this one was not without its strains and sensitivities. The challenge for ASEAN in handling its Communist suitors was to keep them all interested while making it clear that marriage, or even betrothal, to any one was out of the question.

Dong's five-day stay in Thailand set the pattern for the entire tour. An advance Vietnamese team arrived with a wad of proposed agreements, the most important of which was a treaty of friendship and cooperation containing a nonaggression and antisubversion clause. While the Thai were prepared to sign minor agreements covering trade and communications, they were firm that a friendship treaty must not be rushed. It was set aside to be considered at some future time.

An antisubversion clause included in a joint communiqué signed by Dong and Thailand's Premier Kriangsak Chomanand was a rewrite of Vietnam's proposed text omitting any reference to a third country, a reference that could have been construed as anti-China. The two countries pledged to refrain from "carrying out subversion, direct or indirect, against each other and from using force or threatening to use force against each other." This amounted to an open and explicit undertaking by Vietnam not to support Communist insurgencies.

As he stumped through the region seeking to allay fears that Vietnam harbored ill will toward the members of ASEAN, Dong repeated his commitment not to support revolutionary movements. The undertaking was appreciated most in Thailand and Malaysia, though observers noted that it was made at little cost to Hanoi, since all the underground Communist parties of any consequence were pro-Peking.

At each stop, Dong reiterated not only Vietnam's peaceful intentions and respect for territorial integrity but its desire to contribute to regional peace and stability. His rather unseemly

haste to defrost relations with ASEAN earned him the appella-
tion "Pelan Pelan Dong"—slang for "Hey, slow down a bit"—
from officials in Jakarta.[1] Everywhere he met cordial hosts, who
welcomed his reassurances but politely rebuffed the proffered
friendship-and-cooperation treaty and anything else that might
be interpreted as deviating from ASEAN's neutrality in the
Vietnam–China dispute.

Little was said publicly about the sensitive issue of refugees.
Malaysia had taken the lead in bringing ASEAN closer to Vietnam, but it was also most affected by the boat people. The Malaysians were fearful that their policy of extending temporary
shelter to Vietnamese refugees would offend Hanoi, whose declared position was to prevent their departure. But the number
of refugees reaching Malaysia was growing rapidly, averaging
3,200 a month from April to September, and along with them a
feeling that Vietnam at the very least was not doing enough to
stem the outflow. As Malaysia's Home Affairs Minister, Ghazali
Shafie, remarked, "To move from one area to another in Vietnam you need documents. Why is it so simple for the boat
people?"

In any event, when Malaysian leaders raised the matter privately, Dong expressed regret at the difficulties the refugees
were causing. He explained their eagerness to leave Vietnam in
terms of the war. Malaysian officials, not wanting to offend
Dong, asked journalists not to question him about the refugees at
his press conference in Kuala Lumpur. When the subject was
raised regardless, Dong said he was "not happy" that the refugees were proving burdensome. "We wish that the international
agencies responsible for this will do their utmost to fulfill their
responsibilities in order to lighten the burden of the Malaysian
government," he said.

While there was obviously a considerable degree of skepti-
cism about Dong's multitudinous promises, especially in Singapore, the prevailing attitude at the conclusion of his rather extraordinary tour was to wait and see. "Only time will tell,"
remarked Malaysian Premier Hussein Onn. The ASEAN countries wanted time to test Vietnam in the terms stated by Dong
himself: "the deed we do today, what we do tomorrow and the
deed we do the day after tomorrow."

They did not have to wait long.

While Dong made the rounds of the ASEAN capitals, a rising tide of boat people continued to engulf the region. In October 1978, a record 12,540 Vietnamese refugees were registered by UNHCR, all but 850 of them in ASEAN territory and more than 80 percent in Malaysia. Following the same pattern, arrivals soared in November to 21,505. To cap it all, the freighter *Hai Hong* dropped anchor in Malaysia that month, bringing with it some 2,500 Vietnamese and the suggestion that their departure was organized, probably with Vietnamese government involvement.

"The so-called refugee problem is now a well-planned and well-organized exercise involving racketeers and profiteers," declared Zakaria Mohamed Ali, Secretary General of Malaysia's Foreign Ministry. Deputy Premier Mahathir Mohamad was unhappy that Vietnam had not done "anything at all" to help solve the problem, though he and other spokesmen stopped short of accusing Hanoi of orchestrating the exodus.

More disappointment was in store for ASEAN. On November 3, Vietnam finally abandoned the evenhanded approach it had maintained for years in its relations with China and the Soviet Union. It signed a twenty-five-year friendship-and-cooperation treaty with Moscow. Although Hanoi had been tilting toward Moscow since its open break with Peking, the treaty took most observers by surprise—none more so than the ASEAN leaders to whom Dong had endlessly professed Vietnam's neutrality and independence. What was particularly worrisome was that a mutual-defense clause binding both sides, in case of either being attacked or threatened with attack, to "immediately consult each other with a view to eliminating that threat," made the treaty a de facto military alliance.

The biggest shock was still to come. On December 25, more than 120,000 Vietnamese troops, as many as 20,000 Kampuchean insurgents trained by Hanoi and a vast number of tanks, supported by aircraft, invaded Kampuchea. Unlike earlier Vietnamese cross-border raids, this strike did not have a limited objective. The invaders kept going until they entered a deserted Phnom Penh—Pol Pot's government had fled—and installed the puppet Heng Samrin administration.

ASEAN's sense of betrayal, in the light of Dong's undertakings, blended with specific security concerns. The ouster of the

Khmer Rouge brought Vietnamese forces to Thailand's—and thus ASEAN's—doorstep.

The realization that Dong had pushed for the tour of ASEAN as part of Vietnam's plans to conquer Kampuchea added to the outrage. According to one report, Hanoi had decided to topple Pol Pot ten months earlier, and Dong's diplomatic initiative to reassure the ASEAN countries, the forging of economic and military ties with the Soviet Union and the creation of a National United Front for the Salvation of Kampuchea were all part of the preparation.[2]

The indignation that swept through the ASEAN countries was reflected in newspaper editorials. Commented the *Bangkok Post:* "The capture of Phnom Penh by Vietnamese-supported rebels should make it clear to any who thought otherwise that Vietnam in fact is an aggressive and imperialistic power." The question, said Singapore's *Straits Times,* is how far, territorially and ideologically, are the Vietnamese prepared to go? Added Malaysia's *New Straits Times:* "Vietnam's pledges are empty. . . . Prudence will require Malaysia and ASEAN to re-examine their relationship with Hanoi."

ASEAN's response was swift—probably its most decisive stand on a current issue since its formation. Meeting in special session in Bangkok—to display solidarity with Thailand—the ASEAN foreign ministers "strongly deplored the armed intervention against the independence, sovereignty and territorial integrity of Kampuchea." They called for the "immediate and total withdrawal" of all foreign forces from the country. Their joint statement, which was sent to the president of the U.N. Security Council for circulation as a U.N. document, urged the council to take the "necessary measures" to restore peace, security and stability in the area.

Although the statement stopped short of naming any country as the invader, the foreign ministers' denunciation of Vietnam was clear. They indirectly implicated Hanoi by "recalling the Vietnamese pledge to ASEAN member countries to scrupulously respect each other's independence, sovereignty and territorial integrity, and to cooperate in the maintenance and strengthening of peace and stability in the region." That, of course, had been Pham Van Dong's pledge—just four months earlier.

166

To make sure there was no misunderstanding, Sinnathamby Rajaratnam, Singapore's Foreign Minister and ASEAN's house hawk, told a news conference the statement was an appeal to Dong, whose credibility was now being questioned. "Withdraw from Kampuchea," he advised Dong. "That will reestablish your credibility."

On the question of refugees, the foreign ministers declared that the outflow had reached "alarming proportions," which would seriously affect the stability of Southeast Asia if allowed to continue. Significantly, their statement singled out Vietnam while referring merely to "other countries of origin" in Indochina, without naming Laos and Kampuchea. The statement urged them all to take "appropriate measures" to tackle the refugee problem "at the source."

Before the Bangkok meeting, the ASEAN countries were subjected to a hard-and-soft routine that was to become Vietnam's standard method of trying to influence them not to involve themselves in Kampuchea. As part of the friendly approach, Vietnamese officials in the region gave interviews to local publications that attempted to soothe ruffled ASEAN feathers. Tran My, Hanoi's ambassador to Indonesia, said, "What we are doing in Kampuchea is not subversion because we are helping a just struggle of the Kampuchean people. There is no reason for our friends in Southeast Asia to be worried." The touch of steel was applied by Deputy Foreign Minister Phan Hien, who called in the four ASEAN ambassadors resident in Hanoi—all five had diplomatic relations with Vietnam, but Singapore had yet to open an embassy there—and delivered a thinly veiled threat to ASEAN not to interfere.

Vietnam continued to blow hot and cold in the following months. Although ASEAN again called for the withdrawal of all foreign forces from Indochina after Chinese troops invaded Vietnam in February, Hanoi accused the five of straying from the path of neutrality and aligning themselves with Peking. Both Vietnam and Laos charged that Bangkok was allowing Chinese supplies to pass through Thai territory to Pol Pot's guerrillas in Kampuchea. Hanoi, however, still insisted that friendship with ASEAN was important to Vietnam.

For their part, the ASEAN countries dug in for a long period of confrontation, as they saw the refugee flow continue and

Hanoi's role in it become more apparent. In retrospect, the five nations could see that while Dong was scattering his promises to the wind, Hanoi had actually been stepping up the export of boat people to Southeast Asia. "Vietnam's credibility is zero," commented one Thai official.

That much was evident when Dong sent a letter conveying greetings to Hussein Onn on the occasion of the Malaysian Premier's 57th birthday on February 12, 1979. In his message, Dong said that Vietnam was trying to solve the refugee problem "in a positive manner" so that it would not create more difficulties for Malaysia and other Southeast Asian countries. He expressed Vietnam's determination to "unswervingly and scrupulously carry out what had been solemnly agreed upon" between the two countries during Dong's visit. Malaysia, noting the arrival of 13,730 Vietnamese refugees in the region in December 1978, 9,931 in January 1979 and 8,568 in February, did not respond publicly. But it quietly shelved plans to provide Vietnam with technical aid, including assistance for the rubber, coconut and palm-oil industries, and called off proposed bilateral talks on trade and other matters.

With boat people flooding the region in ever-increasing numbers—13,423 in March, 26,602 in April, 51,139 in May and 56,941 in June—ASEAN switched tactics and went on the offensive. Vietnamese ambassadors in Southeast Asia were informed that a continuation of Hanoi's policies would seriously impair its bilateral relations with the ASEAN countries. Some Southeast Asian leaders, led by Singapore's Prime Minister, Lee Kuan Yew, denounced Vietnam for deliberately trying to destabilize the region. Lee charged that Hanoi's "pitiless, cruel, barbaric methods of political blackmail" were making use of unwanted ethnic Chinese to stir racial animosities and put pressure on Vietnam's non-Communist neighbors.

When the ASEAN foreign ministers gathered for their annual Ministerial Meeting on Bali in late June 1979, Vietnam was almost the only topic. Understandably, all five ASEAN countries were becoming increasingly frustrated and angry. Vietnamese were seeking refuge at the rate of nearly 60,000 a month, ten times the pace of a year earlier, and tens of thousands of Kampucheans and Laotians were escaping or being evicted to neighboring lands. Resettlement efforts by the developed world were

168

not coping with the problem. The number of Indochina refugees in transit camps in Hong Kong and Southeast Asia awaiting permanent settlement abroad had risen in four months from 218,-000 to 350,000, and their ranks were swelling daily. With ASEAN's resources being "strained to the limit," in the words of Philippine Foreign Minister Carlos Romulo, all five had announced that they would accept no more refugees.

In addition, an estimated 80,000 Vietnamese troops in Kampuchea were massed along the Thai border trying to wipe out Khmer Rouge guerrillas. With Hanoi, on the one hand, offering assurances that Vietnamese forces would not cross the Thai border, and with the Hanoi-controlled Phnom Penh Radio, on the other hand, accusing the Thai of assembling forces to create tension, Thailand's Foreign Minister Upadit Pachariyangkun described the border situation as "fraught with the gravest danger."

The three-day Bali conference revealed differing perceptions of the upheaval in Indochina and differing views on how ASEAN should respond. Singapore's Rajaratnam, in a fiery seventy-five-minute address, further developed Lee Kuan Yew's thesis—that Vietnam's primary motivation was the use of Sino-Vietnamese to destabilize non-Communist Southeast Asia. Ascribing the blackest motives to Hanoi, he equated Vietnam with the Mafia and accused it of a "policy of genocide." Warning his fellow ASEAN members against "accommodation," against treating Vietnam as "an essentially peace-loving neighbor," he said Hanoi was planning to take over all Southeast Asia, backed by Soviet arms and using the flood of refugees to soften up its intended victims. "Today it is the Chinese Vietnamese," he said. "The Kampucheans have already been added to the list of people who are going to die. . . . Why not Thailand tomorrow, and Malaysia, Singapore and others who stand in the way of Vietnam's dreams?" To Rajaratnam, the refugees represented "political warfare" by Hanoi, which was packing them into "floating coffins" and sending them as "time bombs to destabilize, disrupt and cause turmoil and dissension in ASEAN states."

Some ASEAN members, including the Philippines, privately agreed with Singapore's analysis. Others, among them Indonesia, were pleased that Rajaratnam spoke out, even though they did not share all his views. None of the four others, however, thought ASEAN's response should be as belligerent as that advocated by Singapore. They favored keeping open the lines to Vietnam, hoping to persuade and pressure Hanoi into a more responsible and neighborly attitude.

Nevertheless, the five closed ranks to arraign Hanoi and place it squarely in the dock. Their joint communiqué, which repeated the demand for the withdrawal of foreign forces from Kampuchea, did not accuse Hanoi of organizing refugee departures, or condemn it for attempting to subjugate Kampuchea and Laos in order to achieve its long-held dream of an Indochina federation—all of which Singapore urged. But the communiqué toughened ASEAN's position by naming Vietnam for the first time. The foreign ministers "agreed that Vietnam is responsible for the unending exodus" and "has a decisive role to play in resolving the problem at the source." They "strongly deplored the fact that Vietnam had not taken any effective measures" to stem the tide of refugees.

The pressures manifest at Bali and elsewhere undoubtedly helped bring about the conference on Indochina refugees in Geneva in July 1979. Although ASEAN got much of what it was seeking in Geneva—Hanoi's agreement to halt boat departures, at least temporarily—the five were determined not to let the matter rest there.

At an informal meeting in Kuala Lumpur in August, the foreign ministers made plans to continue their opposition to the Vietnamese takeover of Kampuchea. In a joint statement, they also called on Vietnam to convert the temporary moratorium on the departure of boat people into a permanent arrangement. They warned that the prospect of widespread famine in Kampuchea—a result of fighting that had prevented the planting of the main rice crop—could stimulate a further flow of refugees.

ASEAN always couched its case in terms of the principle of territorial integrity, but there was no doubt that what worried the group most was the loss of the Kampuchean buffer between the mutually hostile Vietnamese and Thai. The fear that Hanoi might use Laos and Kampuchea to encroach next on Thailand sent tremors through the ASEAN region.

Hanoi might not have achieved a formal federation of Indochina, but its overthrow of Pol Pot gave it undoubted sway over all three states. Vietnam quickly concluded a treaty of friendship and cooperation with the Heng Samrin regime, similar to the one it had signed with Laos in 1977. They legalized the presence of Vietnamese troops in both countries. The pacts established a "special friendship" between the two countries and Vietnam, in practice making both Laos and Kampuchea client states. Phnom Penh and Vientiane tightened the three-way relationship—and Hanoi's domination of Indochina—by signing a similar treaty.

ASEAN's active diplomacy to remind the world of Hanoi's aggression in Kampuchea met its share of success. Prodded by ASEAN, the U.N. General Assembly voted in 1979 and again in 1980 to allow Pol Pot's government to continue representing the country. The assembly also passed an ASEAN-sponsored resolution calling for cessation of hostilities in Kampuchea, withdrawal of foreign forces and a political solution to the conflict.

But if ASEAN derived some satisfaction from keeping the heat on Vietnam, its approach cut both ways. At times it was closely and uncomfortably aligned with China, which had demonstrated a willingness to use force in Vietnam in pursuit of political objectives. It was also in the uncomfortable position of seeming to defend Pol Pot's regime, regarded by many as on a par with Hitler's. ASEAN ran the risk, too, of seriously alienating Hanoi and further polarizing Southeast Asia, when its declared policy still was to foster closer ties with Hanoi.

What the future held was unclear. But while there was no end in sight to the occupation of Kampuchea, and the refugee flows, an early reconciliation between the two warring blocs seemed unlikely. In any event, Vietnam would take a long time to live down its reputation for unpredictable behavior, foreign adventurism—and above all, duplicity.

NINE

Late at night, before the boat reached international waters, the water pump broke and the overloaded vessel began to sink. Nguyen Dinh Thuy hugged his children. His son was hot and ill in the stuffy darkness, and his daughter was soaking wet and cold. "We are going to die for sure," he thought. For the first time he no longer regretted that his second stepbrother had been unable to accompany them. His mother would have one surviving son at least.

An ethnic-Chinese woman removed a scarf from her head. She too knew what fate was in store. A relative of hers on the top deck, a former naval officer, heard the ethnic-Chinese crew talking. If the boat capsized, they planned to cut loose the two life rafts, abandon the passengers and save themselves. The woman tore the scarf into small pieces and bound the hands of her six children to her own. She wanted the family to be together in death. . . .

ONE JAPANESE DIPLOMAT based in Southeast Asia used a friendly Sunday-afternoon American-style barbecue as a model to describe the collective approach to taking care of the Indochina refugees. The barbecue is successful, he said, when every participant contributes something he finds most suitable and appropriate. One friend makes his home available, because he has the space and facilities in his backyard; others bring the meat and salad, while someone else bucks in and does the cooking. Similarly, some nations were giving temporary shelter to Indochinese, while those with the room and conducive social conditions accepted them for permanent settlement and others provided the funds to do the job.

The envoy's prime point was to answer criticism of Japan, to explain why the affluent Japanese did not open their doors to the refugees but gave money instead. His analogy might have held if a joint humanitarian operation had been mounted in which every country pulled its weight. But the ideal and the reality never met, never came close. Guests are usually eager to attend a barbecue; all but a few nations had a previous engagement when invited to the cause of the refugees. For a long time there was only a reluctant host in search of unwilling friends to make up the numbers, and not nearly enough to eat. Some of those invited never did put in an appearance. From the start, picking up the pieces in Indochina was an exercise in global selfishness, irresponsibility and shame; it was no picnic.

The responsibility for rescuing, rehabilitating and resettling the victims of the postwar turmoil clearly rested with the developed world. Yet the industrial democracies demonstrated a reluctance to do anything to alleviate the problem that they could possibly avoid. Some played a numbers game, imposing small refugee resettlement quotas and hiding behind a flurry of dismal statistics on employment, growth and balance of payments. Others, including critics of American involvement in Vietnam whose humanitarian concern at the height of the war had been strident, made almost as much noise with their silence over the fate of refugees languishing in camps and drowning in the South China Sea.

Dick Clark, U.S. Coordinator for Refugee Affairs, at one stage warned that not enough was being done to ease the burden carried by first-asylum countries placed by geography in the refugees' flight path. The inadequacy of resettlement programs, he said, constituted a "human crisis" that went far beyond what the international community had anticipated. While it is true that the dimensions of the problem had not been foreseen, the response of the wealthier nations for the most part remained mean and grudging when the tidal wave of human misery broke across the beaches of the region.

The Asian Wall Street Journal, in a lengthy editorial that was reprinted in *The Wall Street Journal,* America's largest-selling daily newspaper, and widely quoted elsewhere in the United States, noted that the leaders of resettlement nations, while keeping the refugees waiting, were squabbling about jurisdiction, fretting over health hazards and worrying about assimilation. Some were even arguing that the Vietnamese refugees were those who had lacked the backbone to defeat Communist aggression and so deserved the fate that had befallen their country. "Such excuses should be seen for what they are," the paper said, "handwringing, buckpassing and demagoguery." The halfhearted reception of the Indochina refugees, it declared, was "a scandal in the house of decent men."

The foot-dragging in the developed world needlessly deepened the anxiety and prolonged the suffering of people who already had experienced more than their share of anxiety and suffering. More serious, it contributed directly to the decisions of Indochina's neighbors to refuse refugees temporary asylum, setting in train a sequence of tragedy. In short, it was a death warrant for thousands.

The pathetic international response can be traced to a failure of leadership in, and by, the United States. After the "fall" of Saigon and the "loss" of South Vietnam, a humiliated United States was on the run in Southeast Asia, retreating and inclined to isolationism. The Congress and the people looked inward. Gerald Ford was a stopgap president, having replaced the disgraced Richard Nixon. He was succeeded by an indecisive Jimmy Carter. Drift and vacillation characterized official Washington.

Anxious to put the Vietnam trauma behind it, the United States simply failed to provide the leadership it would normally assume in a major humanitarian crisis. Ford told the American people when the last helicopters lifted off from the rooftops of Saigon, "Our long national nightmare is over." But as more than one observer has noted since, another nightmare was just beginning for many of the people of Vietnam, Laos and Kampuchea.

It is true that the United States acted with dispatch to accommodate 134,000 persons who fled as the Thieu and Lon Nol regimes collapsed. About 130,000 of them were Vietnamese, the rest Laotians and Kampucheans—diplomats and their families from around the world and a few others who had worked for the United States in Vientiane and Phnom Penh. They were paroled into the United States by the Attorney General, who had the authority to do so for emergency or public-interest reasons under the 1952 Immigration and Nationality Act. Immigration restrictions were waived so that they could all be accepted, including bar girls, businessmen and an entire fishing village evacuated by mistake from Vietnam in the confusion of the final days.

Equal to the occasion, Congress approved almost immediately most of the $507 million Ford requested for an initial refugee program. The funds were to cover transport, maintenance, resettlement, medical aid, welfare and social-service benefits as well as language and vocational training. By December 1975, the last of the 134,000 had left restaging centers on military bases to take their places in the American community.

Once the Indochinese were out of sight, the nation was pleased to forget Vietnam and all it stood for. But the United States did not ignore developments in Indochina altogether. It announced successive ad hoc measures to admit more displaced Indochinese as the problem grew consistently and remorselessly: 3,500 Laotians in 1975–1976; 11,000 later in 1976, again mostly Laotians; a limited program of about 100 boat families a month in early 1977; 15,000 extra places in July, 7,000 of them for boat people, the rest for land refugees in Thailand; a further 7,000 boat places in January 1978.

In every case the Attorney General exercised his parole authority—supposedly an emergency mechanism, but one that was becoming standard procedure—to admit the refugees to the United States. In every case the response was totally inadequate. By the time the Carter administration, in March 1978, proposed a permanent refugee program, the ASEAN countries were inundated with refugees and becoming alarmed: there were 100,000 in Thailand, 7,000 in Malaysia, smaller numbers elsewhere.

Carter's solution was to recommend to Congress that the Immigration and Nationality Act be amended to permit up to 50,000 refugee admissions to the United States each year, half of whom might be Indochinese. Pending authorization, the administration intended to implement the policy immediately by having the Attorney General continue using his parole powers to admit 25,000 Indochina refugees in the year May 1, 1978, to April 30, 1979.

Within months the proposed legislative program, like the earlier piecemeal measures, had been overtaken by events before it was implemented. Said one leading refugee activist: "The movement planned over a twelve-month period has not yet started: no funds have as yet been made available for the transportation and resettlement of the refugees. But there are already more *new* refugees waiting in the camps than the new U.S. program was devised to accommodate."[1] Southeast Asia's camp population had risen by 30,000 while the 25,000-place American program awaited activation.

Measured purely against the task at hand, the contribution of the United States was puny. But considering the country's strong tradition of openness, its past acceptance of the victims of war, famine and oppression and its annual immigrant intake, its efforts appeared positively resentful. It had accepted 160,000 Indochina refugees by April 1978, more than 80 percent of them within weeks of the takeovers of Saigon and Phnom Penh. The 26,000 admitted in the three subsequent years contrasted, for example, with 25,000 to 30,000 immigrants admitted each year from the Philippines and South Korea.

The failure of the United States to respond more warmly is even more glaring because it occurred largely during the presidency of Jimmy Carter, who had sought to elevate human rights to a major plank of American foreign policy when he took office in January 1977. The cause of the Indochina refugees was urgent and compelling, a matter of concern for the civilized world, the more so for the United States, which presumably had moral obligations stemming from its long involvement in the three countries.

But the human-rights gospel being sung in Carter's America was both extremely general and extremely selective. It seemed largely to ignore the barbarism of the Khmer Rouge in Kampuchea and the attempted annihilation of the Hmong in Laos at the same time that it purposefully took to task some of the ASEAN member countries for the fact that they were holding political prisoners. And it did so while only lamely supporting the refugee-rescue efforts taking place in these non-Communist Southeast Asian nations. Reinforcing the impression of a one-eyed, slightly jaundiced administration: the period of lowest intake, from the summer of 1976 to the spring of 1977, occurred when the refugee admissions program was administered by the Assistant Secretary of State for Human Rights and Humanitarian Affairs.

On several occasions the White House publicly connected the upheaval in Indochina with its cherished human-rights cause. Three years after the Khmer Rouge came to power and sixteen months after he assumed office, Carter condemned Democratic Kampuchea as the worst violator of human rights in the world. And on a visit to Thailand in May 1978, Vice President Walter Mondale said, "There is no more profound test of our government's commitment to human rights than the way we deal with" the Indochina refugees. If this was the test, Washington failed it—initially, at least.

The United States set out to define its obligations in Indochina within the context of the small overall admission quotas it set from time to time. Criteria were laid down to guide the selection of refugees to fill eagerly sought places in the United States. Four categories were enunciated by the State Department, priority being given to refugees with close relatives in the United States and to unaccompanied minors. The second category included former U.S. government employees who had held their positions for a certain period, and others who had been so integrated into the U.S. structure that they appeared to have been American employees.

The first two categories were directed primarily at Vietnam, where the United States had maintained a significant overt presence for more than a decade. But their imposition, though well intentioned, seemed to assume the existence of some hitherto-unknown refugee statute of limitations: all Vietnamese

177

were a special American responsibility if they had managed to scramble into fleeing helicopters and planes and onto boats and rafts when the Communists took over in 1975; but the rest were now of no particular concern.

The distinction was both arbitrary and, in some cases, repugnant. Thousands of those who had escaped as Saigon changed hands had bought their seats with corrupt gold and cash; others had used their connections to get out. They had all been automatically admitted into the United States. What of those Vietnamese who had been unable to escape until 1978 or 1979 because they were undergoing forced reeducation? They were effectively punished for having supported the American war effort, or at least having been cogs in the machine that Washington had built to sustain successive South Vietnamese leaders. Some of them had died in reeducation camps; what of their families?

The ethnic Vietnamese who subsequently found their own way out of the country despite Hanoi's tight controls surely deserved the same kind of sympathy as the 134,000 who had escaped in 1975 and whom the United States had accepted without question. Their claim to political-refugee status was equally strong.

As for the ethnic-Chinese refugees from Vietnam, they were at best driven to intolerable lengths so that they would leave, encouraged to go or at worst, evicted. The element of expulsion breaks down the equivalence with "normal" political refugees from a totalitarian regime. The Sino-Vietnamese, especially those from the North, were not simply like the middle class Castro threw out of Cuba, but were rather—as Singapore's Rajaratnam, Romulo of the Philippines and Vice President Mondale said—comparable to the Jews thrown out by the Nazi government of Germany.

Although the bulk of the ethnic Chinese often had little direct connection with the past American activity in Vietnam, they too were entitled to a compassionate response on humanitarian grounds. Various attempts to brand them as "economic emigrants," rather than refugees, were spurious. Such attempts were made by many a politician and editorial writer on the ground that the refugees had paid to leave and had had their departures approved by the government. But such talk was more often than not an excuse to avoid having to help these people—as though they were somehow different from the millions of refugees throughout history who, seeking to escape persecution, oppression and danger, had also paid to reach safety.

There was, of course, a particularly disturbing feature about the boats that left Vietnam between mid-1978 and mid-1979: since the government decided who should go and who should stay, Hanoi was dictating the immigration policies of other nations. But this involved a wider issue of one nation's behavior within the international community. It could not be resolved simply by punishment of the victims, nor should it have been.

As for economic motives, the boat people and indeed the lowland Lao of Laos may have moved and been moved in part by a desire for a better life. But for the most part it was coupled with the denial of freedom to pursue their daily lives or to follow their occupations in peace. And in this sense they were no different from the millions who had poured out of Europe at the close of World War II.

UNHCR accepted almost all the people who left the Indochina peninsula in the first six years after 1975 as refugees or displaced persons who were entitled to asylum, care and protection. There was little practical choice.

Democratic Kampuchea, until it ceased to exist for all practical purposes early in 1979, slaughtered those caught trying to escape as well as returnees. The position of the Lao People's Democratic Republic was less certain. Although Vientiane reaffirmed a commitment by the previous administration to facilitate the return of Laotians, refugees were often shot when trying to get out or after they had been forced back. Somewhat ominously also, the government made a habit of listing seven categories of persons fleeing the country, including "imperialist lackeys," "profiteers and parasites" such as brothel and opium-parlor keepers, and "Vang Pao mercenaries." For its part, the Socialist Republic of Vietnam used guns and prison sentences to deter departures, except for the year when Hanoi got in on the racket, and it refused to give safe-repatriation guarantees at any time. Indeed, Hanoi stated that anyone who left could return "only with the formal and individual authorization of the Vietnamese government."

If the refugee selection criteria in the first two categories specified by the United States were discriminatory and unfair to some Vietnamese, they missed the mark completely with most Kampucheans and Laotians. Few Kampucheans could qualify because the United States had conducted mainly an air war in that country and merely equipped and supplied the former government's forces. Consequently, there were almost no former employees seeking a home in the United States. Without any history of migration between the two countries, even fewer had relatives in the United States to qualify for family reunion. Of the 8,000 overland refugees from Indochina admitted to the United States in 1977, only 181 were Kampuchean.

Yet the Kampuchean refugees, especially those who escaped from 1975 to 1978, had some claim on the United States too. While the destruction of Kampuchea was chargeable in the direct sense to the genocidal policies of the Pol Pot regime, the fact that events could reach this pitch was surely due in substantial measure to the American invasion of Cambodia in 1970 and subsequent American military actions that made its essentially civil war so bloody and divisive.

Similarly in Laos, where Washington had bankrolled the former Royal Lao government forces and conducted an intensive air war, there were few former direct employees of the United States among the tens of thousands of refugees, and a limited number with relatives in the United States. More unreasonably, the CIA's role with the Hmong and others, being covert, was not officially acknowledged, though it had been widely documented in the Pentagon Papers and elsewhere. Although the Special Guerrilla Units had been raised, trained, equipped, paid and fed by the United States, the former irregulars were not considered employees.

Technically, in the case of the Hmong, the funds were channeled to their leader, Vang Pao, who disbursed the money. But morally, the Hmong and other former guerrilla fighters had a particularly strong claim to U.S. attention. Not only had they carried arms in place of American troops, but the CIA had placed them in a position in which Communist victors emerging from the war might have tried to eliminate them. And that is precisely what was happening.

For both Kampuchean and Laotian refugees who seemed to

be unfairly treated by categories 1 and 2, the State Department had a ready answer: categories 3 and 4.

Category 3 covered refugees who had been persecuted or feared persecution because of their previous close association with the United States. On the surface it looked all-embracing, but in practice it was narrowly defined—by detailed instructions. For example, to qualify for admission, former employees of U.S. foundations, voluntary agencies or business concerns had to have held supervisory positions for a year, or other posts for five years.

Category 4 was particularly favored by American officials who were called on to answer criticism of the selection criteria. It was touted as a catchall: "other refugees who because of obviously compelling reasons should be granted parole on humanitarian grounds." When it comes to the crunch we can take anyone, the bureaucrats liked to say.

The snag was the limited overall numbers being admitted to the United States—and the lengthening queue at the door. Successive quotas announced by the United States were immediately filled from category 1, and sometimes category 2. Only a few category 3 were admitted. Category 4 never got a look in. The catchall was catching no one.

The U.S. refugee quotas had to be cut another way as well, between so-called land cases and boat cases, which in the early days came down to a trade-off between the conflicting demands of the two first-asylum countries at the center of the storm, Thailand and Malaysia. While mindful of other considerations, Washington often made the split with the idea of saving lives that were in immediate jeopardy. By limiting its intake so severely, Washington narrowed its options so that on occasion it was in the uncomfortable position of seeming to contradict its declared policy by rewarding the country least hospitable to the refugees.

On top of all this, the United States weeded out refugees who met its selection criteria but were unacceptable for other reasons. It continued to admit Indochinese under the Immigration and Nationality Act, but it no longer waived the immigration restrictions as it had done for the initial intake of 134,000. More than 30 categories of persons were excluded under the act, including criminals convicted of crimes of moral turpitude, revolutionaries advocating the violent overthrow of the government, the mentally defective, the sexually deviant, chronic drinkers, the dangerously diseased, professional beggars and polygamists. The departments of State and Justice both screened applicants, using computerized files in Washington, including South Vietnam's old criminal records.

Much to the consternation of first-asylum countries, other major resettlement nations also imposed selection criteria and immigration restrictions. The others, unlike America's, were sometimes role-oriented and emphasized education and language skills. It encouraged the belief that the developed countries were "skimming off the cream and leaving the dregs," and "abandoning the scum."

As Malaysia's Deputy Prime Minister, Mahathir Mohamad, told one visiting American congressional delegation, a first-asylum policy which the United States was trying to persuade Southeast Asia to adopt would force Malaysia to accept all incoming Indochinese immediately, "with no questions asked." The United States, he pointed out, "then has the luxury of spending several months asking the refugees if they have tuberculosis, if they speak English, and so on, before it decides whether to accept them or not."

Washington is known to have failed fewer than 1 percent of refugees from Malaysia on immigration tests, but the number was far less important than the principle. It was one more inconsistency that materially weakened the position of the United States when it belatedly sought to come to grips with the Indochina exodus in 1979.

What the ASEAN governments sought in order to maintain their first-asylum policies was an assurance that "every single refugee would be resettled within a reasonable time," as Mahathir expressed it. They wanted to avoid being left with what they called a "residue," particularly as they all suspected, as did Mahathir, that any refugees left over at the end of the day when all available resettlement places had been filled would consist of "prostitutes, criminals and other social undesirables." The avoidance of a "residual problem" became the crux of Malaysia's policy on the boat people, and it was central to the attitude of the other Southeast Asian countries as well.

Leaving aside obligation, the assurances sought by South-

182

east Asia were obviously beyond the capacity of most individual nations. Presumably, though, it was well within the ability and resources of the United States to arrange such guarantees in conjunction with its allies. The contradiction of the U.S. position was that Washington wanted to "internationalize" the Indochina rescue effort. In theory, that entailed not getting too far ahead of the pack in case other developed nations failed to play their part and the United States ended up carrying the load. But because Washington did not seem overly enthusiastic about taking the lead in what was seen as the aftermath of a mess of its own making, the others were decidedly reticent about signing up.

The result was that by the time the United States had accepted 160,000 Indochinese, France had admitted 42,446, Australia 7,595 and Canada 7,057. At this stage these four were the only countries that had resettled more refugees than Malaysia, which, in addition to bearing the brunt of the seaborne invasion, had permanently accepted 1,500 Kampuchean Moslems. A second tier of resettlement countries trailed a long way behind: Belgium 1,057, West Germany 1,043, New Zealand 663, Britain 576, Denmark 352, Norway 249, Austria 232, Italy 216, Switzerland 210, the Netherlands 203 and Israel 66. All others had taken fewer. America was also helping to pay for the upkeep of the refugees still in camps, contributing nearly half UNHCR's Indochina budget, which amounted to almost $18 million in 1975 and 1976, and $14.4 million in 1977.

Altogether it was hardly a sparkling performance by the world's richest and most powerful nations; scarcely a ringing declaration of man's concern for his fellowman, and something less than a reaffirmation of fundamental democratic principles.

Although it would be unfair to accuse Washington of attempting to lead from the rear, it was not far enough out in front to impress upon others the seriousness of its commitment. A more constructive and productive course would seem to have been for the United States to set a bold example and bring its considerable powers of persuasion to bear on its allies, instead of relying on exhortation alone.

As early as mid-1977, the United States had been trying to persuade Japan, among others, to be more forthcoming, but without noticeable success. Specifically, it was pressing Tokyo to be more liberal in granting temporary permits for refugees who arrived in Japanese ports after having been picked up at sea by Japan-bound ships, to reconsider its decision to impose a ban on permanent asylum and to increase its contribution to UNHCR. But by early 1978, Japan had not agreed to resettle a single refugee, though it had somewhat relaxed its attitude toward temporary asylum.

One possible solution, and one favored by some longtime critics of American involvement in the Vietnam war such as *The New York Times*, would have been for the United States to declare its readiness to accept all Indochina refugees, alone if necessary. However, the Carter administration did not share the view of most other countries, that it was dealing with an American problem. One Washington official, briefing newsmen in Southeast Asia in late 1978, said that the United States felt no obligation to help purely because of its involvement in the war. "We have humanitarian considerations for helping these people," he said.

The administration preferred to emphasize that the "overwhelming majority arriving now are leaving not because of past direct ties with the United States, but because they wish to escape the ravages of continuing armed conflict as well as persecution and maltreatment stemming from the general restructuring of society imposed by the new Communist regimes."[2] The harshness of the governments in Hanoi, Phnom Penh and Vientiane was beyond question and was undoubtedly a primary reason for the outflow. But to what extent the policies they were pursuing were a consequence of long American intervention in Indochina was also relevant.

Apart from the worry that other developed nations might shirk their general humanitarian responsibilities toward the refugees, the main argument against the United States' signing a blank check, as opponents liked to put it, was that it might encourage more to leave their homelands, some to die en route, in hopes of finding a better life abroad. No less an authority than Lee Kuan Yew, the astute Prime Minister of Singapore, contended that welcoming any refugees at all was cruel because it encouraged others to leave. A push factor was undoubtedly at work in Vietnam, Laos and Kampuchea. The debate centered on whether there was also a pull factor, which might considerably boost refugee flows. It worried first-asylum and resettlement countries alike.

Indeed, for this reason Malaysia and Thailand always had mixed feelings about resettlement: they wanted to be rid of the refugees as quickly as possible, but they feared their prompt transfer abroad might induce others to flee. The Malaysian government initially took the extreme step of prohibiting refugees sending letters from camps because it believed news of their safe arrival would persuade friends and relatives in Vietnam to follow them.

Experience turned up little evidence that an increase in U.S. or other Western quotas stimulated the exodus from Indochina in the first four years to any significant extent. Indeed, although the U.S. refugee office in Bangkok closed after June 30, 1976—most refugee personnel left Thailand and the functions were assumed by a single officer in the consular section of the American Embassy—refugee arrivals increased. The refugees came, as officials discovered, even though there was no publicity about resettlement and they did not know what their chances might be of going abroad.

The U.S. government observed that the pressures inducing the outflow stemmed directly from the policies of the Indochina governments toward large segments of their populations. "The flow therefore can be expected to continue as long as these regimes continue to restructure their societies and do not stop escape or emigration," it concluded. "The fact that asylum areas exist does not so much contribute to the decision to flee as give it direction."[3]

A U.S. congressional fact-finding mission that addressed itself directly to the issue reached much the same conclusion:

> The question of whether the refugees came out because they would go anywhere rather than stay in their homeland, or because they knew there was somewhere relatively comfortable to go, seems to have been resolved. Despite the cramming of tens of thousands of boat people into small quarters in Malaysia, they still come out. Despite the risk of drowning, rape and pillage by the pirates of the South China Sea, refugees still set out. Despite the difficulties of the first ship, the Huey Fong,* both the Hai

* The Hai Hong had in fact preceded the Huey Fong.

Hong and the Tung An still came filled with thousands of refugees. Despite official Thai attempts to shut the Laotian border in November to January 1977–78, refugees still sought to come across, although in reduced numbers. Despite Khmer Rouge patrols on the inside and Thai patrols on the outside of Cambodia, a trickle of refugees has continued into Thailand.[4]

Prior to 1975, there were no significant numbers of refugees leaving Indochina, despite the devastation of war. Before the Communist victories in the three countries, there was always somewhere else to go without leaving Indochina: to a "liberated" zone held by the Communists, to a city under anti-Communist government control or even across a national frontier—say, from Vietnam to Kampuchea, where the fighting might not be so intense. That choice disappeared in 1975.

To that extent it seems reasonable to conclude that the West encouraged Indochinese to become permanent refugees only by offering some hope of rescue and resettlement in the first place. But, as Leo Cherne once commented, "if we are concerned lest we raise the hopes of the most wretched of the earth, we ought to then take down the Statue of Liberty."

The point is that the industrial democracies had little choice but to maintain and widen their humanitarian measures. Not to deal with the outflow, whatever its size, would have been inconsistent with the basic principles for which all these nations stand. In the case of the ethnic Chinese, it also might have put them in a position that Britain, the United States and others were in when the Jews were being evicted from Nazi Germany—of an obduracy that appeared to condone Hanoi's very reasons for the evictions.

Given that lack of choice, and the tragedy that flowed from constantly dwindling quotas, it would have been infinitely more constructive for Washington to have capitalized on an inevitability and provided the assurances that first-asylum countries desperately needed. Although it would have committed the United States to opening its doors and its heart a lot wider, it did not mean it had to go it alone.

That it was possible for the United States and its allies to assume such an undertaking was demonstrated in 1979 when a

186

decision was made to establish an international refugee-processing center on the Indonesian island of Galang. The idea was to transfer up to 10,000 refugees to the center, including some from other ASEAN countries, to relieve some of the pressure on first-asylum nations. Before the Indonesian government turned over the refugee-processing center (not to be confused with a first-asylum camp also established on Galang) to UNHCR, it required a guarantee that all the refugees admitted to the center would be resettled within a reasonable period of time; that there would be none of the feared residue of misfits. That guarantee was promptly forthcoming, as it was again later when the Philippines made space available on the Bataan Peninsula for a processing center to hold 20,000 or more refugees.

Admittedly, the guarantees of no residue extended to these refugee-processing centers, whose establishment the United States encouraged, were limited and fell well short of any blank-check acceptance of all people who left Vietnam, Laos and Kampuchea. The most important difference was that refugees admitted to the processing centers were already prescreened, leading some American officials to call them "reprocessing" centers. Only those refugees most likely to be accepted were transferred to them. Any who were ultimately rejected by the screening country would be picked up by the other resettlement nations.

Although under different ground rules, this is more or less what eventually happened in the general selection of refugees from first-asylum countries. There was little sign of a residue—persons rejected by every resettlement country—as the United States and its allies worked their way, slowly and painfully, through the Southeast Asian camps. The problem was the overall limits on admissions. Once the openings were available, everything else fell into place. Minor resettlement nations often tailored their intakes to admit those rejected by the major programs. So while defecting Communists from Vietnam were not welcome in the United States, Australia and Canada, some West European countries willingly accepted them. Other Europeans specifically sought out handicapped refugees, or the certified insane, who might otherwise have had difficulty finding a permanent home. Still others offered "open" places: they were willing to take anyone.

It seems apparent that the United States, with a little imagination, a more logical application of its own human-rights creed and a strong and more effective leadership, could have provided life-saving assurances to the ASEAN countries. As it was, Washington and its allies were going about the selection of refugees in a way that had the opposite effect and generated doubts about their long-term intentions.

As has been explained, it would not have been necessary to set huge quotas to satisfy the first-asylum countries. In any event, setting forth numbers, even large ones, had a drawback: they had a habit of soon appearing grossly inadequate in terms of the problem, and nobody could foresee how the situation would develop in the future. All in all, the numbers game seemed self-defeating.

The downplaying of quotas in favor of a serious commitment to come to terms with the growing crisis would also have made political sense for Jimmy Carter. A Gallup Poll released on April 30, 1975, had reported that 54 percent of Americans interviewed nationwide opposed resettlement in the United States of the Vietnamese being evacuated from Saigon, while only 36 percent favored it. Opposition to the continued admission of the refugees certainly still existed in 1977 and 1978, and the announcement of successive and ever-growing intakes could have triggered alarm and led to organized resistance to the Indochina program. However, domestic criticism and the undeniable economic problems facing the United States, including high unemployment, hardly constituted grounds for the administration's limited and unimaginative response. It would have had a good case, and it was not without public support.

One of the main concerns was that the refugees would remain on unemployment relief, or take jobs from Americans. But within two years the record showed that 94.5 percent of employable Indochinese in the first wave had jobs, compared with 93.1 percent for the United States as a whole. Starting at the bottom like other immigrants before them, the Indochinese demonstrated what one observer called "an astonishing work ethic." With their large families, they sometimes had to turn to public assistance such as Medicaid and food stamps to supplement their meager incomes. But the United States was not dealing with a major welfare or economic problem.

The Indochinese continued to improve their performance. Philip A. Holman, Director of the Office of Special Programs of the Social Security Administration, reported in 1979 that in just over three years the refugees "have demonstrated a determination to build new lives for themselves and their families and have established a record of diligence in employment."

As for edging Americans out of jobs, the American Federation of Labor–Congress of Industrial Organizations called it a "false issue." The biggest U.S. labor group supported a more open-ended policy toward Indochina refugees:

> No organization is more concerned about the problem of unemployment than the AFL-CIO. But that problem will hardly be affected by the number of Indochinese we are talking about—an estimated 25,000 a year—or even by the 50,000 political refugees the administration proposes to admit annually. In any case, these refugees do not take jobs away from steelworkers, metal workers, retail clerks, public employees, plumbers, carpenters, farm workers or any others. To portray these political refugees—who like our immigrant ancestors take jobs no one else in our society seems to want—as a threat to our jobs, in the same class with unfair international trade, excessive interest rates and misguided government economic policy, is a travesty.

A significant section of the deprived black community, which also might have resented the refugee influx, took the trouble to point out that it favored their admission to the United States. On March 19, 1978, in an advertisement in *The New York Times*, 89 black leaders urged the administration and Congress to welcome "our Asian brothers and sisters in the refugee camps." It was signed by the leaders of the National Urban League, the Southern Christian Leadership Conference and the National Association for the Advancement of Colored People, as well as by Coretta King and mayors Richard G. Hatcher of Gary, Indiana, and Kenneth Gibson of Newark, New Jersey.

Convinced that American efforts to be receptive to the Indochinese were grinding to a halt, the New York–based International Rescue Committee, Inc., a leading U.S. voluntary agency providing relief and resettlement services for refugees escaping persecution and violence in totalitarian countries, stepped forward. Alerted, unofficially, by a frustrated senior State Department official who despaired of action by the White House, it set about immediately bringing the matter to the attention of the American conscience.

In late 1977, the International Rescue Committee sponsored an organization called the Citizens Commission on Indochinese Refugees, consisting of 13 Americans representing a range of views, including some who had opposed U.S. involvement in the Vietnam war and some who had supported it. Leo Cherne, chairman of the International Rescue Committee, and William J. Casey, a lawyer and former Under Secretary of State for Economic Affairs, became cochairmen.

The Citizens Commission embarked on an intensive lobbying campaign to rally support for a more liberal and sympathetic approach. Members visited Southeast Asia in two groups, spending time in Thailand, Hong Kong, the Philippines, Taiwan, South Korea, Indonesia, Macao and Singapore. At the end of their field tours, they called a news conference in Bangkok and advanced a seven-point program. The first four points, going to the vacuum at the heart of U.S. policy, included a call for a "coherent and generous long-range" program and a better deal immediately for Kampuchean and Laotian refugees.

Back in the United States, the Citizens Commission blitzed Congress, the administration and religious and secular groups. As a direct result of its lobbying, the AFL-CIO supported the Citizens Commission's recommendations, and the black leaders took their stand in *The New York Times*.

Meanwhile, the administration instructed a special interagency task force, chaired by the National Security Council, to review its entire Indochina-refugee policy. On March 29, 1978, Carter approved the task force's recommendations, principally the proposal to admit 25,000 Indochinese annually by parole while waiting for legislation to be adopted.

As we have seen, even this step was overtaken by events before it could be implemented. And in Southeast Asia the policy of first asylum was under serious strain. Numerous incidents beginning in 1976 indicated that there was a limit to the generosity and patience of Malaysia and Thailand.

The authorities of both countries started regularly turning

190

away boats, the refugees being allowed to land only when their vessels were considered unseaworthy. This led to the dangerous but common practice of refugees' scuttling their own boats near landfall or offshore oil rigs. The refugees tried to inflict enough damage to ensure that the vessel could not be repaired and sent back to sea while timing the destruction for the last minute so that all occupants, including aged persons and mothers with babies, could get ashore. Casualties were inevitable.

The Malaysians were responding to the resettlement performance of the West. After Carter in July 1977 announced a new intake of 15,000 Indochinese, Kuala Lumpur temporarily eased its attitude toward asylum. On the other side of the coin, the selfishness, apathy and indifference in far-off places sometimes had a lethal application on the spot. Such was the case with rescue at sea. Merchant vessels that picked up boat people in distress, sometimes short of food and water and more dead than alive, found it an expensive exercise to try to unload them. Without resettlement guarantees in advance, many countries refused to allow them ashore.

In one celebrated instance, Tel Aviv finally accepted 66 refugees after an Israeli freighter that had rescued them off the Vietnamese coast had tried without success to land them at various Asian ports. Another group of 51 Vietnamese became the first boat people to reach Africa, when the Greek ship that had plucked them from their foundering craft arrived in Mombasa, Kenya.

The humanitarian concern of ship owners and operators turned out to be thin when the threat arose of impingement on profit. In many cases they warned masters plying the South China Sea to ignore refugees who, if rescued, might be responsible for long and costly delays while the vessel sailed from port to port seeking government permission to unload them. Others had a stronger conscience about violating their legal obligations and a traditional law of the sea: they regularly directed masters to sail hundreds of miles off course to reduce the odds of encountering boat people.

But even for the best intentioned, the boat people could present problems. Some masters reported refugee boats proceeding normally in calm weather and not in obvious danger—until they sighted a potential rescuer. They would then disable

191

their boat and start issuing distress signals in hopes of being taken on board. Another complicating factor was the prevalence of flags of convenience being flown by ships in Asia. In many cases the flag or ownership state of the vessel that rescued refugees was either unwilling to provide a resettlement guarantee or for practical reasons, unable to do so quickly.

East European ships sometimes followed the Soviet example in getting out of a tight spot and at the same time demonstrating their fraternal solidarity: they answered signals for help from boat people—and then promptly returned the escapees to Vietnamese authorities.

By late 1978, about 14,000 refugees, representing 15 percent of the 95,000 boat people registered with UNHCR, had been rescued at sea. Thousands of others had died unrecorded on the ocean, some after being sighted, ignored—even, on occasion, resupplied, but ultimately abandoned—by nameless passing ships.

Although the United States seemed semiparalyzed and incapable of the initiatives needed to ensure the maintenance of temporary asylum by the countries on the rim of the South China Sea, Washington remained acutely aware of the deteriorating situation. One warning, among others, was sounded by the U.S. House of Representatives Subcommittee on Asian and Pacific Affairs. After a series of hearings in 1978, subcommittee chairman Lester L. Wolff, pointing to the looming crisis in Thailand and Malaysia, reported that "a time bomb may be waiting to explode."

It ticked away through the second half of 1978—numbers multiplying, the ethnic-Chinese factor emerging, suggestions of Vietnamese government complicity surfacing—culminating in the arrival in Malaysia in November of the *Hai Hong*. The rusting old tub focused world attention on the Indochina refugees, but any hopes that it might give the international community a guilty conscience were misplaced.

The United States twice more, in June and December, had expanded its quota for the year through May 1979—more than doubling it to over 51,000. And after expressions of support in both houses of Congress, the State Department had added a fifth category to guide the selection of refugees. Category 5 provided for 625 Kampucheans a month, a total of 7,500 a year, to be admitted to the United States from October 1, 1978. Although eligibility was still to be in accordance with the factors specified in categories 1 through 4, the creation of the subgroup met the special circumstances of one particular segment of the Indochina refugee population. The Hmong and other former CIA guerrilla fighters waited for similar recognition.

But all this still had amounted to mere tinkering with a problem that required a major overhaul.

Under pressure to find a solution, the U.N. High Commissioner for Refugees, Poul Hartling, called an international conference on December 11–12. Officially titled a "Consultative Meeting with Interested Governments on Refugees and Displaced Persons in Southeast Asia," it brought together thirty-eight nations in the marble-walled Palais des Nations in Geneva.

In the days before the gathering, U.S. Deputy Assistant Secretary of State Robert Oakley toured Southeast Asia to confer with local officials and assess the situation. The meeting was doomed when it became apparent from Oakley's talks that the United States had not prepared any specific plan of action to present to other industrialized nations. Having just boosted its proposed intake yet again, it was hoping others would follow. More of the same; Washington had learned nothing.

A Note prepared by Hartling spelled out the gravity of the situation. By November 30, 1978, some 200,000 persons had arrived overland in Thailand, and 134,000 of them were still in camps awaiting resettlement. More than 50,000 of the 95,000 registered boat people also had still to be resettled abroad. In November, 7,131 land refugees had arrived, a daunting load considering that their 1978 monthly resettlement rate was under 1,700. As for boat people, 21,505 had checked in during November, against an average resettlement figure for the year of under 2,300 a month.

In addition, UNHCR was running out of funds. The rapid increase in its case load had necessitated several revisions in its projected spending for the period between January 1, 1978, and February 28, 1979, to $39.5 million, nearly three times the 1977 budget. With some $29.6 million pledged, the agency was short about $10 million.

Apart from pointing to the yawning and obvious gap between arrivals and departures, the Note stressed the "strong hu-

193

manitarian tradition" in favor of admitting those seeking asylum, going to some lengths to point out that it was not limited to conventions dealing directly with refugees. It found "particularly relevant" the principle that if one country was burdened by the granting of asylum, others should consider measures to lighten its load. "The attitude of states in the region is clearly affected by a variety of important factors including the prospect for durable solutions outside their territories," the Note said. "The question of temporary asylum cannot, therefore, be considered in isolation."

In the oblique and deadening language of international bureaucracy, it was an appeal to the developed world to stand up and be counted, to help Thailand and Malaysia in order to avert tragedy. It fell on deaf ears.

Throughout 1978 a number of resettlement countries, notably Australia and France, while disturbed by the trend of events in Indochina, had questioned the wisdom of scheduling an international refugee conference before the climate was right to produce results. They feared that a forum which drew attention to the problem without finding any "durable solution" would do more harm than good. And so it came to pass in Geneva in December 1978.

It was clear from the outset that most governments, including some of the wealthiest in the world, were more concerned with explaining why they could not help than with trying to come up with answers.

Vietnam did nothing to help. Its representative, Vo Van Sung, placed Vietnam in the same category as the non-Communist Southeast Asian nations—an innocent country battling the problems posed by an influx of people from a neighboring land. He said Hanoi understood fully the complaints of countries admitting Vietnamese because Vietnam, as of October 1978, was host to 426,459 such persons from Kampuchea. Denying "rumors" that the Vietnamese government was involved in any way, Sung said that Hanoi did not welcome the exodus but was powerless to prevent it. He appealed for more substantial economic aid and greater financial assistance through UNHCR to help redress the devastation caused by war and successive natural disasters, "the principal cause" of the outflow.

Hartling termed the meeting, held behind closed doors, a

194

diplomatic success: it had raised $12 million, and participants had agreed to accept 82,350 refugees over a one-year span. But the conference itself yielded only about 3,500 new places, compared with a total camp population of about 200,000. No fewer than 51,000 of the 82,350 places were those offered by the United States, and they had already been filled at the time of the meeting. As for the additional funds, $5 million of which was pledged by the United States, they would see UNHCR through for a further eight weeks at the most.

One official U.S. report put the conference results in distressing perspective. As of January 16, 1979, UNHCR had received 88,000 resettlement offers for 1979. If American, Australian, French and Canadian contributions were subtracted, "fewer than 7,500 resettlement offers have been received from all other participating governments." Moreover, most of these offers "have been made on a one-time basis and cannot be relied upon to be annually renewable."[5]

Of Japan, the wealthiest nation in Asia and one that profited from the Vietnam war but did not participate in it, there was no sign. The Japanese representative contented himself with restating the position disclosed earlier in the year: under U.S. pressure, Tokyo had contributed $10 million to UNHCR in 1978 earmarked for Indochina programs; it was "considering" bilateral aid to the countries affected by the outflow; it was providing unconditional temporary admission to refugees rescued at sea by foreign-flag ships and it was offering permanent resettlement, "under certain conditions," to an unspecified number of Vietnamese admitted temporarily "if it [was] their desire to stay." The representative did not say it, but the "certain conditions" imposed by Japan, together with Japan's traditional cold-shouldering of foreigners seeking to enter its society, would ensure that no more than a handful of Indochinese ever settled in the country.

So much for the Japanese diplomat's international effort; so much for the Sunday-afternoon barbecue.

TEN

REPORTERS LIKE Mahathir Mohamad, Malaysia's Prime Minister, a former medical practitioner; he usually has a quotable quote ready for delivery. Even before July 1981, when he was still Deputy Prime Minister, they trailed him everywhere—to the airport to greet state visitors, or to inconsequential meetings in the countryside, where their only interest was "Dr. M." and what he might be persuaded to say. So even as Deputy Prime Minister, Mahathir was rarely off the front pages, a situation that owed much to the country's shy, self-effacing Prime Minister at the time, Hussein Onn, who seemed just as determined to shun publicity. Mahathir sometimes surprised himself with his willingness to comment on just about anything. Cautioned once by a ministerial colleague on the political pitfalls of opening his mouth so often, he admitted to some anticipation as he read the morning papers to see what he had said the previous day.

When he glanced at the racy Malaysian daily tabloid *The Star* on June 16, 1979, the headline screamed: "SHOOT ON SIGHT

196

ORDER." He was the source of the report. After opening a seminar at a university near Kuala Lumpur, Mahathir had given his shadowing journalists a startling story. Malaysia had reached the end of the line with Indochina refugees. No more boat people would be allowed to land. Those who managed to reach the shore would be put aboard boats, built by the government if necessary, and kicked out. More than 70,000 Vietnamese in camps in the country were also to be shipped back to sea. Further, the government would pass legislation to give it the authority to shoot on sight any refugees attempting to enter Malaysian waters.

There had in fact been no need to wait for the next day's newspapers. The story had traveled around the world via the international wire services within hours of being issued by Bernama, Malaysia's national news agency. It burst at U.N. headquarters in New York, in Washington and in a host of other capitals. The time bomb had exploded.

Some controversy lingered over what Mahathir had actually said, or meant to say, on the question of shooting.[1] But there was no doubt about the thrust of his remarks. It was government policy, confirmed three days later by Premier Hussein, himself replying to a cable from U.N. Secretary General Kurt Waldheim expressing concern over the "alarming" reports of Malaysia's intentions. While drawing the line at shooting, Hussein said that Malaysia would no longer provide asylum.

It turned out that the decision to get tough had been made not only by Malaysia but by all five ASEAN countries, acting in concert if not as a formal organization. While Malaysia cordoned off its east coast and began expelling boat people, Thailand started to forcibly repatriate about 85,000 "new" Kampucheans; not in formal camps, they were classified as "illegal immigrants" rather than refugees by the Thai, who used January 7, 1979, as the cutoff date to make the distinction.

Indonesia was reacting as much to the hardening policies of Bangkok and Kuala Lumpur as to internal pressures when its Defense Minister, General Mohammad Jusuf, announced that it too would accept no more boat people. While pointing to social and economic costs, he acknowledged that the crackdown in Thailand and Malaysia would funnel the boat people to Indonesia unless they were checked. Indonesia's proposed solution was

197

to follow Malaysia's lead in mounting a naval blockade to turn them away.

Singapore had maintained a firm stand all along. For its part, the Philippines, though not so greatly inconvenienced and distressed as the others, would go along as an act of solidarity. And so the doors slammed shut.

Although the denial of temporary asylum chilled and shocked the West, it was the predictable, almost inevitable, outcome of events over the preceding twelve months. Perhaps it was thought that Thailand and Malaysia were crying wolf. Because both had not only threatened but announced bans earlier, they were suspected at least of exaggeration in order to turn up the pressure for speedier resettlement. But they were deadly serious this time—well, almost.

The ASEAN countries had never really been happy about extending asylum. Their original decisions were largely passive, since they could not stop boat people from landing along their far-flung coastlines or, in the case of Thailand, police lengthy land borders. In the early stages, most of the refugees were allowed to remain, except in Singapore, where a combination of geography and callous-hearted leaders made it possible to rigidly control their entry.

Affected in varying degrees and in different ways, the ASEAN member states initially did not think in terms of a coordinated response to the influx. That came later when they diagnosed a threat to the region and pondered Hanoi's possible stake in instability. For the most part, their individual reactions amounted to reluctant acceptance of the refugees while quietly hoping the passage of time would take care of the problem.

Only Singapore formulated a policy that would adequately protect itself should the refugee flow not subside. Boats arriving from Vietnam were intercepted, reprovisioned, refueled and sent on their way. Those which refused orders to leave Singaporean territory were towed back to international waters. Leaking and listing boats were often towed around the back of Singapore Island so that the refugees could land near UNHCR camps in southern Malaysia. Pulled at high speed, these boats would take on more water as the cork-sealed planking vibrated and opened. At least a few refugees are known to have died at the hands of an uncompromising Singapore Navy.

198

When in February 1979 the *SB-001*, carrying 269 refugees, was intercepted for the second time trying to sneak into Singapore harbor and refused to attach a towline, it was pinioned by two Singapore Navy patrol boats. The *P-81* maneuvered along its starboard side and the *P-74* nosed it amidships at right angles on the port side in a constant ramming action. The heavy swell lifted the *P-74* high in the air, and its steel bow came crashing down on the stern of the wooden *SB-001*, killing one Vietnamese instantly; 14 others either were thrown overboard or jumped into the sea to avoid the impact. The patrol boats released a life raft capable of carrying about 10 people and left the scene. Although the *SB-001* was taking on water and had to abandon the 14 and make a dash for the Malaysian coast, almost miraculously only 1 of them drowned. The 13 others were fished out in four groups by other Singaporean government patrols and fishermen, 3 of the refugees after being together in the water for more than twenty hours.

UNHCR, Britain, Australia and the United States all expressed concern over another incident, in May 1980, when a Singapore Navy boat stood by and refused to rescue 18 Vietnamese whose small boat had broken up and sunk in heavy seas. A 3-year-old boy at one point was taken on board the patrol craft, but soon returned by sailors to his mother in the water; both drowned. The Singaporean government decided not to release the findings of an official inquiry into the episode.

Singapore also set strict limits on refugees who could disembark from merchant ships that had rescued them at sea. They were not allowed on Singaporean soil until another country had agreed to take them within ninety days. In late 1978, Singapore tightened its controls by imposing a ceiling of 1,000 refugees to be allowed in at any time. Countries that accepted in writing, but failed to remove refugees within the time limit were subject to a system of penalties, while other refugees wanting to go to the offending country were not permitted to land until the backlog was cleared. The penalties applied even before the ceiling was reached.

UNHCR protested that the new provisions would make ships' masters more reluctant to answer the call of refugees in distress at sea. Singapore, the second-busiest commercial port in the world, is at an international crossroads. Many of the vessels plying the South China Sea pass through it. If Singapore were their next port of call, they would face unacceptable delays in trying to discharge rescued refugees. The government refused to back down.

Although Singapore's attitude was not characterized by flexibility and humanitarianism, it was nevertheless linked to the resettlement efforts of the industrial nations. Premier Lee Kuan Yew complained that once refugees were given temporary shelter, the world tended to forget its "responsibility" to provide permanent homes for them. Questioned about the possibility of a more liberal first-asylum policy, Lee answered: "We are prepared to take as many as possible in transit if we have pledges made to us. I've told this to the Americans; I've told this to the Australians. They have made no pledges to us."

Singapore's stand on refugees, like its posture on other important issues, was pragmatic and hardheaded to the point of being ruthless. It was based entirely on self-interest, with little room for sentiment or sentimentality. Lee summed it up succinctly: "You must grow calluses on your heart . . . otherwise you will bleed to death."

The policies of the four other ASEAN countries were more ambiguous. Thailand and Malaysia were essentially humane and resilient while trying their best, for various reasons, to disguise the fact. Considerable confusion existed at any time over what precise course they were following.

With Thailand, it was often a case of government spokesmen sending out conflicting signals, as they are wont to do on any controversial subject, or local authorities interpreting policy to suit local needs and conditions rather than the dictates of Bangkok. All Indochinese were regarded as "displaced persons" and, according to a Cabinet decision of June 3, 1975, were to be prevented from entering the country. If they could not be driven out, they were to be detained in camps and treated as "illegal immigrants."

With the approval of UNHCR, the government in November 1977 also started enforcing a policy that attempted to distinguish between "political" and "economic" escapees. Those judged economic were forced from Thai territory at the point of a rifle. For Laotians, both Hmong and Lao, this sometimes meant instant death: they were executed by Laotian forces on the banks of the Mekong, within view of the Thai officials who had made the decision on the spot to force them back across the river. Enforcement varied widely from district to district, however, and the Thai came under strong American pressure to abandon the policy. In early 1978, the newly installed Prime Minister, Kriangsak Chomanand, said that Thailand would continue to treat arrivals in a humanitarian way. Many provincial officials, when faced with a choice, took their cue from the Premier, though some based along the Mekong still made determined efforts to discourage arrivals.

In Malaysia, the government deliberately preached a hard line while practicing a more humanitarian policy. Like its ASEAN partners, Kuala Lumpur wanted to discourage further arrivals and avoid offending Hanoi. Word of its policy was carried back immediately to would-be refugees in Vietnam, who diligently monitored Voice of America and British Broadcasting Corporation broadcasts for every new development.

Officially, Malaysia's policy was little different from Singapore's: boats were provided with food, water and fuel and ushered on to other destinations. In reality, the few patrol craft of the Royal Malaysian Navy could not prevent their landing, but there was an important escape clause in Kuala Lumpur's edict as well. Those boats that were unseaworthy were allowed ashore and to stay, as were any ill persons.

Some boats were turned away between 1975 and 1978, but most were allowed to land. Even some of those towed back to sea managed to get ashore farther south. The occupants met the qualifications to become refugees by disabling their craft. State officials, in whose hands their fate rested until a national refugee task force took over in 1979, were happy enough, in the early days, to go along with this informal arrangement.

Although Malaysia started emphasizing in November 1977 that all boat people were "illegal immigrants," the government did not quibble with UNHCR for calling them "refugees," since this classification entitled the Vietnamese to full maintenance by the U.N. agency, thus relieving the country of the burden. It seemed that the "illegal immigrant" appendage, used faithfully ever after by the Malaysian press, was largely psychological, designed to reassure Malaysians that the intruders were in the country only under sufferance, and only temporarily at that. But no doubt both the Malaysian and Thai governments wanted to make the point that they were not bound by the Convention of 1951 or the Protocol of 1967 relating to the status of refugees and would safeguard their sovereignty only as they saw fit.

Much the same system applied in Indonesia. Vessels intercepted by the navy, made seaworthy and resupplied often turned up later on the north coast of Australia. Those which landed in the Indonesian islands and were unable to proceed were permitted to disembark their passengers, who entered one of several camps.

Altogether, the asylum arrangements for Indochina refugees in Southeast Asia were at best fragile and, as developments such as Thailand's temporary ban of November 1977 indicated, never far from the breaking point. The drowning of several hundred persons off the Malaysian coast, some after being denied entry and stoned by villagers, together with horrifying tales of pirate attacks, were constant reminders of just how precarious was the situation.

The arrival of the *Hai Hong* in Malaysian waters in November 1978 persuaded Kuala Lumpur to change tactics. After years of treading softly where the refugees were concerned, the government decided to hype up the issue. Stung by Western press reports that it was all but guilty of murder for refusing to accept some boats that subsequently overturned, Malaysia set out to pressure the developed world into taking more refugees. Editors of local newspapers and other news organizations were summoned, informed of government thinking and bidden to play their part. They immediately unleashed a sustained attack on the United States and other resettlement countries. Hanoi did not escape criticism, but the main target was Washington.

Although the campaign was highly emotional, it reflected rising public resentment. If it appeared that government leaders themselves were contributing to the mood of anger, the government had reason to want to be seen as doing something about the refugees: political opponents were sniping at it for allegedly being soft on them. The main threat came from the theocratic Partai Islam, a Malay opposition party, but the government also had to heed rumblings within the ranks of its own United Malays National Organization, the dominant partner in the ruling National Front. Government members of Parliament representing coastal constituencies were demanding an end to the influx. One went so far as to suggest that Malaysian waters be mined to keep the refugees out.

Thai patience was also starting to run out. Newspapers, politicians and the public called for the expulsion of the refugees. Leading the outcry was Thanat Khoman, a former Foreign Minister who was sitting in Parliament as leader of the centrist Democrat Party. Thanat was highly critical of the government's handling of the issue and said, among other things, that if Vietnam was using racial background as the benchmark for expelling ethnic Chinese, Bangkok might be equally justified in shipping its Vietnamese residents back to Vietnam because they were not ethnic Thai.

By November 1978, Thailand's Premier Kriangsak was echoing Malaysia's hardening sentiment toward boat people. The Thai would receive them, he told the *Bangkok Post*, only long enough to resupply them before returning them to open waters. "If any boat needs repairs this will be permitted, but it will have to leave with the refugees as soon as repairs are completed," he said.

It was in this uncertain but assuredly souring atmosphere that the 38 nations gathered in Geneva on December 11 and 12 to see what could be done. Malaysia was represented by the forceful and flamboyant Ghazali Shafie, who is known in the country as "King Ghaz." He had been assigned the refugee headache as much for his reputation as a troubleshooter as by virtue of his Home Affairs portfolio, which covers internal security. Ghazali proposed an island processing center away from Southeast Asia, possibly on U.S. territory in the Pacific, where refugees could stay while awaiting resettlement. It was a specific strategy to cope with the worsening situation, a concrete undertaking by Malaysia to remain a country of "first transit" if the West would match it with a pledge of resettlement. "Malaysia is prepared to be the staging post and assist in transporting them to the processing center," Ghazali said.

There were no takers. The American delegation cited legal problems with establishing a refugee-processing center on American soil, and the relative high cost of reopening Guam or using some other distant land, as opposed to processing in Southeast Asia.

203

A month later, on January 15, 1979, Premier Hussein announced a ban on refugees' entering Malaysia. It was just as difficult as ever for the thinly stretched navy to blockade the east coast. But patrol craft made a serious effort, often firing over the bows of refugee boats to deter them. Hundreds of military observation posts were established along the shores to watch for intruders.

Kuala Lumpur left it to the military to implement the ban. The government said all refugee boats were given food and water before being sent out to sea, but refugees frequently claimed the navy had taken their maps, compasses and other navigational aids and left them with engines out of order, helpless on the high seas. Patrol craft were frustrated by the ploys of the refugees: some would allow themselves to be towed into international waters, but would head for the Malaysian shoreline again as soon as the navy cut them loose and moved on.

With Vietnamese boats being stalked down the east coast by both Thai pirates and the Malaysian Navy, one of the most controversial incidents of the entire Indochina refugee sága took place—the sinking of the *MH-3012* with the loss of 104 lives. As pieced together from interviews with survivors, it amounted to an accusation of sadistic murder against the officers and crew of a Malaysian Navy patrol boat, while suggesting that a general policy was being practiced that was cruel to the point of indifference to human life. Two separate reports, one prepared by UNHCR, the other by officials of a Western diplomatic mission in Kuala Lumpur, agreed on every significant detail. According to the account by survivors:

The *MH-3012*, a 59-foot wooden fishing boat, set out from Ca Mau, in southern Vietnam, on March 19, 1979, carrying 237 refugees, most of them ethnic Chinese. It was a typical government-sponsored departure, the passengers having registered and paid in advance. The *MH-3012* headed south until it met the *Kris*, a 103-foot Malaysian Navy patrol boat, near the Thai–Malaysian border on March 22. The *Kris* towed the boat south for thirty-six hours before cutting the connecting wire and telling the Vietnamese to head toward Indonesia, only six hours away. The UNHCR report commented: "The Vietnamese boat was in very bad condition, water pump was broken and engine could not be started. No water was available . . . a baby was born on board in the meantime . . . All the facts were known to the naval officers who had been on board."

As the Vietnamese boat drifted for the next four days, 10 persons died of dehydration—1 elderly man and 9 children, 2 to 6 years of age. With a small desalination plant on board producing only 1.3 gallons of water a day, each survivor was limited to 2 teaspoonfuls of water daily. On March 31, when 4 of the Vietnamese began swimming in search of land, 2 of them were picked up by the navy patrol craft *Renchong,* a sister ship of the *Kris.* The 2 men were "thrown unconscious in a corner." After they recovered and the *Renchong* located the refugee boat, navy officers refused Vietnamese requests to land anywhere and insisted on towing the boat farther south. The UNHCR report said: "When the Vietnamese refused to tie the rope to their boat, naval officers fired shots and one Vietnamese, Hua Trac Thanh, was hit in his left arm." The second report said that the refugees had heard a burst of gunfire as the man was hit. The navy sent men aboard the refugee boat to attach a towline. The Malaysians removed Thanh, 1 sick woman and some children and took them on board the *Renchong.*

The *Renchong* towed the *MH-3012* farther south at high speed on a zigzag course, causing it to take on water. "After one hour into the tow the boat was very low in the water and in danger of sinking," the second report said. The Vietnamese signaled the *Renchong* to stop, but the only response was shouts of laughter from the crew, some of whom took photographs. The refugees were "wailing . . . for mercy," UNHCR said.

During one of the turning maneuvers, when the *MH-3012* was 40 miles off Mersing on the southern Malaysian coast, it rolled over, "the obvious result" of the exercise, throwing the refugees into the water. The *Renchong* quickly cut the rope and slowed, and naval officers began taking photographs of "floating Vietnamese." The refugees who tried to reach the patrol craft were prevented from boarding by naval officers and crew who pulled up the ship's ladder. The *Renchong* circled the Vietnamese for half an hour before it began picking up survivors, 122 of them in all. But by then it was too late for many who had floated away.

The Malaysian government reacted angrily to the allegations and immediately ordered an investigation. Ghazali Shafie said in a statement that the *MH-3012* had been in good condition, with adequate provisions, and had been requested to leave Malaysian waters. Without specifically denying the shooting, his statement suggested otherwise. A preliminary government inquiry had shown that the "alleged gunshot wound" was a "jagged laceration without any trace of gunpowder." The inquiry also revealed that the boat had been pirated three times before reaching Malaysian waters. As for the rescue, about 50 navy and police personnel and local fishermen had rendered assistance to the sinking boat "as an effort to save human lives at the risk of their own."

As an explanation, it was unconvincing. But more damaging, the Malaysian Cabinet decided not to make public the findings of the official investigation. Allegations of the most serious nature remained unanswered, and as a result Malaysia's reputation was blemished.

One way or another, Malaysian authorities pushed back more boats and more refugees in early 1979. But because the refugee tide was rising, more also managed to land. In March, 5,088 refugees in 29 boats were repelled, compared with 4,959 in 50 boats for all of 1978. Expulsions rose to 7,412 refugees in 71 boats in April and 13,462 in 86 boats in May.

At the same time, some Malaysian states, notably Johore, introduced an unannounced policy of expelling boat people who had landed. In a ten-week period about 1,200 Vietnamese were held under guard on the beachfront, packed into boats that were often not the ones they had arrived in and pushed out to sea again.

Apart from following Malaysia's example in cracking down on boat people, Thailand began to move against the "new" Kampucheans. On April 13, the Thai gave notice of what was to come when they forced back into Kampuchea 1,700 persons, mostly women and children, who had crossed the border since January 7. On a visit to Thailand the following month, U.N. Secretary General Waldheim told Premier Kriangsak that in the eyes of the United Nations all persons arriving from Kampuchea were refugees and not to be repatriated against their will, despite Thai refusal to grant them refugee status. If it had any effect, the protest seemed to annoy the Thai, who were convinced that the rest of the world did not care about their massive problem and was leaving them to face it almost alone.

The situation became more acute when a lack of funding due to congressional delays cut the American intake of Indochina refugees by half. Although the United States was supposed to be admitting 7,000 a month, fewer than 3,500 were flown out in April and again in May. American officials called the setback temporary and said Congress would rectify it quickly. But it arose at a most inappropriate time, adding to the mood of isolation, panic and desperation that was enveloping Southeast Asia.

A meeting in Jakarta on May 15 and 16, 1979, to discuss the establishment of a refugee-processing center on Galang Island further convinced the ASEAN countries of their helplessness and inability to control events. Attended by UNHCR and twenty-four nations, including the ASEAN five and Vietnam, the meeting decided to go ahead with the proposal.

But feasibility studies had to be commissioned and financed, and the center obviously would not be ready to receive refugees for some time. Most developed countries were unwilling to advance funds until the project was shown to be feasible. And when it was completed, perhaps in a year or two, it would hold a maximum of 10,000 persons. To put that figure into some perspective, it should be pointed out that in the week during which the meeting was held, 10,000 boat people landed on Asian beaches and thousands more streamed overland to Thailand.

Another depressing aspect of the meeting was the continued intransigence of Vietnam. The arrival of a three-man delegation from Hanoi led by Vu Hoang, Director of Consular Affairs in the Foreign Ministry, raised some hope that Vietnam might follow through on the statement by Premier Pham Van Dong that the refugee exodus was not intended to inconvenience Southeast Asia. But it was Tran My, the Vietnamese ambassador to Indonesia, who spoke for the country, and all he did was recall Dong's pledge that ". . . we are doing our utmost, whatever that can lessen the difficulties to other countries in this region, and are cooperating with the UNHCR to find out the best solution to this problem."

Vietnam's idea of cooperation—though unconfessed—was to authorize and arrange the departure of at least 51,000 fare-paying passengers in that month of May 1979. Tran My's comment was regarded as the same unhelpful kind of talk the Vietnamese had indulged in privately in Geneva the previous December. Vu Hoang added to the despondency. He told journalists that 600,000 more ethnic Chinese might want to leave the country. He also spoke of Hanoi's willingness to allow up to 10,000 residents a month to leave directly for recipient countries under an orderly departure program negotiated with UNHCR and said that for openers, the government intended to deliver to the U.N. agency the names of 20,000 potential émigrés.

In early June, the Thai Army swung into action, for four days emptying makeshift camps occupied by "new" Kampucheans near the border districts of Aranyaprathet and Ta Phraya, and busing the refugees 290 miles north to Sisaket province.

> The parallel with the Jews being led to the showers was close. When the first group of the 42,000 Cambodians were loaded on to buses by Thai soldiers . . . they were told they were being taken off for resettlement. Instead, after a six-hour drive with stops to pick up a two-day supply of rice, they were dropped off near the disputed temple of Preah Vihear, marched to the Cambodian border and pushed at gunpoint across it. They were then told to follow a narrow trail down a steep hillside. Those who wandered off it were blown up by mines. Those who attempted to climb back up the hill were shot at.[2]

How many of the deportees died was never established with certainty, but it is known to have been in the hundreds, perhaps thousands. Many were middle-class merchants, professionals and intellectuals, and as many as 1,500 had been selected for resettlement by American officials who had no time to rescue them before the pushback started. The victims included the wife of Tan Kim Huon, a former president of the National Assembly of the Khmer Republic; she was killed in a road accident.

One of those expelled, the wife of a former cabinet minister executed by the Khmer Rouge, later told of seeing up to 100 people blown up by mines when they were first shoved across the frontier. On another occasion, when food rations ran low, the Kampucheans died at an average of 30 a day. "It was a true

208

nightmare," she wrote. "Never has the feeling of being abandoned by man and by God been so strong."

The woman, accompanied by her 3 children, ended up walking 375 miles in five weeks before arriving, fatigued and badly emaciated, at her native village back near the Thai border. She reported that along the way the miserable masses had been stopped once by Vietnamese soldiers to allow Hanoi Television to film them. She also detailed numerous instances of discrimination against Sino-Khmer in their ranks. The ethnic Chinese were made to cross rivers behind Khmer, Lao and ethnic Vietnamese, and were given less to eat.

The deluge of international criticism that the mass expulsion provoked infuriated Thai leaders. Kriangsak, a pro-West former army general, retorted: "This is our business; it is done to protect the national interest"—a reference to Hanoi's threat over Thai sanctuary for the Khmer Rouge. Alluding to the sore point of resettlement, he turned on Western critics: "They're ready to talk about human rights, but why don't they do something about it?"

Kriangsak countered protests by President Carter and Secretary General Waldheim by firing off appeals to both for more help in moving the refugees out of Thailand. However, he agreed to suspend the repatriation exercise, much to the relief of about 50,000 "new" Kampucheans still in Thailand.

Foreign correspondents and cameramen who flocked to Malaysia to see refugees being machine-gunned on the beaches after Mahathir's outburst were disappointed. As the policy was clarified by Premier Hussein, even the 76,000 refugees in UNHCR camps would not be sent out to sea immediately; their fate rested on "definite pledges and programs" for resettlement being given within some unspecified "reasonable time frame." But sitting in their old haunt, the Pantai Motel in Kuala Trengganu, the newsmen could once again sip drinks and watch the dramatic movement of overcrowded and leaking Vietnamese fishing boats—leaving this time, not arriving.

Most of the boats denied entry in Malaysia were allowed to land in Indonesia, despite Jakarta's announced ban. Had Indonesia enforced the ban, thousands of boat people almost certainly would have perished: the only alternatives were onward to Australia or reverse to the Philippines, distant lands beyond the reach of all but a few of the disintegrating boats and their deteriorating passengers.

The formal denial of asylum by ASEAN left Hong Kong as the only publicly proclaimed haven for boat people. As befits a territory that has granted asylum to such personalities as Philippine independence hero José Rizal and, ironically, Ho Chi Minh, Hong Kong refused to say "No more." Having tried to shut refugees out and found it could not do so without endangering life, Hong Kong backed off.

It paid a price for its humanity, in terms both of refugees attracted by its attitude and of resettlement nations rushing off to assist countries threatening mass murder. By the end of July, 35 percent of the boat people to reach landfall in 1979 had found shelter in Hong Kong, but the colony had been allocated only 13 percent of resettlement places. ". . . one cannot blame people in Hong Kong for drawing the conclusion that help would be greater if policies were harsher," commented the Chief Secretary, Sir Jack Cater. "Nor, unhappily, can you blame those who apply harsher policies for concluding that they have paid off."

Still, anachronistic and capitalistic Hong Kong, lambasted endlessly for its preoccupation with the fast buck, a tiny enclave with standing room only and more moral right to protection against an inundation of strangers than almost any place else, did not call time out. "We have turned none away," said Cater. One former resident, in a letter to a Hong Kong magazine, suggested that in happier times the words be engraved on a slab of the granite that makes up so much of the colony's estate: "WE HAVE TURNED NONE AWAY."

ELEVEN

A former boat owner among the passengers saved them. He took over, turned the TB-41979 around and headed back to the Vietnamese coast. About 2 A.M. on February 28, they arrived near Tra Cu, still in Cuu Long province, 130 miles south of Ho Chi Minh City. At 6 o'clock they leaped ashore, grateful for the chance to stretch their legs and surprised to be alive.

Tra Cu was their home for the next week and a half while the water pump was repaired. Some of the refugees contacted their families. Those who could afford to bribe local police were able to arrange for their relatives to visit them. Nguyen Dinh Thuy did not have the money. . . .

ON A CRISP summer morning, several hundred Vietnamese are demonstrating outside Geneva's Palais des Nations. They stand silently with placards on a neat strip of lawn opposite the en-

211

trance, through which pass delegates gathering for the second international conference on Indochina refugees. The demonstrators have come from France, West Germany, Belgium, the Netherlands and Britain to join Swiss compatriots in denouncing the government of the Socialist Republic of Vietnam. They include 9 saffron-robed monks sitting cross-legged on the grass and Phan Dinh Cuong, a 19-year-old former student and professional table-tennis player, who arrived in Paris as a refugee only two weeks ago from Malaysia's Pulau Bidong camp. The flag of old South Vietnam is held aloft by several protestors, though not all of them supported the Thieu regime; some say they backed the National Liberation Front during the war but have since become disenchanted with the new government.

Apologetic Swiss police in plain clothes arrive with a request. They have received a complaint from the Vietnamese mission about one particular banner; while it remains on display the Vietnamese will not attend the conference. The demonstrators obligingly remove the offending sign, which, to the casual observer, looks no more pointed or insulting than the others. It reads, in French: "TOUT LE PEUPLE VIETNAMIEN CONTRE LA CLIQUE DE HANOI"—all the Vietnamese people against the Hanoi clique. Soon after it disappears, two black limousines appear on the street, swing into the entrance and disappear up the driveway. It is 10:02 A.M. on July 20, 1979. Two minutes late, the Vietnamese representatives, led by Deputy Foreign Minister Phan Hien, arrive, the last of 65 national delegations taking part in the largest refugee meeting in history.*

The road back to Geneva was littered with guilt, strewn with regret. A second meeting was necessary because the nations that attended the first had turned their backs on the issues. In the seven months since then, the situation had deteriorated into what U,N. Secretary General Kurt Waldheim called "one of the most tragic experiences which the world has faced." The International Committee of the Red Cross termed it "potentially the biggest tragedy" since World War II.

This time around it was not left to UNHCR but was backed with the full authority of the United Nations. After an initial ap-

* Several other governments attended as observers, while a number of intergovernmental concerns and groupings of nongovernment organizations were also represented.

212

peal in May, Waldheim invited the international community to try again at a two-day ministerial-level conference. "ALTHOUGH THERE ARE VERY MANY SERIOUS REFUGEE PROBLEMS IN OTHER PARTS OF THE WORLD," he said in his 288-word invitation cable, "THE ALARMING PROPORTIONS OF THE CRISIS IN SOUTHEAST ASIA REQUIRE IMMEDIATE AND SPECIAL ATTENTION."

By the time the delegates assembled in Geneva in July, 372,000 refugees were in UNHCR camps in Asia awaiting resettlement: 202,000 boat people, the rest overlanders. In the first six months of 1979, 209,000 Indochinese had crossed national boundaries, but permanent homes had been found for only 54,-000 of them. These were the dimensions of the tragedy:

—Malaysia was host to 74,408 boat people, Hong Kong 66,065, Indonesia 44,247, the Philippines 4,938, Macao 3,211, Singapore 821, Japan 557, South Korea 42 and Brunei 20. Small numbers were scattered elsewhere.

—Thailand was providing camp shelter for 169,167 land refugees from Laos and Kampuchea as well as 7,000 Vietnamese and Kampuchean boat people. In addition, about 50,000 "new" Kampucheans denied refugee status remained on Thai territory, their fate uncertain since the forcible repatriation of the others in June.

—China had received 250,000 from Vietnam, 200,-000 of whom the government had resettled. The 50,000 others were still without shelter, some of them ethnic Vietnamese waiting for an opportunity to be resettled abroad.

—Vietnam had taken advantage of Pol Pot's overthrow to repatriate most of the 150,000 or more nonethnic Vietnamese from Kampuchea. About 30,000—some Khmer, but most ethnic Chinese—remained in Vietnam; some of them were being encouraged to integrate into the local community, though others continued to emigrate.

Poul Hartling, the U.N. High Commissioner, in a Note prepared for the conference, explained the breakdown in the system: Southeast Asian countries had lost confidence in the ability of the international community to control the problem; in turn, the accepted principles of asylum and nonrefoulement had been breached; the nations of the region were thus reluctant to pro-

213

vide local permanent solutions where these might otherwise have been possible. There was a funding problem, too, which was not surprising after the way the collection plate had been generally ignored at the December conference. UNHCR spending in Southeast Asia was now running at $10 million a month, and it appeared that the agency would be short $56 million in 1979, excluding costs related to processing centers to be built in Indonesia and the Philippines.

Despite the gravity of the situation, a note of hope and expectation had been injected late in the day by the United States. Belatedly, Washington had shrugged off its attitude of all-together-or-not-at-all in favor of a leadership role. No doubt the administration was spurred by ASEAN's denial of temporary asylum, which raised the specter of tens of thousands more deaths. But officials also detected a softening in public sentiment, influenced by the focus of television and newspapers on the plight of the boat people, which encouraged the White House to act.

In February, Carter created the position of U.S. Coordinator for Refugee Affairs, to which he appointed Dick Clark, a former Iowa senator, with the title of ambassador-at-large. The aim, according to Clark, was "to raise the refugee issue to a level of higher visibility and authority." Among other things, he was responsible for developing an overall U.S. refugee and resettlement policy, and he reported directly to the President and the Secretary of State.

In March, the administration sent to Congress new legislation, the Refugee Act, which would regularize American refugee policy and admission procedure. The legislation proposed the adoption of the U.N. definition of a refugee and the removal of narrow geographic and ideological criteria in determining admissions. It set a "normal" refugee inflow of 50,000 a year, with the President able to admit more in an emergency after consultation with Congress.

In April, Carter approved the admission of Indochina refugees at the rate of 7,000 a month, raising the annual intake from about 53,000 to 84,000.

When Carter flew off to Tokyo in late June for a state visit to Japan, to be followed by a meeting with the leaders of the world's six other major industrial nations, he termed the refugee issue the most important, after energy, that they were to consider. He indicated that he wanted a "clear, specific and substantive" declaration on the matter from the summit on June 28 and 29.

Apart from a greater effort to resettle the refugees, the United States was seeking support for a campaign to show that it was Vietnam's policies that were forcing Indochinese to flee. It believed that if it could mobilize international opinion, it could put enough pressure on Vietnam to force it to modify its policies. Convinced that Moscow would not use its influence with Hanoi, Washington wanted to divert the $1.7 billion in economic aid that non-Communist sources had promised to grant or lend on soft terms to Vietnam for its Second Five-Year Development Plan.[1]

The seven heads of state and government, representing West Germany, Britain, Canada, France and Italy as well as Japan and the United States, duly issued a "special statement of the Tokyo Summit on Indochinese Refugees," separate from their communiqué. In it they declared that the plight of the refugees was "a humanitarian problem of historical proportions" and a threat to the peace and stability of Southeast Asia. Pointing the finger at Hanoi, they called on Vietnam and other countries of Indochina to take "urgent and effective measures so that the present human hardship and suffering are eliminated."

Urging all nations to join in, the seven leaders said: "Given the tragedy and suffering which are taking place, the problem calls for an immediate and major response. . . . The governments represented will, as part of an international effort, significantly increase their contributions to Indochinese refugee relief and resettlement by making more funds available and by admitting more people." But there were no specific numbers or contributions, and the leaders wrote themselves an escape clause. Using language that was depressingly familiar, they said they would boost their efforts "while taking into account the existing social and economic circumstances in each of their countries."

Some reports suggested that Britain's Prime Minister, Margaret Thatcher, was primarily responsible for qualifying the commitment. Her Conservative government had shown little interest in the refugees since its election the previous month. In any event, Thatcher's fellow summiteers endorsed her May 31

215

call for a new international conference on the subject, thus ensuring that it would take place.

Shortly after the release of the joint statement, Carter announced that the United States would double its intake of Indochina refugees to 14,000 a month, adding $150 million to the resettlement bill, largely for job retraining and the operation of relocation centers in the United States, bringing it to $400 million. Carter's announcement, that he had acted out of "the compassion that has traditionally characterized the United States when confronted with such situations of human crisis," rang a little hollow in view of Washington's earlier reluctance to act until others were willing to do so. But there was no denying the grand gesture of 168,000 refugee places a year, or the challenge it represented to other nations to match it proportionately. Eyes immediately focused on Japan, whose refugee policy had become an international embarrassment.

One U.S. official implicitly acknowledged Washington's new approach. "The President's decision was based on the fact that there are people fleeing, losing their lives," he said. "It was not based on actions other countries may or may not take."

Bold as Carter's initiative was, it came almost too late. The foreign ministers of ASEAN, meeting on the Indonesian island of Bali at the same time as the Tokyo summit, formalized their closed-door policy on refugees. The annual gathering of foreign ministers, known as the Ministerial Meeting, is ASEAN's highest decision-making authority. The twelfth Ministerial Meeting, held June 28–30, 1979, welcomed the declaration of the Tokyo summit, but expressed disappointment over resettlement efforts nevertheless. In a communiqué, the ministers vowed to take "firm and effective" measures, including urgent coordinated action, to block the arrival of refugees.

Moreover, adopting the thrust of a Malaysian position paper, they reserved the right to return the refugees to Vietnam, Kampuchea and Laos. Further, they proposed that Vietnam establish UNHCR-run transit camps within its borders to administer the legal emigration of would-be refugees, and to hold any refugees repatriated from the ASEAN region. They also called for refugee-processing centers to be established outside the region, in addition to those being built in Indonesia and the Philippines. Further, the ASEAN countries would "send out" the 350,-

000 refugees on their soil, "should they not be accepted by re-settlement countries, or by the respective Indochinese countries, within a reasonable time frame, and in the absence of any arrangements to the contrary."

The ASEAN position was coupled with a strong demand that Vietnam halt the refugee outflow and withdraw its troops from Kampuchea. The five states were heartily fed up with Hanoi, being especially irked by its latest maneuver in dispatching a senior diplomat, Mai Van Bo, allegedly to help Southeast Asia solve the problem caused by the Vietnamese refugees. When Bo visited Indonesia and Malaysia in June, it was obvious that he had no authority to negotiate and was interested only in restating Vietnam's position. He denied that Vietnamese officials were accepting bribes, he claimed that most of the refugees were from China, not Vietnam, and he declared that Vietnam would refuse to accept any refugee sent back home. To top off his assertions, he insisted that only 4,000 refugees had left Vietnam in May, rather than the 51,139 registered as arrivals by UNHCR.

Two days after their meeting, the ASEAN foreign ministers began conferring on Bali with their counterparts from the United States, Japan, the European Economic Community, Australia and New Zealand. The two-day series of meetings, at ASEAN's invitation, was billed as an exchange of views among allies. But it rapidly became a joint U.S.-Japanese diplomatic offensive to convince ASEAN that refugee relief was on the way.

Under considerable pressure, Japan had decided to support with concrete action the sentiment expressed in the special statement of industrial leaders. Although accepting large numbers of refugees for permanent settlement was still out of the question, Tokyo decided to play its part by providing the funds. Sunao Sonoda, the Foreign Minister, saved the announcement for his address to the ASEAN foreign ministers. Japan would step up its contribution to UNHCR's 1979 Indochina budget from 25 to 50 percent—an offer that turned out to mean $65 million. Japan would also fund half the $13 million cost of the first of the refugee-processing centers, to be established on Galang Island.

The U.S. officials attending, led by Secretary of State Cyrus Vance, employed a fairly open and friendly carrot-and-stick approach in trying to persuade the ASEAN countries to reinstitute first asylum. Vance stressed that they could "count on continuing American help in dealing with the refugee crisis." But he also implied that the growing international effort which the United States and Japan were leading might falter if first asylum were not maintained.

Dick Clark, who was accompanying Vance, told newsmen that the U.S. Congress was likely to scrutinize ASEAN's policies on first asylum before voting more funds for refugee resettlement. He also hinted that the United States might take more refugees from countries with liberal asylum policies. The implication was that those which did not cooperate might find themselves left out in the cold and stuck with refugees for a long time.

However, the United States was in no position to dangle the carrot or brandish the stick with any moral force. It had forfeited that authority by hesitating too long before acting out of "the compassion that has traditionally characterized the United States." The ASEAN states knew that they were finally commanding attention because they were getting nasty. Humane policies had got them nowhere—nothing but ever-swelling refugee camps. With a second Geneva conference looming, they were not about to let the United States and Japan off the hook.

After the talks, Indonesia and the Philippines indicated that they would probably continue to accept boat people. But the key first-asylum countries, Malaysia and Thailand, would not budge. And the ASEAN communiqué, though it contained a certain amount of posturing, since Indonesia in practice was taking thousands of refugees turned away from Malaysia, stood—at least as a declaration of intent.

Nevertheless, the U.S. announcement and the rapid follow-up by Japan seemed to generate the momentum American officials were seeking. As the conference approached, other nations joined in. Italy dispatched two navy cruisers and a supply ship to the South China Sea to rescue about 1,000 boat people it would accept permanently, while others pledged resettlement places or funds. Canada, which was taking 12,000 Indochinese in 1979, said it was ready to treble its monthly intake to 3,000, beginning in August, and accept 50,000 by the end of 1980. Most countries knew what was expected of them, since U.N. High Commissioner Hartling had approached them individually, suggesting "indicative numbers," as the UNHCR jargon had it.

Somewhat ironically, the mounting international effort enveloped Britain, whose indicative number was 10,000, which would involve trebling its intake. Thatcher had issued the call for an international conference only when she found that Britain was expected to take more than 1,000 refugees rescued by the British freighter *Sibonga*, which had put in to Hong Kong, in addition to regular numbers. Her government argued with Hong Kong authorities for five days before agreeing to accept the *Sibonga* passengers "on humanitarian grounds." Thatcher expressed her displeasure by disclaiming the establishment of any precedent.

Britain's niggardly attitude toward Hong Kong irked American officials. To reward the colonial government's humanitarian policies they stepped up their intake of refugees from Hong Kong, but there was a point beyond which they would not go until London accepted more responsibility for what is, after all, its colony. The pressure on Britain was heavy: not to be seen to be pulling its weight was doubly embarrassing—for wailing so loudly about the problem and at the same time doing so little, even when Hong Kong's interests were at stake. Days before the conference, Britain announced that it would take 10,000 more boat people from Hong Kong.

The number of resettlement places officially pledged to UNHCR and immediately available over a one-year span had risen from 53,500 in October 1978 to 125,000 in May 1979. Significantly, the tally had soared to 209,000 in the seven weeks before July 19. The aim of the conference, opening the following day, was to push it over 250,000.

While most quarters agreed on the need for an international conference, there was no consensus on the format or participation. It boiled down to two main schools of thought: those who wanted the meeting confined to humanitarian aspects of the refugee outflow, and the others who favored a more wide-ranging discussion that would examine political issues, including the reasons for the exodus, as well.

Vietnam, at the center of the debate, took the same steps to avoid being placed in the dock and chastised as it had on earlier occasions: it simply threatened to boycott anything other than a

219

humanitarian discussion. A statement issued by Hanoi in late June said the agenda must be restricted to an agreement signed a month earlier by Vietnam and UNHCR providing for the orderly departure of persons from the country.

Vietnam was protected to a certain extent by the system. The organizers of any international conference where contentious issues are to be debated realize that an unbridled discussion can easily bog down in name-calling and rhetoric, and fail to produce the results needed to proclaim some sort of success. Thus in May, Indonesia's Foreign Minister, Mochtar Kusumaatmadja, ruled out politics at the conference to discuss the proposed Galang Island refugee-processing center. So neither the ASEAN countries nor other participants replied to the Vietnamese delegates, even when they delivered what were considered blatant untruths and distortions.

Kurt Waldheim did the same in Geneva. Inviting governments, he said he envisaged a meeting "of a humanitarian character, designed to produce additional support" for UNHCR. He stressed the point again in his opening remarks to the conference itself. While acknowledging that the problem had political roots, he appealed to delegates to "refrain from acrimonious debate" and "concentrate on the elements of solution rather than on areas of disagreement."

As for participants, Waldheim declined to invite Kampuchea because of the vexed question of representation, which had snarled several international gatherings such as the nonaligned movement. The United Nations recognized Pol Pot's Khmer Rouge administration, though the Vietnamese-installed Heng Samrin regime had occupied Phnom Penh since January. Hanoi would not tolerate the presence of Khmer Rouge. For all practical purposes, Waldheim's decision meant that Laos also would not be invited because China would object to Laotian representation without a Kampuchean presence. So two of the three countries of origin, accounting for about one-third or more of the permanent refugees from Indochina, did not participate.

Despite their threat not to appear in Geneva, the Vietnamese made extensive preparations for the conference. A 12-member delegation was assembled, headed by Phan Hien, the suave Deputy Foreign Minister who is one of the country's ablest negotiators. Also on the team were Vietnam's permanent representatives in Geneva and New York; its ambassadors to France, West Germany and Britain; Vu Hoang, the Foreign Ministry official who had attended the Jakarta meeting in May, and Mai Van Bo, who had handled the consultations with Indonesia and Malaysia in June.

Questioned at a news conference the day before the meeting, Hien issued the standard denials of Hanoi's responsibility for the refugees and its involvement in the traffic. It did not have a policy of expelling anyone, it did not extract fees from boat people and it did not authorize them to leave. But he went one step further than the usual claim that the Vietnamese authorities were unable to stop the outflow. He said that the agreement with UNHCR provided for safe, orderly and legal departure; "illegal departures" were prohibited, and persons caught trying to leave "illegally" were being punished.

Journalists exchanged knowing smiles and irreverent comments about the cynicism of a government prepared to publicly brand "illegal" an activity it privately not only condoned but authorized and profited from. After all, 56,941 boat people had reached neighboring countries in June, so there could not have been much deterrent effect in the punishment being handed out by the Vietnamese authorities. But what the journalists did not realize was that Hien's claim at that time was technically true. He did not use the term "illegal" carelessly. Though presented to give the impression of ongoing, unchanged policy, it in fact represented a departure whose significance would become apparent only in the days ahead.

Indeed, Vietnam in its own obscure way had signaled a new course a month or two earlier when it began issuing reports of a crackdown on refugee trafficking. On June 18, Hanoi Radio had said that a Greek cargo ship, the *Nikitas F*, had been detained in Ho Chi Minh City for being used to organize the "illegal departure" of many Vietnamese. The authorities had found the ship packed with military officers and policemen of the old regime, it said. Western wire-service reports noted that it was the first significant example cited by Vietnam as evidence that it was attempting to discourage the refugee outflow.

Four days later, Hanoi Radio reported that the ship and 3 of its officers and crew had been fined for trying to smuggle 69 refugees out of Vietnam. The prosecution was quoted as saying that

221

the incident clearly indicated the existence of a racketeer organization because the refugees belonged to different social classes and came from many places.

When the 8,403-ton *Nikitas F* arrived later in Hong Kong, the Greek master, Samothrakitis Komniwos, told an intriguing tale. He said the ship had gone to Vietnam on May 26 to drop off 11,400 tons of wheat it had collected in India; later, it had planned to proceed to Shanghai to load rice for Africa. The *Nikitas F* had remained berthed in Ho Chi Minh City while the wheat was being unloaded by Vietnamese dock laborers, who were mostly women. On June 12, two days before the unloading was complete, Komniwos had noticed more men working. Suspecting that some of them intended to stow away, he had ordered the crew to search the ship. They had found some Vietnamese hidden in the engine room and others completely immersed in bilge water in the shaft tunnel with only their mouths and noses above the surface. None of them could be persuaded to go ashore.

Komniwos had made a full report to port police the same day and requested their assistance to remove the stowaways. Two days later, about 70 police boarded the vessel and rounded up 34 Vietnamese. When some of the crew intervened to prevent the stowaways from being beaten, they were threatened by the police, who wielded automatic weapons.

Later in the day, Komniwos was taken ashore and held responsible for the stowaways. He argued that since he had reported them previously and since there were 4 armed Vietnamese guards on his ship at all times, he could hardly be blamed. But his argument was not accepted, and he was informed that his ship was under arrest. Over the next few days the police made frequent visits to the *Nikitas F* and carted off a total of 69 Vietnamese. The ship remained under arrest until June 21, when the chief engineer, Elias Katsanis, agreed under pressure to sign a confession.

Katsanis, as well as an assistant cook and a sailor, were summoned to appear in a people's court the following day. Katsanis was charged because most of the stowaways had been found in the engine room and the assistant cook and sailor because it was they who had intervened when the police were roughing up the stowaways. Captain Komniwos attended court

on behalf of the ship's owner. All were charged with "illegally harboring many Vietnamese citizens aboard the ship *Nikitas F* to smuggle them abroad." The defendants were allowed to consume beer and sandwiches during the afternoon session of the one-day hearing. Although represented by a private lawyer, they were each asked only one question during the trial: "Have you ever been to Ho Chi Minh City before?" The answer was no in every case.

Found guilty, the ship was fined $5,000, Katsanis $3,000 and the assistant cook and sailor $1,000 each. Komniwos was ordered to pay $300 court costs and $1,500 police expenses. Although none of them had the money to pay the fines, the vessel was allowed to sail within two days.

If the master's story was true—and Hong Kong marine authorities were convinced it was—the Vietnamese government was almost desperate to persuade the world it was doing its best to prevent the "illegal departure" of refugees. It had either arranged the stowaway incident on the *Nikitas F* or taken advantage of a genuine stowaway attempt at the expense of the ship, its officers and crew, simply to stage a meaningless trial for the benefit of the international community.

On July 5, Hanoi Radio gave another example of the war being waged on the refugee racketeers. Dang Thanh Dong, the leader of a gang arranging escapes from Vietnam, had been jailed for ten years for his "crimes." The director of a fishing enterprise in Tien Giang province, Dong had been caught using his concern's boats to smuggle people out of the country. A people's court in the Mekong Delta province had tried Dong and his accomplices for organizing the "illegal departure" of 32 Vietnamese. Hanoi Radio continued to report other convictions in different parts of the country.

When he addressed the conference in Geneva on July 20, Phan Hien repeated that his government was determined to work closely with UNHCR to ensure that people leaving Vietnam departed "in a legal and organized way." The government hoped that the agreement it had signed "will dissuade persons who still want to leave Vietnam illegally," he said.

Most of the outside world, familiar with the Vietnamese government's role in the refugee traffic, dismissed the Hanoi broadcasts as more propaganda. Similarly, delegates who lis-

tened to Hien in Geneva, like the journalists at his news conference the previous day, thought they were hearing a restatement
of Hanoi's old position. Such was Hanoi's credibility.

The talkathon continued, speakers taking the floor for ten
to fifteen minutes one after another for two days, breaking only
for lunch—defending their records, making pledges, suggesting
solutions. Simultaneously, delegations staged news conferences,
held press briefings and distributed an avalanche of printed
propaganda. The Vietnamese took it all impassively except for a
blistering attack by China, whose Vice Foreign Minister, Zhang
Wenjin, accused the Hanoi leaders of "practicing genocide."
Vietnamese delegates brought the proceedings to a halt by rap-
ping their wooden nameplate on the bench in protest, but Zhang
was allowed to complete his tirade. He left no doubt what solution Peking favored when he quoted an ancient Chinese saying,
"To stop a pot from boiling over, it's better to take out the fire-
wood than to pour on cold water."

As the conference closed, Poul Hartling summed up the results of the pledging session:

> —A "truly dramatic" increase in the number of re-
> settlement places from 125,000 at May 31 to more than
> 260,000 on July 21.
> —New pledges totaling about $190 million in cash
> and kind, some earmarked for 1980.
> —An offer of a new site in the Philippines for a pro-
> cessing center to accommodate at least 50,000 refugees.
> —$25 million offered for a proposed fund to extend
> resettlement to developing countries ready to receive ref-
> ugees but without the resources.

The political results, less tangible than the pledges but
overshadowing all the rhetoric and high-minded cadences in the
Assembly Hall, were hammered out elsewhere. Delegates hud-
dled in U.N. briefing rooms, diplomatic missions and gilded hotel
suites overlooking placid Lake Geneva. Most efforts centered on
a French initiative for a moratorium, a period during which
Vietnam would halt the outflow to provide a breathing space for
all concerned, especially the hard-pressed front-line countries.

The Vietnamese said they were willing, repeating what
they had been saying for a month or more to a disbelieving audi-

ence: they really were putting an end to the boat traffic. Most diplomats and officials remained skeptical, even when late reports from Asia showed that the arrival of Vietnamese refugees in the first half of July had slowed to half the rate of June. It might be a negotiating tactic by Hanoi; certainly the decline could be traced almost to the day the conference had been set.

In the end the solution was to invest Vietnam's undertaking with the prestige and honor of the office of Secretary General of the United Nations. Waldheim's announcement, which he portrayed as a major breakthrough, electrified the final minutes of the conference:

> As a result of my consultations, the government of the Socialist Republic of Vietnam has authorized me to inform you that for a reasonable period of time it will make every effort to stop illegal departures. In the meantime, the government of Vietnam will cooperate with the UNHCR in expanding the present seven-point program designed to bring departures into orderly and safe channels.

| TWELVE

ITEM: THE REFUGEE crisis in Malaysia reached a turning point in July 1979, when the number of displaced Indochinese in the country declined for the first time in eighteen months. The total fell from 74,817 at June 30 to 66,222 at July 31.

Item: Tran Minh Chau, a Thieu-regime soldier and leader of a gang that tried to smuggle refugees out of Vietnam aboard a stolen fishing boat, was sentenced to death on August 6, 1979. A people's court, which was told that the gang had killed a guard while seizing the boat, also jailed his accomplices and convicted some of the passengers who had paid in gold for a voyage to Hong Kong.

Vietnam's undertaking to stop the outflow was a questionable breakthrough. Hanoi might have begun choking off the traffic to earn points at the Geneva conference, but it was nevertheless serious about stopping it altogether. During the fairly unimpeded flow from January to July 1979, refugees arrived by boat throughout the region at the rate of more than 25,600 a month. From August to December, when the ban was officially imposed, the average was just over 4,400—not counting some 5,000 two-timers who reached Hong Kong after spending more than six months in China. The decline was dramatic from the time the Vietnamese authorities clamped down on "illegal departures": June, 56,941; July, 17,839; August, 9,734; September, 9,533; October, 2,854; November, 2,209; December, 2,745.

Intensive interviewing confirmed that the new arrivals were genuine escapees. They were overwhelmingly ethnic Vietnamese from the southern part of the country, mostly fishermen and other rural folk or those from small towns. They dribbled in, usually about 30 or 40 to a boat. Although some bribed minor officials to let them go, there was no evidence of systematic government complicity in the escapes. Some of the refugees who did not pay off local cadres and officials put to sea under fire and were pursued. For the boat people, the wheel had turned full circle. "All we're seeing at present," observed one Western refugee official in Malaysia early in 1980, "is the same sort of clandestine departure that has been going on since 1975."

How long the moratorium would last was a matter of conjecture. France had suggested six months. Asked to interpret the meaning of "a reasonable period of time" specified by Hanoi, Waldheim said no deadline had been set by the Vietnamese. "But the understanding is several months," he said. Nguyen Co Thach told a U.S. House of Representatives study mission which visited Vietnam in August 1979 that the policy was permanent. "We will keep it forever," he said. The Vietnamese comments had to be evaluated against the accuracy and sincerity of their earlier pronouncements.

In any event, the Geneva conference had the positive result of saving lives immediately. With vastly reduced numbers putting to sea, fewer lives were at risk. Refugees in distress, often after being towed out to sea by the Malaysians, were sighted and picked up by the aircraft and ships of several nations involved in rescue work. The three-ship Italian task force collected more than 900 boat people, some of whom were towed into the path of the Italians by the Malaysian Navy.

With arrivals rapidly dwindling, camps emptying steadily and continued lobbying by the United States and others, it was only a matter of time before first asylum was reinstated. Within a month and without fanfare, Malaysia began transferring 4,000 boat people in limbo encampments on beaches to camps run by UNHCR. Kuala Lumpur first eased its tow-out practice, then, in October, abandoned it altogether, again without any official announcement. Boat people also landed without obstruction in southern Thailand, an important haven once more when the continuing trickle of boat people changed direction in late 1979. Thai pirates literally made a killing. An estimated 166 refugees died in a two-month period as pirates went on an orgy of rape, pillage and murder.

With temporary and permanent asylum assured for refugees, merchant ships showed a new willingness to rescue boat people. Masters returned to their old routes, no longer worried that a chance encounter with a sinking refugee craft would involve them in long delays that would anger owners and operators and jeopardize their careers. Some of the merchantmen cooperated with military planes and vessels on rescue missions, though the role of the U.S. Seventh Fleet remained controversial.

In Geneva, Vice President Mondale had announced what amounted to a major rescue effort ordered by Carter as commander-in-chief of the armed forces. American navy vessels had always had standing regulations requiring them to render assistance to persons and ships in distress. In mid-1978, moreover, they had been specifically directed to assist boat people they encountered and take aboard those facing undue hardship or death. Carter's orders, however, meant the start of a new and aggressive phase to locate and help refugees.

Rescue opportunities were improved within normal operations in a number of ways, including modification of ship schedules and port visits to increase the amount of time spent off the coast of Vietnam. Special air patrols were flown daily by navy P-3 Orions, which reported their findings to a communications control center set up for the purpose at America's Clark Air Base in the Philippines. The center would then alert military, merchant or other ships in the vicinity of the boat people.

Within three weeks after the presidential directive was issued on July 21, the Seventh Fleet had made eight rescues involving 168 refugees, based on sightings by P-3s and ship-based aircraft. Over four months the number of rescued refugees edged up to 846, which compared with 540 picked up by the Seventh Fleet in all 1977, 589 in 1978 and 544 in 1979 up to July 20. The P-3s also coordinated their operations with merchant ships in rescuing 991 others.

The timing of the rescue effort left Washington open to criticism on several counts. From a humanitarian standpoint, it seemed tragic that American aircraft and vessels had not been around when they were desperately needed earlier, when tens of thousands of boats and refugees were being tossed at the mercy of the elements on the open ocean. Now they were systematically sweeping the area in search of a mere handful of boat people.

To friend and foe alike, it also looked as if the United States were encouraging the further flight of refugees and thus sabotaging the agreement for orderly departure. Malaysia and Indonesia criticized the activities of both the Seventh Fleet and the Italian ships. A statement by the Vietnamese Foreign Ministry, calling for an immediate end to the Seventh Fleet's operations, said they were clearly aimed at instigating Vietnamese to leave the country illegally and at obstructing the arrangements made in Geneva.

No other single event epitomized so well Washington's handling of the Indochina refugee crisis: ultimately generous, but so late that much of the potential benefit was dissipated and the goodwill squandered.

There was a negative and disturbing side to the Geneva conference that had nothing to do with the peripheral efforts of the United States or any other party outside Vietnam. By accepting the moratorium, the international community recognized Hanoi's right to suspend free emigration, which is proclaimed in the Universal Declaration of Human Rights adopted by the General Assembly in 1948. Waldheim acknowledged the potential conflict when he opened the conference: "The United Nations of course stands for the proposition that individuals wishing to leave their country have the right to do so. At the same time, as a practical matter, we obviously do not wish to see an exodus of persons anywhere in the world who depart from their countries in a manner which would put their lives in jeopardy." Faced with the imperative of ending the watery deaths,

Waldheim went along with Hanoi's plans to stop all refugees except those passing through official channels. "There is a dilemma; there is certainly a contradiction," he conceded at a postmeeting news conference. "But these people are drowning in the sea. We've got to do something about it."

The issue was more than academic to large segments of the Vietnamese population. The first to feel the sting of the policy reversal were the middlemen and organizers of the refugee traffic. Where their activities had been overlooked, condoned or encouraged, they were now condemned—on pain of severe punishment. The Vietnam News Agency and other official media carried numerous reports of gangs being busted, racketeers brought to trial, their boats, gold and other possessions confiscated. Those identified as ringleaders typically were jailed for ten to twenty years, accomplices for lesser terms.

Nguyen Co Thach told members of a U.S. House of Representatives study mission led by Benjamin S. Rosenthal in early August that 4,000 cases had been brought to trial since the beginning of the year.[*] "Very drastic measures" had been taken against persons plying the trade, he said, the courts handing out "some death sentences" to those responsible for sinking boats and killing people. The Hanoi-based representative of UNHCR, Anders B. Johnsson, confirmed that the government had begun to stop boats by all means, and to jail and execute persons committing serious crimes while attempting to get passage on boats. Foreign residents in Vung Tau, mostly engaged in offshore oil exploration, reported seeing parachute flares used at night to illuminate the water and hearing machine guns fired at fleeing boats.

As the record showed, the harsh measures ended the flourishing refugee traffic fairly abruptly and effectively; organized departures, a way of life and death, soon became a thing of the past. A bamboo curtain was lowered on the country. Only in the more remote coastal locations was it sometimes possible to sneak

---

[*] Thach's figure seems exaggerated, to say the least. Although he sought to give the impression that the 4,000 trials had been spread over the first seven months of 1979, the crackdown almost certainly had not started seriously till June. The authorities would have had to bring more than 60 cases to court every day for two months to reach 4,000 by early August.

230

past the guns. Most of those who desperately wanted to leave lived in the cities.

How many potential refugees were trapped in Vietnam by the ban was not known with any certainty and in fact was the subject of considerable confusion. It was not necessarily a static figure. An informed estimate ranged from a minimum of 400,000 to a maximum of 3 million. These were the limits set forth at various times by Vietnamese officials, though it should be pointed out that they often possessed little more accurate information than outsiders.

United Press International, in a dispatch from Hanoi in August 1979, presented the thinking of Nguyen Co Thach after he went into the question of refugees in some detail with American newsmen. "Thach did not specifically say how many potential refugees there are in Vietnam," UPI reported. "But he indicated some three million Vietnamese may want to leave, depending on the political situation."

At much the same time, Thach left Daniel K. Akaka, who was visiting Vietnam with the Rosenthal delegation, with the impression that 2 million would go if they were allowed. The figure came up repeatedly, Akaka said, and when Thach was asked if it was accurate, he replied that it could well be. Thach's arithmetic produced a totally different picture a few days later for a delegation of the U.S. House Subcommittee on Asian and Pacific Affairs, headed by Lester L. Wolff. "Thach said that if the legal outflow could be set at 10,000 per month the problem could be taken care of in one or two years," the mission said in its report. "It would take that long to clear out the ethnic Chinese and U.S. 'collaborators.'" Far from 2 or 3 million, Thach now seemed to be saying there were only between 120,000 and 240,000 possible emigrants in place of the chaotic boat traffic.

The inconsistency defied ready explanation. If it was deliberate, the objective was obscure. Much more likely, the Vietnamese had no way of knowing, and their estimates fluctuated as they made propaganda points about the need to restrain China and attract international aid for Vietnam.

The starting point in any calculation, however it was made, had to be the ethnic-Chinese community, estimated to be still more than 1 million strong in mid-1979. It was hard to conceive of any Sino-Vietnamese believing they had any future at all in

Vietnam, even though the free market was thriving once more in Ho Chi Minh City. The Hanoi leadership had shown it did not trust them when the chips were down. Prospects for reconciliation were dismal even if tension between Vietnam and China disappeared, which was unlikely in the short term. If generations of residence and twenty-five years of socialism in the North had not removed the doubts and distrust, it was difficult to imagine what would.

The second identifiable group consisted of the military, police, civil servants and others who had directly served the Thieu regime, together with professional, intellectual and middle-class elements that might find Communist austerity and restrictions most uncomfortable. It was widely assumed there were about 1 million in this group also.

Much as the government did not like to admit it, some ordinary folk were also ready to run if and when the opportunity presented itself. Thach might protest that "peasants don't leave," but the 22,000 boat people who dodged bullets to depart in the last five months of 1979 before confronting the persisting dangers of pirate attack and drowning included a high percentage of rural dwellers.

Presumably there existed in the first two categories a disaffected core of perhaps 1.5 million who did not want to remain in Vietnam under any circumstances. For many others, in all three categories, whether they stayed would depend to a great extent on how they were treated. Whether hard-core or waverer, opportunity to get out would doubtless be a key factor.

How many would have the chance to go through the front door—legally—was not clear, though the number appeared limited. The seven-point agreement signed by UNHCR and the Vietnamese government on May 30, 1979, was narrow, restricted to "family reunion and other humanitarian cases." The Vietnamese, in their undertaking at the Geneva conference, had promised to cooperate with UNHCR to expand it, but just how this might be done was not specified.

The genesis of the agreement was Vietnam's announcement on January 12, 1979, of a new emigration policy. Under relaxed conditions, Vietnamese were to be allowed to go abroad in order to rejoin their families or "to earn a living." Three categories would not be permitted to emigrate: people liable for compulsory military service, persons with access to state secrets and those occupying important jobs in production and public service for whom there were no replacements at present, and convicted criminals and others subject to judicial processes.

It was subsequently issued as a Cabinet decision dated March 14, to take effect "the day of its publication." Containing ten articles, it elaborated on the January 12 announcement. The only important difference was that one category prohibited from emigrating had been deleted; those of draft age were now free to leave.

One article stated: "Persons leaving Vietnam in a manner contrary to the stipulations of this decision will be severely punished in conformity with the laws of the Socialist Republic of Vietnam."

As for the seven-point "memorandum of understanding," its preamble simply said it was agreed that UNHCR would help implement Vietnam's January 12 announcement to permit the orderly departure of persons wishing to live abroad. Applicants were to be selected on the basis of separate lists prepared by the Vietnamese government and the receiving countries: "Those persons whose names appear on both lists will qualify for exit." Names appearing on only one list would be subject to discussions between the various parties.

If the agreement was meant to provide a substitute arrangement for the former chaotic outflow of boat people—and that is the way it was presented by both Vietnam and UNHCR—its deficiencies were all too apparent. It might have the virtue of ending the unacceptable loss of life at sea and eliminating first asylum from the process, but it also changed the role of the participants from refugees to emigrants. If the West was reluctant to resettle boat people once they were stranded in other countries, it would scarcely come running for the chance to accept them directly from Vietnam.

Should the Vietnamese authorities, for their part, want to prevent residents from leaving, they clearly could use the agreement for that purpose; it was a matter of ensuring that the names on the lists did not match. Alternatively, if they chose to discriminate against certain types of people and push them out,

233

the way was at least theoretically open. Asking the victims of persecution and others tormented by the system to voluntarily register for departure was in itself not without some risk.

Even with goodwill, the agreement was hardly the answer to the problem. Although Nguyen Co Thach in August, like Vu Hoang in May, had spoken optimistically of 10,000 persons a month leaving Vietnam under the orderly departure program, numbers of this size were never a possibility. According to UNHCR's Anders Johnsson, when the program was in full swing one special aircraft would be leaving Ho Chi Minh City each week carrying about 120 people. In other words, the best that could be hoped for was 480 emigrants a month—fewer than 1 percent of the 57,000 refugees who had been gushing from the country each month until they were forcefully restrained. At that rate it would take 260 years to complete the evacuation of the disaffected hard core alone.

In practice, even 480 a month proved difficult. Matching names turned out to be an elusive art, a game for bureaucrats who often had conflicting aims and motives. By the end of 1979, seven months after the agreement took effect, only 1,174 persons had left Vietnam for a new life in the West. By the end of 1980, the total had edged up to 5,880. It was hardly reassuring for ethnic Chinese and others who were being asked—rather, compelled—to wait their turn instead of putting out to sea.

When Nguyen Co Thach was asked by some American visitors after a few months why Vietnam was taking so long to respond to the 5,000 names submitted by the United States, he replied: "We have red tape here just like you do in the United States." He had a question of his own: Why had the United States accepted only 10 immigrants from 228 recently offered by Vietnam? The explanation was dismissed by Thach as inconsistent with Western pressure for orderly departure.

The explanation was that only those people who qualified under regular immigration procedures would be accepted by the United States directly from Vietnam: close relatives of American citizens or permanent residents. No exception could be made for applicants from Vietnam as potential refugees. On the contrary, priority was to go to the occupants of refugee camps awaiting resettlement throughout Asia. The orderly departure program

234

was not to encroach on the 168,000 places a year Washington had offered at the Tokyo summit.

Obviously expecting the United States to be more flexible, Hanoi initially handed Washington two lists containing the names of some 30,000 persons it was prepared to allow to leave, with almost no supporting details. American officials came to refer to the listings as the Cholon Phone Directory: most of the people were Sino-Vietnamese with no family connections in the United States. Vietnam followed up with two more lists containing 3,500 names, this time including names and addresses of relatives. On its side, Washington provided the names of 17,000 Vietnamese it probably would be willing to accept, and was preparing to add 100,000 more.

Vietnam's unflagging determination to rid itself of undesirables was displayed nakedly in dealings with Canada, with which it had negotiated a restricted family-reunion arrangement before the seven-point UNHCR agreement was signed. After some Vietnamese emigrants had settled in Canada, Hanoi suddenly trotted out the one-for-one formula: it insisted the Canadians ignore their immigration law and take one independent candidate nominated by the Vietnamese government for every one who qualified under family reunion. A senior Vietnamese official brazenly reinforced the demand with a chilling threat: if the Western nations were not prepared to accept people directly from Vietnam on the same conditions under which they took them from refugee camps, Hanoi was ready to send them once more to the coasts of neighboring lands. That official was none other than Vu Hoang, the Foreign Ministry's Consular Affairs Director, who had attended both the Geneva and Jakarta conferences.

With negotiations bogged down, the legal movement of people out of Vietnam all but stopped. Fearing a new wave of boat people, the United States informed Hanoi it would be willing to accept up to 1,000 persons a month from Vietnam who would not normally qualify under immigration procedure. They would be selected according to refugee criteria, though they would still need to prove a close association with the United States. Their numbers would be deducted from the 14,000-a-month quota.

The first special planeload of Vietnamese to go to the United States under the orderly departure program did not leave Ho Chi Minh City until December 1980. At that stage, the Vietnamese and the Americans, working through UNHCR because the two countries still did not have diplomatic relations, had managed to agree on only 1,758 persons who could go to the United States. In 1980, 75,823 boat people escaped Vietnam and survived to register with UNHCR.

The international community was left to reflect on the fact that while Hanoi did not modify its internal policies, Vietnam for many continued to be a vast prison, for clearly when the back door was slammed shut and locked, the front door was not thrown open. The orderly departure arrangement was like using a spigot in place of an open valve to drain a huge water tank.

If the Geneva conference produced only mixed results over Vietnamese boat people, it failed altogether to tackle the issue of land refugees engulfing Thailand from Laos and Kampuchea. The Laotians especially continued to be the forgotten ones, though of course they also benefited from additional resettlement places pledged in Geneva.

To a certain extent, the focus on the Vietnamese was understandable. Malaysia had screamed the loudest and shocked the world into action with its throw-out, tow-out policies and threats to shoot boat people. Thailand also had taken drastic action, but the victims of its push-back policies were blown up by mines and died of disease and starvation beyond the sight of television cameras and reporters.

Thailand's attitude toward temporary asylum remained crucial: not only were Laotians still streaming across the Mekong at the rate of 5,000 a month, but ongoing conflict and impending famine in Kampuchea threatened a massive new influx from that country. The critical question was whether the Thai government, having recently repatriated a total of about 48,000 "new" Kampucheans, would permit the returning survivors of those groups and tens of thousands of others to join some 50,000 who remained just across the border on Thai soil.

The looming hunger was widely foreseen well before the conference in Geneva that was supposed to discuss the refugee situation in all Indochina. "Famine on a hideous scale threatens occupied Cambodia," Dennis Bloodworth said in *The Observer* of London in early May. Warned *The Asian Wall Street Journal:* "Famine may soon give Southeast Asia the largest flow of Indochinese yet—a stream of hungry people for whom no international aid is being organized."

The immediate cause of the famine, as noted by the ASEAN foreign ministers at their meeting in August, was the widespread failure to plant the main rice crop in June and July. Farmers who ventured into paddy fields risked being shot, while masses of Kampucheans continued to mill around the nation trying to avoid the fighting, locate relatives and return to their native villages.

Part of the problem was that the unknown Heng Samrin and his equally obscure associates met little success in trying to persuade their countrymen and -women to participate in the rebirth of the shattered nation under the banner of the People's Republic of Kampuchea. Some survivors of the Khmer Rouge bloodbath were wary of volunteering to help in case they became victims next time around. Others saw a contradiction in trying to build a new Kampuchea under the leadership of Khmer so obviously beholden to Hanoi. No one of any standing rallied to Heng Samrin, who was in any case a Khmer Rouge defector and shared at least some of their blood-soaked past.

For months the central leadership consisted of no more than a couple of dozen officials, the main administrative work being performed by Vietnamese and so-called Khmer Viet Minh, Khmer Communists who in 1954 joined Vietnamese troops in South Vietnam for repatriation to North Vietnam under the terms of the Genva Agreement. The recruitment of meagerly talented and roughly trained Kampuchean cadres gave the administration a poor record and an even poorer image. The absence of any sense of identification with the Vietnamese-controlled regime was matched only by the lack of unity among Kampucheans generally.

Heavy monsoonal rain that set in during May allowed Vietnamese troops, by now 200,000 strong, to consolidate their position and prepare for what was apparently intended as a decisive dry-season attempt to wipe out the Khmer Rouge guerrillas, who were pressed up against the Thai border. When the monsoon eased in late August, earlier than usual, the Vietnamese

237

conducted sweeps against food-growing areas, guerrilla bases and villages suspected of being under Khmer Rouge control. According to Thai military intelligence, they ruthlessly enforced population- and resource-control policies in northeast Kampuchea, in contrast with a more orthodox and less repressive approach elsewhere.

By September, the country was in the grip of the predicted famine, another national travail to mark almost a decade of man-made disaster for the country. The search for sustenance provided the impetus for new migrations, primarily in opposite directions—to Phnom Penh and other cities on the one hand, and to the Thai border on the other.

After ten months of Heng Samrin control, only 40,000 civilians had been allowed back to work and live in Phnom Penh. Some 600,000 others were encamped in a 5-mile zone outside the city limits, unemployed and barely able to survive. The few foreign visitors saw groups of ragged, hungry people foraging like animals. It was the same around other towns, despite a declared policy to resettle the masses in surrounding provinces.

The people were drawn to the towns by the distribution of food that was starting to trickle in from the Soviet Union, Vietnam and Western relief agencies. Much of it was delivered up the Mekong River from Ho Chi Minh City to the port of Phnom Penh, though Soviet vessels began unloading in Kompong Som, from where supplies of rice were transported to the capital by the recently restored railway service.

A 4-member team representing the World Council of Churches and the Christian Conference of Asia, which visited Kampuchea in early October, found that workers in Phnom Penh were being issued 28.6 pounds each of imported rice a month. The ration dwindled with the distance from the capital. As close as 50 miles from Phnom Penh, even adults were getting as little as 3.3 to 8.3 pounds. Apart from personal consumption, in the absence of currency this rice also had to be used for bartering in order to obtain small amounts of fish, meat and vegetables.

Recent arrivals from the northern half of the country and western districts under the control of the Khmer Rouge resistance were grossly undernourished and ill, leading the team to conclude that hunger in those areas was "truly serious." Those left behind were reported to be dying of malaria and diarrheal disease as well as starvation. The capacity of the hospitals and health centers was severely limited, the team noted: "Equipment for the simplest and most basic laboratory tests is lacking. Intravenous therapy with fluids and blood is very restricted. Almost no surgery can be done due to lack of equipment and anaesthetics."

Despite the rampant disease and catastrophic state of medical care, Ros Somay, Minister of Economy and People's Welfare, told the team: "More than medicines and any other form of aid, we need food."

Food was also desperately needed by the civilians who headed for the Thai border. Those under Khmer Rouge control had no choice but to keep walking at gunpoint. But weary columns of others voluntarily trudged to the frontier, attracted by a black market that was operating in areas occupied by small groups of armed anti-Communist Khmer Serei. Kampucheans dug up gold, diamonds and jewelry buried in 1975, and recovered animal ornaments of beaten silver, for which the country is famous, to barter with Thai merchants for food and clothes. Thai bankers estimated that $15 million of precious metal was being traded monthly. Beginning at mid-year, Thailand-based relief services also began to distribute food, medicine and clothing to Kampucheans clustered along the border. The flourishing black market and the aid gave birth to trading, a constant movement on foot and bicycle across Kampuchea to and from the Thai border that became the country's major economic activity.

A typical trader was Neang Sotha, aged 30 and the father of 5, who walked the 70 miles from Battambang to the border. He sold some gold and silver objects for baht, the Thai currency, then purchased a shiny new bicycle, brightly painted blue and white, its twin headlamps still encased in plastic wrappers. He pedaled it back home, using it to carry some clothes he had also bought. In Battambang he bartered the clothes for rice from truck drivers in charge of transporting relief supplies. The drivers in turn used some of the clothes to bribe officials to close their eyes to the sacks of rice missing from the trucks. And so the cycle continued.

Between 130,000 and 300,000 civilians were spread along

the 500-mile border by early October, some up to 50 miles inside Kampuchea, perhaps 20,000 straddling the ill-defined boundary. Those in border sanctuaries were held in check by a combination of Vietnamese pressure, Khmer Rouge discipline and Thai vigilance. More than half the total were under the tight control of the Khmer Rouge: they were strung out south of Aranyaprathet all the way to Khlong Yai, on the Gulf of Thailand.

The rest of the civilians were more concentrated immediately north of Aranyaprathet, where several different groups of Khmer Serei could muster about 5,000 poorly armed and equipped fighting men. One Western refugee official called it "the last stand of Kampuchea's middle class." Among the people in rags were the survivors of the country's educated elite, including professional and commercial ranks.

The Kampucheans in the Khmer Serei areas, who had built themselves flimsy thatched shelters under the trees, were generally in better physical shape than those to the south. Although there was not enough food and medicine, and people had little treatment for malaria, dysentery, typhoid and war wounds, they managed to cope, mainly with the help of the black market.

In the Khmer Rouge areas, where soldiers and cadres were fed first as a matter of policy, civilians were dying by the hundreds. In a dispatch for the Associated Press after a tour of the area, Denis Gray quoted escaping refugees as saying that large numbers of civilians herded into a jungle clearing were sleeping on the rain-soaked ground and subsisting chiefly on roots, leaves and bamboo shoots.

The amount of relief required for the Kampucheans was disputed. The United Nations Food and Agriculture Organization estimated the food deficit for all Kampuchea from August to December 1979 to be 350,000 tons of milled rice, while the Phnom Penh authorities put it at about 108,000 tons. Others calculated somewhere in between. The differences were due to the use of different population figures and varying estimates of daily requirements, though the Heng Samrin administration and Vietnam also sought to underplay the disaster for political reasons. But by the most conservative count—4 million people eating one-third of a pound of rice a day—600 tons of rice were needed daily for six months to avert tragedy.

With minimal transport and communications and little other infrastructure, the logistical problems were immense. But the relief effort was well within the resources and technical competence of the international community. It was—or should have been—an advantage to know of the approaching famine well in advance.

On October 10, Bill Herod, Indochina consultant for the U.S.-based Church World Service, told the House Subcommittee on Asian and Pacific Affairs: "Thousands, perhaps hundreds of thousands, will die even if proposed relief operations were to begin today."

In looking back at what went wrong, it is obvious that blame lay in several directions in what was a bureaucratic and political tangle. The core of the problem was that only Vietnam, the Soviet Union and a few of their allies had diplomatic relations with the Heng Samrin authorities. The United Nations still recognized the Khmer Rouge under Pol Pot as the legal government of Kampuchea.

Hanoi and Phnom Penh insisted that all aid be channeled through the Heng Samrin regime, doubtless hoping it would lead to de facto recognition of the puppet administration. Indeed, not until late June did the regime allow representatives of the International Committee of the Red Cross and the United Nations Children's Fund, known as UNICEF, to visit Phnom Penh to assess the situation, despite requests. And only on September 26 did the two organizations receive permission to establish offices in the capital.

UNICEF, named the lead agency by U.N. Secretary General Kurt Waldheim, while mounting a combined operation with the Red Cross, tried to insist on monitoring its aid to see that it did not go to combatants instead of civilians. The Heng Samrin authorities rejected such supervision. They also reacted angrily to plans for personnel based in Thailand to assist Kampucheans along the border, because the Khmer Rouge and the Khmer Serei would benefit. The regime turned down an American proposal for a so-called land bridge, a convoy of trucks to cross the Thai border and distribute food along highways on the way to Phnom Penh.

Western countries such as the United States could have

moved faster if they had capitulated politically. But for a host of foreign-policy reasons, Washington was not about to let the Vietnamese and their Soviet backers score political points.

So once again the health, welfare and very existence of the people of Indochina were subordinated to political considerations. The game of nations came first, keeping people alive a poor second. "Some issues transcend politics," said U.S. Secretary of State Cyrus Vance. "This is one of them." He was right and he was wrong. Clearly the plight of the Kampucheans should have been above politics. But it was not, and that it was not was nothing less than a blight on civilization.

When the international relief effort finally got under way, it was organized as planned on two fronts—one operated within Kampuchea and the other, headquartered across the border in Thailand, operated on both sides of the border. By the end of 1980 the bill would amount to $500 million, making it one of the most expensive relief exercises in history.

But for a start, with Phnom Penh itself attempting to distribute the supplies sent its way, food piled up in warehouses, especially in Kompong Som. Officials denied that this was deliberate, explaining the bottlenecks as "technical and structural problems." Western correspondents who visited Kampuchea reported no evidence of willful obstruction or obvious diversion of food. But who or what was responsible was less important than the fact that food was sitting in storage and not being rushed to those who needed it as a matter of life and death.

Jockeying among relief agencies for the right to save dying Kampucheans did not help. The World Council of Churches and the Christian Conference of Asia declined to join a broad nongovernmental aid consortium proposed by Britain's relief and development agency Oxfam. Recommending against joining, the 4-member team that visited Kampuchea in October pointed out that it was the second delegation representing the two organizations that had gone to Phnom Penh "promising aid as an expression of the interest and concern of the world community of Christian churches." If this assistance were to become indistinguishable in the general flow of nongovernmental aid, "the churches will lose considerable face and credibility in Kampuchea and Indochina," the team said in a confidential report.

With the forces of both sides in the Kampuchean conflict

contending for recognition, territory and legitimacy, some food inevitably went to military personnel. It was impossible to stop supplies from seeping through to Khmer Rouge soldiers along the border, just as surely as it was to prevent Vietnamese troops from getting their hands on some elsewhere in Kampuchea. Khmer Rouge couriers merely lined up at distribution points on the border and carried rice back to their camps deeper in the country, where it was often held in communal stockpiles.

In advocating cross-border assistance, the Thai government hoped to keep most Kampucheans inside Kampuchea, as well as covertly to support the Khmer Rouge. But this proved impossible too. Taking advantage of the dry weather, Vietnamese forces in early October began attacking Khmer Rouge positions south of Aranyaprathet, supported by heavy artillery and mortars. The onslaught sent some 50,000 people across the border, most of them civilians, but including Khmer Rouge cadres, rear service personnel and their families.

They were in a pathetic condition, tottering on reed-thin legs and ridden with disease. Some fell and died by the roadside as they staggered into Thailand; their friends and relatives were too weak to help them. Others succumbed within sight of medical assistance, unable to summon the energy to crawl the last 50 yards. A number among the ones who made it were beyond help: children of a few years or a few months shriveled like prunes as if they were dying of old age; their parents lay feverish with malaria and barely conscious.

They were remnants of the 80,000 who had passed through Thai territory six months earlier; and they were the lucky ones, if the sick and dying can be said to be in luck. The 25,000 or so slaves who had been accompanying the Khmer Rouge columns were no more. When one cadre was asked about them, he gestured back toward Kampuchea: over there in the jungle, he said, there are thousands and thousands of dead.

On October 19, Premier Kriangsak Chomanand, after a highly publicized tour of the area, reversed his previous stand and announced what amounted to an open-door policy: Thailand would provide shelter for all the victims of war and famine from Kampuchea until conditions allowed them to return home. But these "new" Kampucheans would still be "illegal immigrants" and not official refugees. Although the decision was

243

widely portrayed as a spontaneous humanitarian reaction, the Thai were motivated by some practical considerations as well.

Among other things, Bangkok concluded that the best way to guard against serious border incursions was through the support of world opinion. It did not possess the men or equipment to do it through military might. And it would not win friends internationally, especially in Washington, if it resorted to expulsion again. The support of the U.S. Congress was needed for both arms and refugee aid.

The Kampucheans reaching Thailand were being joined by a trickle of refugees from Vietnam. Their departure by boat blocked by Hanoi's edict, the Vietnamese had opened a new escape route overland from Ho Chi Minh City. They were usually bribing officials to leave the country by truck for Phnom Penh, catching a lift to towns in western Kampuchea and then joining the flood of Kampucheans heading for the border on foot.

These Vietnamese, like the "new" Kampucheans they accompanied to Thailand, were denied refugee status. They were not put under UNHCR protection, nor were they allowed to resettle abroad. Both the Thai and UNHCR feared that their inclusion in the resettlement stream would attract many more of them. Held near the border in a Thai Army–supervised camp known as Northwest Nine, they numbered several thousand by early 1981. A few hundred with close relatives abroad were later allowed to resettle. Some defectors from Vietnam's occupation army in Kampuchea were also held in Northwest Nine with the refugees.

The Thai hurriedly prepared contingency plans to accommodate up to 300,000 "new" Kampucheans in six holding centers well clear of the frontier. The first was to be at Sa Kaeo, 45 miles west of the border, to hold the Khmer Rouge refugees who had fled the Vietnamese assault. But Khmer Rouge leaders decided that 20,000 of them, after eating and resting, should return to Kampuchea to continue the fight.

Dithering by relief agencies, principally UNHCR, resulted in a total lack of preparation to receive the remainder at Sa Kaeo. When the first busload arrived on October 24, bulldozers were just starting to prepare the site for the camp in which they were to live. Within days, more than 31,000 Kampucheans were dumped on the spot in the blazing sun, some so frail they died during the short bus ride.

They continued to die at the rate of 20 to 30 a day as they were forced to erect the most basic shelter for themselves on the freshly turned earth, using twigs and branches and plastic sheeting. Some lay helpless in bundles of rags, unnoticed by overworked staff and too weak to ask for rice and medical treatment. Heavy rains turned the camp, in reality 35 acres of flat, bare ground ringed by barbed wire and Thai soldiers, into a quagmire. As they lay in the mud, it was difficult to tell who was dead and who was alive. When the death toll in the camp topped 370 after three weeks, authorities in the nearby Buddhist temple reported no more room; the burial ground was full.

At the height of the debacle, several coachloads of camera-toting tourists arrived—insensitive foreigners eager to snap the walking scarecrows to show the folks back home. A Thai travel agency was thoughtfully running special day tours from Bangkok: come and see the Kampuchean refugees before they all fall down.

Within a week or two, UNHCR and others had pulled the center, almost miraculously, into shape. But it remained an eerie place, unlike any other refugee camp in Southeast Asia. Still under the control of Khmer Rouge cadres who were sent to accompany them to Sa Kaeo, the occupants did not return to life as they recovered their strength and health. A sullen silence hung in the air, the refugees taking in everything with their eyes but revealing little. They were reluctant to admit to outsiders that the dreaded Angka held sway in the camp. Eventually, UNHCR withdrew its chief representative from Sa Kaeo after the Khmer Rouge leader reportedly threatened to kill him.

UNHCR was more prepared for the second intake of "new" Kampucheans, who were to be drawn from Khmer Serei encampments. Another holding center was built at Khao I Dang, farther north and only 10 miles from the border: row after endless row of neat huts, separated by wide roads, toilets and other lots staked out for schools, churches and recreational facilities. The only drawback was the lack of water, which had to be brought in by road tanker from a source 60 miles away at a cost of almost $15,000 a day.

245

But the refugees, expected to enter at the rate of 8,000 to 10,000 a day when the center opened in November, were reluctant to move. Many of the destitute Kampucheans did not want to lose their access to the black market and the opportunity to earn a few dollars by trading. Khmer Serei leaders, most of them thugs growing rich by exploiting starving fellow Kampucheans, employed any number of tactics to deter others. They held rallies, appealed to patriotic instincts and spread stories that Khao I Dang was a Thai prison where inmates would be poisoned—a powerful propaganda line after the grim repatriation exercise earlier in the year by the Thai. In some cases the leaders and their henchmen set up roadblocks and threatened to kill refugees when they tried to leave.

The Thai were going cold on the idea of holding centers anyway because of the rapid refugee buildup on the border. By December, the population of Khao I Dang had reached 85,000, making it in effect the largest Kampuchean city in the world. That it was outside Kampuchea said a lot for the state of the nation and its people. But scattered in less formal settings along the border there were said to be about 700,000 other civilians, though it was impossible to count them accurately and official estimates were almost certainly exaggerated. "Now there are too many; we can't handle seven or eight hundred thousand," said Air Chief Marshal Siddhi Savetsila, the minister in charge of Thai refugee affairs.

Instead of trying to attract Kampucheans to the holding centers, the Thai concentrated on feeding and caring for them in the border encampments. So the Kampucheans continued their precarious existence, vulnerable to Vietnamese military probing, unsure of what tomorrow would bring.

The extent of their exposure was brought home to them in the whine and explosion of mortar and artillery shells in early November. The attack came not from the two potential aggressors, Vietnamese regular forces and the Khmer Rouge, but from the Royal Thai Army. Apparently in retaliation for a dispute that left at least one Thai soldier dead, the Thai assaulted a camp containing 40,000 Kampuchean civilians at Sra Srong, about a mile from the small Thai village of Kok Sung. For six hours they systematically shelled the area, using marker rounds to pinpoint the densely crowded center of the camp, killing more than 100 and leaving dozens wounded and dying among the trees. Under American pressure, the Thai government promised an investigation, but it apparently came to nothing.

On other occasions, artillery rounds from the warring parties fell around the Kampucheans, though the mass panic and stampede into Thailand feared by relief officials did not occur. At the end of 1979 there were, by official count, more than 1 million displaced persons being cared for from Thailand: 147,-000 refugees in camps run by the UNHCR, almost 130,000 "new" Kampucheans in holding centers and 800,000 other Kampucheans roaming the borderlands.

By early 1980, Kampuchea seemed to have pulled back from the brink, at least for the time being. Enough supplies were getting through, one way or another, to keep most people alive. With a return to reasonably stable conditions during the year, most Kampucheans left the border zones and went back to their homes and farms, though thousands continued to trek regularly to the frontier to trade and collect rice handouts.

Thailand at mid-year undertook a voluntary repatriation exercise under UNHCR supervision, but only 9,000 Kampucheans in holding centers were willing to go, more than 80 percent of them followers of the Khmer Rouge from Sa Kaeo. The Vietnamese expressed their displeasure at what they regarded as provocative Thai support for the Khmer Rouge by sending some troops across the border on a limited incursion; they were repulsed by Thai forces in fierce fighting.

The future of the 170,000 "new" Kampucheans who entered holding centers remained uncertain. Although Thailand insisted they were all to return home when conditions permitted, surveys confirmed the presence of large numbers of Phnom Penh bourgeois in Khao I Dang who were single-minded about going to live abroad. The Thai at first allowed only a few thousand who had close relatives overseas to be resettled, partly because they wanted resettlement places to go to Laotian and Vietnamese refugees who had been in Thailand for years. But after the limited results of the June repatriation, and anxious that at least some others be resettled while the outside world was still interested in receiving them, they relaxed their attitude. Thai authorities also began trucking volunteers, mostly farmers, back to the border, though almost as many other Kampucheans, usually middle-class defectors from the Heng Samrin regime in Phnom Penh, continued to sneak into the holding centers. By the end of February 1981, more than 19,000 "new" Kampucheans had gone abroad, and 39,000 others were about to follow. For more than 100,000 others, however, there appeared little alternative to either returning to Kampuchea or spending an indefinite period in camp.

AFTERWORD

The TB-41979 put back out to sea in the early hours of March 9, 1979. Around midday on March 12 it arrived off Kuala Dungun, in Malaysia's Kuala Trengganu state. Pushed back by Malaysian authorities, the Vietnamese holed the boat and wrecked the engine. By 3 P.M. they were allowed ashore. After being held in a local encampment for more than a week, they were admitted to the Pulau Bidong refugee camp on March 25.

Within weeks, Nguyen Dinh Thuy and his children had been accepted for resettlement in Australia. They planned to return to Perth, where Thuy had once attended the University of Western Australia, played chess on the state team and been known to his friends as Peter. After four years of frustration and a harrowing escape that took them to the brink, they were relieved and happy. But in many ways their ordeal was just beginning.

Thuy's son was too young to think of the future, of the

249

adjustments that would be necessary. His daughter, an Australian citizen with the name of Liz, remembered nothing of the land of her birth. She imagined Australia "full of skyscrapers" and "with lots of green trees and full of fruit and kindhearted people." The reality was an alien landscape, full of unemployment and full of people who spoke English, foreign to both children.

One man, his son and daughter had torn themselves adrift from everything Vietnamese, from everything that was familiar and comforting. Extended family life, with its insulation and sense of belonging, in different circumstances might have provided the cocoon. But it no longer existed. Their family was blown to the wind, scattered across four continents: Hung, Thuy's stepbrother, went to Canada to join his sister. Thuy's mother and stepfather received permission to emigrate to West Germany, where another of his sisters lived. And still in Vietnam, in her own shattered world, was Phi Yen, now his wife in name only.

THE INDOCHINA REFUGEE crisis was, at its core, not a simple humanitarian issue but a serious political problem that threatened the peace and stability of one corner of the globe. It was a problem the international community faced reluctantly, and then with only limited success. All told, it points to a fairly bleak future, in an age of refugees, unless the world can somehow profit from the experience.

Neither can one seek comfort in the thought that the Indochina situation is exceptional. True, it was the result of extraordinary circumstances and became one of the most dramatic and complex refugee crises of modern times, one unusual characteristic being the high proportion of refugees requiring relocation in third countries. But in today's interdependent world, any large-scale refugee crisis is a danger to established order and thus no different in its essential elements.

The crisis in Southeast Asia was precipitated by a breakdown in acceptable standards of behavior, primarily in the way the post-1975 governments of Vietnam, Laos and Kampuchea treated their peoples, and by the tardiness of the developed world in relieving the pressures brought by the refugees on

250

countries of temporary asylum. As we have seen, the circumstances were never simple and did not occur in a vacuum. But a tragedy occurred when these essential, if unwritten, international obligations were breached: the first created the refugees; the second all too often condemned them to further suffering and death.

Some argue that revolution must inevitably produce a stream of losers, some of whom just as surely will become refugees in the political upheaval that follows. While that may be so, it should in no way diminish the responsibility of victorious movements, revolutionary or reactionary, for the welfare of the people they liberate or conquer.

The record in Indochina contains nothing that can be said in defense of the Khmer Rouge, who managed in just forty-four months to eliminate almost one-third of Kampuchea's population. Led by French-educated intellectuals, they pursued policies that were senselessly brutal and violent. In addition to their former enemies, they slaughtered many innocent people as well, people with the education, skills and training to help build a better future. In this insanity, the relatively few escapees who reached neighboring countries and gained official refugee status were the fortunate ones.

Although the extreme cruelty of the Khmer Rouge can be attributed in part to the brutalizing effects of the war that brought them to power, their approach denied not only humanity but common sense and survival. In the end, they left a sad and empty land—one vulnerable to Vietnamese invasion and occupation.

Similarly, there is no evidence that the Pathet Lao ever sought a serious accommodation with the admittedly independent Hmong who had fought for Vang Pao and the CIA. On the contrary, they seemed to see their victory as allowing them to suppress the troublesome Hmong once and for all. With the ongoing help of Vietnamese troops, and using harsh and questionable methods, they did just that.

Toward the rest of the population the government was more restrained, but scarcely bent on national reconciliation. Its reforms alienated many Laotians who initially welcomed the end of the war and the chance to build a better life or at least were prepared to go along with the changeover.

Nowhere, however, was the reservoir of goodwill squandered so recklessly as in Vietnam. By the end of the war, Hanoi had won wide sympathy with its long struggle for independence. Especially during the American phase of the conflict, it had been able to mobilize world opinion in support of its cause: a peasant-society David battling an American Goliath which was prepared to obliterate it, if necessary, to prevent a Communist victory.

Vietnam in 1975 was not just a model for revolutionary movements trying to overthrow pro-Western regimes around the world. It enjoyed almost heroic status in the nonaligned movement for having endured so much, persisted so long and eventually triumphed against great odds. Just over four years later, Vietnam stood isolated internationally, subjected to censure in the U.N. General Assembly and repudiated by the nonaligned nations. By all but a few Soviet-bloc members, it was judged guilty of practicing racist policies at home, of exporting its people for profit and of pressing the military occupation of Kampuchea.

There was no shortage of extenuating circumstances that Vietnam could call on in its own defense. Grave economic difficulties in the aftermath of war were compounded by successive seasons of droughts, floods and typhoons. China, a wartime ally, turned hostile in peace, increasing tension on Vietnam's northern border. China also armed Kampuchea and incited the Khmer Rouge in their encroachments on Vietnam's southwestern flank. Peking aroused the Sino-Vietnamese inside Vietnam, stopped its aid and finally resorted to the invasion of Vietnam. As for the United States, it made little effort to heal the terrible wounds it had inflicted on Vietnam and, while leading the campaign to deny Western economic assistance to Hanoi, came uncomfortably close to encouraging China's belligerence and determination to "bleed Vietnam white."

Altogether, a limited refugee outflow probably was to be expected after 1975. Once it started and word got back to Vietnam that the escapees who survived were being resettled in the West, a pull factor no doubt entered the equation. Though offset to some extent by reports of high losses at sea, this pull factor ensured that escape by boat would remain a viable alternative.

However, the vast upsurge in people deserting Vietnam in 1978 was neither natural nor unavoidable.

Vietnam, more than a little arrogant after defeating the French and the Americans, frustrated by the difficulty of absorbing the South and angry at being denied what it regarded as the proper fruits of victory, allowed racism to prevail over reason and resorted to all-too-familiar violence. Its suspiciousness turned to paranoia. Hanoi first set up an organization to reap profit by allowing residents to become refugees under conditions that endangered their lives. Then it forced its ethnic-Chinese minority out of parts of the country and into their quest for refuge. Not content to defend itself against the Khmer Rouge, who undoubtedly were being provocative but were hardly a serious threat to Vietnam, Hanoi solved its border irritation with a major invasion that overnight wiped out its hard-won reputation as a victim of aggression and branded itself an aggressor.

It was more than a case of the Socialist Republic of Vietnam's being isolated within the community of nations. The government in Hanoi was isolated from large sections of its own people, and its policies were alienating Kampucheans and Laotians from Hanoi's yes men in Phnom Penh and Vientiane. They protested in the most dramatic and extreme way—by flight.

The developing countries on the rim of the South China Sea were never enthusiastic about accepting the refugees, even temporarily. But their response was basically humane and remained so as long as they were supported by the more affluent nations. Only Singapore refused shelter to the Indochinese from the outset, and it too subsequently linked a more liberal asylum attitude to the willingness of the developed world to resettle them. As long as the offtake kept pace with the rate of arrival, tragedy was averted; when arrivals overwhelmed departures, tragedy surely followed.

Although temporary asylum is an absolutely essential first step in meeting the needs of all refugees, it is not a one-sided obligation that falls on the nations that happen to find themselves near a refugee-producing situation. Various principles derived from U.N. declarations and conventions have produced the concept of international solidarity, under which the rest of the world community should ensure that countries offering asylum to refugees do not have to pay an unbearable price. It can be argued that Thailand and Malaysia were asked to pay an unbearable price.

Such an argument in no way seeks to minimize such outrages as towing listing boats full of men, women and children out to sea, or forcing refugees on foot back to the scene of their persecution. The countries that did so proclaimed limits to their humanity, and they will have to live with the knowledge and the consequences. But, it has to be stressed, they found that cruelty brought concern as well as condemnation from an otherwise indifferent world. Only when first-asylum countries abused refugees, or threatened to mistreat them, were they given the international support they had every right to expect.

Little can be said in defense of the response of the industrial democracies to the plight of the Indochina refugees and the burdened countries of temporary asylum until mid-1979. A few performed better than others, but as a community they simply were not interested—with dire, sometimes fatal, consequences, during years when their attention should have been riveted on the area.

While a roll call of offenders hardly serves any purpose, the United States inevitably invites criticism. Washington's reluctance to go to the rescue of displaced and distressed Vietnamese, Laotians and Kampucheans reflected poorly on a country that had long championed their cause. Years of intervention in Indochina had surely left the United States with a responsibility over and above that of being the leader of the non-Communist world, which in itself required the United States to act. Those responsibilities, if anything, were heightened by America's pursuit, in the years following its defeat in 1975, of policies designed to ensure that conditions in Indochina, or within Vietnam at least, did not materially improve.

If the United States is singled out for being dilatory, however, it must be praised wholeheartedly for its ultimate leadership and generosity. Once it made the decision to mobilize and help underwrite the international humanitarian effort to cope with the refugees, it did much to restore its record and reputation for welcoming the "homeless, tempest-tost" masses "yearning to breathe free." By February 1981, in just under six years, more than 1 million Indochinese had settled abroad, including

254

263,000 who went directly to China (see Table 1). America's share was 481,000, which probably would top 600,000 by the end of the year, and Washington was spending $2 billion a year on refugee programs, most of it for Indochinese.

The U.S. ambassador to Thailand, Morton Abramowitz, once complained that America's role in the refugee drama had been "insufficiently understood and grossly underestimated." More than "saving countless lives," he said, "it has also contributed fundamentally to the security of every nation" in Southeast Asia. In the final analysis, that was an accurate assessment.

The response generated by the Geneva conference in 1979 brought results. Temporary asylum became more assured as the pace of resettlement quickened to 25,000 a month and camp populations fell. It was tempting to believe the problem was in the process of being solved, but long-term factors were at work that almost guaranteed it would persist. A report in August 1980 by the Office of the U.S. Coordinator for Refugee Affairs showed that net gains in the twelve months since Geneva were limited. While the life-threatening aspects had been relieved, it said, "the situation remains volatile and virtually in the state of crisis which existed one year ago."

The international community was treating the symptoms and not the disease. Being humanitarian in nature, the conference had done nothing to remove the people's underlying reasons for flight; the outflow was continuing from all three countries, though most Kampucheans were not being accorded refugee status and were not eligible for resettlement. What is more, as the numerous national refugee programs became established, they took on a momentum and life of their own, changing the composition of the refugee flows and increasing the pull factor. A study prepared for the U.S. Congress in late 1980 noted that almost anyone who left Laos and Vietnam was likely to find safe haven in a neighboring country and could expect fairly rapid resettlement. "This prospect tends to encourage future refugees," it commented, "even those who are not fleeing immediate threats to life and property."[1]

Although the Laotian government had liberalized economic reforms and injected elements of flexibility and pragmatism into many of its policies, Laotians were continuing to cross the Mekong at the rate of more than 3,000 a month. Critics of

TABLE 1

INDOCHINA REFUGEES SETTLED ABROAD, 1975–81

COUNTRY	NUMBER ACCEPTED
Argentina	1,281
Australia	47,637
Austria	1,553
Belgium	3,636
Brazil	68
Canada	72,484
China	265,588
Denmark	1,991
Finland	115
France	71,011
West Germany	17,179
Greece	95
Hong Kong	9,474
Iceland	34
Ireland	212
Israel	366
Italy	2,842
Japan	991
Laos	34
Luxembourg	97
Malaysia	2,137
Netherlands	4,218
New Zealand	3,634
Norway	2,334
Paraguay	31
Spain	917
Sweden	2,290
Switzerland	6,816
United Kingdom	13,996
United States	480,913
Others	620
Total	1,014,596

SOURCE: UNHCR and Office of the U.S. Coordinator for Refugee Affairs. Totals cover the period April 1975 through February 1981.

In addition, there were 193,626 refugees in camps and processing centers awaiting resettlement and an estimated 150,000 "new" Kampucheans in holding centers in Thailand facing an uncertain future.

continuing large-scale resettlement liked to point to the relatively few "add-on" cases: a Lao male from Vientiane would cross alone to the Nong Khai refugee camp and register for resettlement processing; after preparing a home in the camp, the refugee would summon his family from Laos, often by phone, adding to the list. And yet for tens of thousands of Laotians the attraction was as a temporary shelter and not as a step toward resettlement; they refused even to register to go abroad.

Arrivals from Vietnam were overwhelmingly ethnic Vietnamese who had the opportunity to escape, such as coastal farmers and fishermen with access to a boat, including some from northern areas of the country. They often turned up with maps on which the locations of UNHCR refugee camps were clearly marked and with practiced answers ready for the questions they knew would be asked in processing. Ethnic Chinese and others with the most compelling claims to persecution were mostly trapped near Ho Chi Minh City. Visitors to the old capital were left with the impression that several million residents desperately wanted to leave, including identifiable groups of ethnic Vietnamese suffering official discrimination because of their wartime associations.

If 1980 was any guide, the world could expect an indefinite outflow from Vietnam and Laos on the order of 120,000 persons a year, some of doubtful refugee status and excluding many with high claims to international help. While such numbers could be contained for the time being and headway made toward whittling down existing camp populations, progress was slower than the mass resettlement of refugees suggested. Moreover, the West was showing signs of suffering from what one American Congressman called "compassion fatigue." If it was true and serious enough, the backlog in the camps might start to build up again. And at any time Hanoi could swamp the entire game plan by once more permitting or encouraging departures, which it threatened to do on at least one occasion. A resurgence of fighting or another round of famine in Kampuchea could have a similar effect.

In 1981 Thailand took the lead among first-asylum countries in introducing humane measures designed to discourage Indochinese from becoming refugees, although it seemed unlikely that such tactics would have more than a marginal effect overall. Lao arriving after January 1 were placed in a detention center, built within the sprawling Nong Khai refugee camp, where conditions were less attractive than usual. Denied resettlement, they were transferred later to a long-term camp that was just as basic. Although the results were far from conclusive, the Thai were encouraged by a decline in Lao arrivals in the first half of the year and announced that the measures would be extended to boat people. Vietnamese were still going to be allowed to land on Thai shores, but they were to be placed in an austere detention center where they were to remain indefinitely, not knowing what the future would bring. Neither UNHCR nor major resettlement nations objected to the Thai policies, regarding them as essentially humane and more acceptable than most theoretical alternatives.

But in at least one case Thailand went beyond what was regarded as humane and acceptable. In an effort to dissuade Vietnamese escaping overland through Kampuchea, they closed the Thai Army–supervised Northwest Nine camp in May 1981 and refused to allow any more Vietnamese to cross into Thailand. Bangkok's position, maintained despite intensive lobbying by American diplomats and international organizations, was that Kampuchea was the country of first asylum for the Vietnamese and they must be processed there. The stand immediately left about 420 refugees trapped in border encampments controlled by the Khmer Rouge and Khmer Serei, neither of which had much time for Vietnamese of any political persuasion. The refugees' acute danger was dramatized in June when a badly wounded Vietnamese youth staggered into Thailand. He reported that he was the sole survivor of a group of 11 who had been tied, blindfolded and gunned down by Khmer Rouge soldiers.

As the United States debated its attitude toward the ongoing Indochina refugee issue, existing programs were vulnerable to domestic criticism on two scores: the high cost and the self-sustaining nature of the flows that brought increasing numbers of people who appeared to be more economic immigrants than political refugees. Administering officials were quick to challenge the notion that economic considerations could be separated easily from a refugee's other motivations in fleeing, or that more than a small percentage were in fact in the economic

258

category. But in any case there are practical reasons for maintaining current policies.

Opportunities for voluntary repatriation and local settlement remain as limited as ever. Although about 60,000 Laotians—two-thirds Hmong and other highlanders—were not interested in resettlement abroad in early 1981, few showed any inclination to go home. While Laotian officials claimed that 8,000 had returned spontaneously to Laos over a five-year period, the figure appeared exaggerated. Certainly only several hundred had volunteered to go back under the protection of UNHCR, and several thousand more at the most were likely to follow in the near future. There were no volunteers to return to Vietnam.

For their part, the Thai were still not prepared to follow through on their earlier indication that they would accept between 10,000 and 20,000 Lao permanently. While conditions remain unstable in Laos, they fear local settlement would attract a large number of refugee Lao to the northeast, which, though poor by Thai standards, enjoys a standard of living well above that of Laos.

If the United States were to attempt to restrict its intake drastically without simultaneously curbing the outflow from Indochina, refugees doubtless would again start to swell camps in Southeast Asia, since other resettlement nations are unlikely to take up the slack. Thailand and perhaps other first-asylum countries, still lacking long-term resettlement guarantees and still fearful of being left with refugees to care for indefinitely, probably would be tempted to push refugees back again. Altogether, it would be an invitation to a reenactment of the tragedy and crisis of 1979. As for discouraging refugees from leaving their homelands—for instance, by attempting to screen out "economic" as opposed to "political" refugees—that would involve a radical departure from established U.S. policy toward Indochina. It would also create a new problem—what to do with the rejects?

But such a change of policy actually started to take place in early 1981 when officials of the U.S. Immigration and Naturalization Service began applying stringently the new definition of a refugee as contained in the 1980 Refugee Act. Thousands of Indochinese who normally would have been admitted to the

United States had their cases deferred. They remained stranded in camps as the Reagan administration debated the issue. Under strong State Department pressure, they were eventually accepted, but not before Southeast Asian governments voiced concern and the American intake dropped to almost half the 14,000 monthly quota.

The problem was solved temporarily by Attorney General William French Smith, who ruled that the old guidelines should apply for the remainder of the fiscal year ending September 30, 1981. The issue was then to be argued again as the administration sought congressional approval for an intake of 120,000 Indochinese, or 10,000 a month, in the following year. The debate would involve such basic issues as the extent of American responsibilities in Indochina and the nation's capacity and willingness to continue absorbing Indochina refugees indefinitely.

The battle lines were drawn mid-year when a Special Refugee Advisory Panel led by former Assistant Secretary of State for East Asian and Pacific Affairs Marshall Green toured the region. The panel endorsed the State Department's stand. It concluded that generally American policies and programs were correct, that the existing course was effective and that no major shifts were warranted for the time being. It said all people fleeing Vietnam, whether by land or sea, should continue to be presumed to be refugees within the meaning of the Refugee Act, "since their voluntary repatriation for the foreseeable future is not possible." As for Lao, Hmong and Khmer, if significant numbers of them could be repatriated voluntarily, they should be screened on a case-by-case basis to determine whether any individuals might properly be deemed refugees.

The panel's findings were hotly disputed by some members of Congress who followed soon after on a similar fact-finding mission. They declared their opposition to continuing large-scale resettlement on various grounds, most of which were among the "mounting criticisms" acknowledged by the Green panel: claims that rising numbers of refugees were motivated primarily by pull factors such as economic betterment; the fact that more and more refugees entering the American program had had no direct connection with the United States in pre-1975 Indochina; a growing tendency among refugees to exploit the U.S. welfare system; and the fact that the United States was absorbing an increasingly large proportion of Indochinese refugees.

The critics in Congress were encouraged not only by the actions of the Immigration and Naturalization Service but also by an apparently authoritative memorandum that said the Indochina outflow "seem[ed] to have the characteristics of a straightforward immigration program." The memo, prepared in April as an internal document by Martin Barber, UNHCR's Bangkok-based Deputy Regional Representative, was leaked to the press. In it he claimed that a high proportion of the Indochinese would not qualify for refugee status if individual eligibility procedures were applied. Mr. Barber contended that Vietnamese were risking their lives on the seas because Eldorado, in the form of California, beckoned. "Once that vision is removed, most will give up and stay at home," he said. He also advanced the view that "certain elements" within the State Department believed the exodus should be encouraged because it showed the Hanoi government in a bad light.

In any event, one area worthy of further study is the possibility of widening the channel of direct departure from Vietnam. The more troubled Vietnamese are able to leave legally and safely, the smaller the pool of potential boat people. If they cannot get out under the orderly departure program, they will continue to leave by the back door, even if for some the undertaking is a form of suicide as they attempt to elude armed patrols and put out to sea in unsafe boats completely at the mercy of the elements and vicious pirates. As things stand, the only chance of relief for most of them is in achieving refugee status.

Ultimately, a solution to the Indochina refugee problem rests on a political settlement of the various complex events that helped create it, especially a return to peace and stability in Kampuchea. Regrettably, prospects are remote for an early improvement in relations between the sets of hostile parties: China and Vietnam, the United States and Vietnam, and ASEAN and Vietnam. In addition, Hanoi has to be convinced—one way or another—that it cannot benefit from the wholesale dumping of its people.

While the United States and other nations ponder their options toward displaced Vietnamese, Laotians and Kampucheans, a serious constraint has always been the need to maintain a consistent and practical global approach to refugees. For as urgent and compelling as is their cause, the Indochinese represent only a slice of a tragic worldwide problem. In late 1979, Mohamed Sharif of Somalia said in the U.N. General Assembly: "It is a sad reflection perhaps as much on ourselves as on the sensation-seeking elements in the mass media that it is held more dramatic to die in a boat in a storm than on foot in the deserts of Africa." He was not carping at the mobilization of resources for Indochinese but pointing out that Africa also has a massive refugee problem and needs assistance constantly.

According to the U.S. Committee for Refugees, there are 12.6 million refugees spread over every continent, "evidence of man's inability to manage himself, his religion, his politics and his hungers with due concern for his fellow man." In the words of Senator Edward Kennedy, "The refugee crisis is of greater dimension and more complex than at any time in modern history." And the sad fact is that the crisis is unlikely to go away. With men, women and children forced to leave their homes and their lands, as Kennedy says, "for as many reasons as there are behind the violence and conflict among people and nations," only the dawning of a stable world order that recognizes human and economic rights and settles disputes peacefully will prevent the appearance of yet more refugees. Few would expect it soon.

In the meantime, reinforced by the Indochina experience, much can be done to improve the care and protection of all refugees and to find durable solutions for them. Perhaps what is first needed is a recognition by most countries that they are not dealing with a passing or temporary phenomenon but with a characteristic of the age. Indeed, while the German novelist Heinrich Böll has described this as "the century of refugees and prisoners," more recently it has been suggested that the 1980s may become known as the "decade of refugees."[2]

Soon after he was appointed the first U.S. Coordinator for Refugee Affairs in 1979, Dick Clark acknowledged the persisting nature of refugees and the need for permanent machinery to deal with them. "In the past," he observed, "all of us have assumed refugee problems to be extraordinary occurrences requiring only ad hoc responses. The unfortunate reality is, however, that refugee problems have become a regular feature of

262

our world. The policies and programs of national governments and those international organizations mandated to cope with refugee problems must be based on recognition of this reality."

While individual governments must decide the most appropriate and effective way to respond, it is obvious that the key international agency providing legal and material assistance for refugees, UNHCR, is in need of an overhaul. Established by the General Assembly in 1951 as the ninth in a series of international bodies set up to handle refugee problems since World War I, it has been stretched beyond recognition recently by the increase in its workload. Given a budget of $350,000 and a small staff originally, UNHCR was expected to go out of business after it tidied up in Europe after World War II. When refugees did not disappear, it had its mandate repeatedly renewed, being funded by voluntary contributions from governments and private sources. Only once in the first twenty years did its annual spending exceed $20 million. By 1975, when momentous changes began to take shape in Indochina, its budget had climbed to $76 million. Then it soared to an estimated $475 million in 1980, its staff also expanding rapidly.

Although UNHCR can claim to have helped more than 25 million refugees, its performance in the Indochina theater provoked a legion of critics. A U.S. House of Representatives delegation led by Lester L. Wolff, a New York Democrat, conducted a study of Indochina refugees in December 1978 and January 1979 and concluded that UNHCR deficiencies belonged on a list of the most compelling problems. "The UNHCR responds slowly to increased challenges of exploding refugee populations," Wolff reported. "By not adding personnel until there is no question that they are necessary, UNHCR's capabilities must almost always be less than the task at hand requires." He said the agency, in its relations with host countries, "is too diffident in pursuit of its aims and of administrative excellence, either by nature of the situation or by design." Potentially more troublesome for UNHCR, the delegation observed, "We are not sure that American dollars, which are a large part of the UNHCR budget, are being well spent."

Although the Wolff mission might be dismissed as an aggregation of instant experts, there is no doubt that members were merely passing on what they had been told repeatedly in the field, especially by the staffs of Western diplomatic missions. Relations between UNHCR and resettlement countries, particularly the United States, were constantly taut in Southeast Asia. One American ambassador based in the region during the crisis confided concern that the tension might impede the overall refugee program. Another American ambassador considered publicly denouncing UNHCR but was talked out of it by embassy staff.

Dale de Haan, the Deputy U.N. High Commissioner for Refugees, has pointed out that there are "constraints on the ability" of UNHCR to deal with emerging refugee problems as quickly as it and others might like. Foremost, he said, is the sovereignty of nations, which means that UNHCR can act only with the consent of governments providing asylum to refugees. "Sometimes this requirement results in what may seem undue delay or inefficiency," he said.

Without doubt, however, a wide gulf separates Geneva, where UNHCR headquarters is located in elegant surroundings, and the faraway refugee camps where squalor and misery are the constants in life. The two worlds rarely meet, despite the assignment of personnel in both directions. During the Indochina crisis, too often the bureaucrats at the head office reacted slowly to urgent requests from the boondocks of Asia.

One example was the failure to cope with the rapid refugee buildup in Indonesia in early 1979. UNHCR was caught napping in a repeat performance of what had happened in Malaysia a year earlier. The result: UNHCR was represented in Indonesia for nearly six months by one international officer, who was responsible for up to 45,000 Vietnamese refugees. For most of the time UNHCR was squatting temporarily in two small rooms in Jakarta, its facilities limited to one motor vehicle, a single telephone and a lone typewriter.

Out in the Anambas Islands, hundreds of miles away, and literally dots on a large-scale map, the refugees were being relieved of their money, gold, jewelry and other valuables by Indonesian officials; the government of Indonesia, a little ironically, was UNHCR's operational partner in the country. The single UNHCR representative of necessity was confined to Jakarta. When a UNHCR registration team eventually arrived on Jemaja Island, members interviewed 1,400 refugees in Letung, each of whom had paid local police a bribe of at least $50 to enter the waterfront town from one of four nearby refugee camps. The refugees were not aware that the team would later visit the camps for registration, and so they paid for fear of being passed over for resettlement.

With staff so thin on the ground, it was not always possible to monitor activities closely enough to minimize waste and corruption, which were rife. UNHCR authorized Indonesian officials to buy a basic four-wheel-drive vehicle for refugee work on Bintan Island. After delivery it was found to be a little better than basic: it was fitted with air conditioning, a quadraphonic sound system that relayed music from a tape deck, a quartz digital clock, a compass and fancy fog lamps.

The distressing thing was that little or nothing had been learned from the experience in Malaysia, where controversy dogged the development of the country's major refugee camp, Pulau Bidong. When the first 121 Vietnamese were transferred to the uninhabited island in July 1978, they had found it in its idyllic, natural state without any facilities at all. Malaysian government officials suggested privately that they had sent the first batch to nudge UNHCR along. If that was the objective, it conspicuously failed. When a further 600 refugees were sent six weeks later, still nothing had been done, except for what the Vietnamese had managed themselves. With about 9,000 refugees descending on Bidong in the next month or so, and 29,000 by the end of the year, it was downhill all the way. When the annual monsoon struck in late October, no proper toilets had been built, supply lines were not organized, storage facilities were nonexistent and no steps had been taken to seal wells to prevent contamination of the water supply.

Another area that demands attention is the need to solve the problem of how to require all countries to give asylum to refugees, at least on a temporary basis. The lack of an arrangement through which this can be done was all too sadly apparent in the mass expulsion of Kampucheans from Thailand and boat people from Malaysia and elsewhere. The Convention of 1951 and the Protocol of 1967 relating to the status of refugees obligate contracting parties not to expel refugees from their territory, especially to a country where they might be in danger of persecution. However, only 60 percent of the countries of the world have ratified either the Convention or the Protocol and are thus bound by them. Many of the rest feel a moral obligation to abide by their provisions, though under pressure they can be tempted, like Thailand and Malaysia, to act otherwise. UNHCR has identified the negotiation of "an international legal instrument" to establish the fundamental right of asylum as one of its targets for the 1980s.

The question of asylum leads naturally to the delicate but crucial issue of defining a refugee. It is pointless to "guarantee" asylum for refugees if a host country simply can circumvent its obligations by refusing to confer refugee status on a particular group of displaced persons. The "new" Kampucheans in Thailand, beginning in 1979, went without the protection of international law because they were denied refugee status—with disastrous results for thousands. The rest were saved from forcible repatriation not by law but by the protests and vigilance of international organizations and Western nations.

The ideal situation would be one comprehensive definition recognized by all countries. Even then, disputes could be expected over interpretation. For instance, while UNHCR by statute must refuse refugee status for "reasons of a purely economic character," gauging the motives of people seeking asylum can be a painful exercise.

As it is, the standard formal definition is the one contained in the 1951 Convention and the 1967 Protocol: persons outside their country unable or unwilling to return because of a "well founded fear of being persecuted for reasons of race, religion, nationality, membership of a particular social group or political opinion." Apart from the previously noted lack of universal support for these documents, critics have pointed to shortcomings in the definition. Among other things, it does not cover internally displaced people. It also fails to include those outside their borders, such as many of the "new" Kampucheans, who fear more general victimization, such as being caught between opposing armed forces. In fact, the widely accepted definition of a refugee already goes beyond the persecuted individual, as contained in the Convention and Protocol, to whole groups of people fleeing from dangerous circumstances.[3] Probably the most important influence has been the Organization of African Unity's Convention relating to the specific problems of refugees

266

in Africa, adopted in 1969, to which 21 African states are a party. It accepts the U.N. definition and includes persons who, "owing to external aggression, occupation, foreign domination or events seriously disturbing public order," are compelled to leave their place of habitual residence to seek refuge outside their country. The definition has changed over time in response to particular developments and must continue evolving to meet new situations.

Essential, perhaps, above all in meeting the challenge posed by refugees is the need to involve more countries. At present, the responsibility for the world's homeless is accepted largely by America, the European Economic Community, Canada, Australia and Japan. They not only take most of the refugees requiring resettlement (see Table 2), but contribute the bulk of funds to refugee-aid agencies (see Table 3). Additionally, their private organizations and bilateral government programs are the most generous in providing relief for refugees.

Notable, though not surprising, is the thin line of assistance from the Soviet Union and its allies, and indeed, from all other Socialist countries. As one official American report recorded tersely, "The Communist countries are sources of refugees and, except for Yugoslavia and Rumania, have contributed virtually no funds."[4] With the exception of Saudi Arabia, the oil-producing nations also are providing little support. Persuading them to be more forthcoming and to shoulder a fairer share of the burden will not be easy, but it is encouraging that both Vietnam* and China asked for UNHCR help for the first time during the Indochina crisis, and Laos and Kampuchea also were pleased to accept the agency's assistance.

Even if some leaders are not moved by humanitarian considerations, it will be sufficient if they take the point that no country can be certain of being completely immune to the destabilizing effects of millions of persons being displaced. Refugees have the unique and unpredictable ability to threaten every nation's patch of the planet, and just about all nations need to pool resources to take care of them in order to take care of themselves. As one recent study concluded, "The scale, the complexity, and the persistence of the problem call for an almost

* The Provisional Government of South Vietnam first asked UNHCR for assistance in 1974.

TABLE 2

Major Refugee Resettlement Countries, 1975–80

COUNTRY	NUMBER RESETTLED	PROPORTION OF REFUGEES TO POPULATION
Israel	105,700	1:37
Malaysia	102,100	1:137
Australia	51,200	1:285
Canada	84,100	1:285
United States	677,000	1:329
Hong Kong	9,400	1:511
Tanzania	26,000	1:715
France	72,000	1:744
New Zealand	4,100	1:781
Switzerland	7,500	1:840
Sweden	7,300	1:1,137
Norway	2,700	1:1,519
Austria	4,300	1:1,744
West Germany	32,100	1:1,903
United Kingdom	27,600	1:2,022
Denmark	2,300	1:2,217
Belgium	3,900	1:2,539
Netherlands	4,700	1:3,000
China	265,000	1:3,679
Argentina	2,800	1:9,679

SOURCE: 1981 World Refugee Survey, U.S. Committee for Refugees Inc., New York.

The majority of the refugees were from Indochina; others came from the Soviet Union and Latin American countries. Israel and Malaysia, which topped the list by ratio, could be considered special cases: Israel accepted mainly Soviet Jews, while some 100,000 of Malaysia's total were Filipino Moslems who fled to Sabah after late 1972 to escape fighting between the government and the rebels led by the Moro National Liberation Front.

TABLE 3

CONTRIBUTIONS TO INTERNATIONAL REFUGEE AID AGENCIES

COUNTRY	CONTRIBUTION (IN $ MILLION)	CONTRIBUTION PER CAPITA (IN $)
Sweden	33.0	3.98
Norway	15.2	3.71
United Arab Emirates	1.9	2.43
Denmark	12.2	2.39
Kuwait	2.5	1.91
Switzerland	9.7	1.53
Netherlands	18.8	1.33
Qatar	0.3	1.30
Saudi Arabia	10.6	1.29
Lichtenstein	0.04	1.23
Australia	13.6	0.93
United States	199.4	0.90
Canada	18.0	0.75
Japan	81.1	0.69
West Germany	40.1	0.66
United Kingdom	29.7	0.53
Belgium	5.2	0.52
Libya	1.3	0.43
Iraq	5.2	0.40
Iceland	0.07	0.35

SOURCE: 1981 World Refugee Survey, U.S. Committee for Refugees, Inc., New York.

Information is limited to assistance through international channels, consisting of 1980 contributions to four U.N. agencies and the 1979 figures for one other body, the Intergovernmental Committee for European Migration. Total donations by governments to the five agencies amounted to $520 million, though the European Economic Community also contributed $117 million for refugees, most of it in foodstuffs. These top 20 countries gave $498 million, or 78 percent of the combined total, while the remainder was supplied by another 105 countries.

Although Arab oil-producing nations made significant contributions, their donations went primarily to the U.N. Relief and Works Agency, an organization assisting Palestinian refugees.

unprecedented degree of cooperation among nations."[5] The agony of the Indochinese refugees, only the latest of an ongoing series of such tragedies, demands that a more intense effort be made to achieve that cooperation. Nothing is more certain than the fact that once again, the lives of thousands upon thousands of human beings will be at stake.

NOTES

Chapter One

1. The term "refugee" shall apply to any person who: "As a result of events occurring before January 1, 1951, and owing to well founded fear of being persecuted for reasons of race, religion, nationality, membership of a particular social group or political opinion, is outside the country of his nationality and is unable or, owing to such fear, is unwilling to avail himself of the protection of that country; or who, not having a nationality and being outside the country of his former habitual residence as a result of such events, is unable or, owing to such fear, is unwilling to return to it. In the case of a person who has more than one nationality . . . a person shall not be deemed to be lacking the protection of the country of his nationality if, without any valid reason based on well founded fear, he has not availed himself of the pro-

tection of one of the countries of which he is a national."
The Protocol uses identical terms to cover refugees created
by events after January 1, 1951.

CHAPTER TWO

1. *Refugees: A World Report*, Facts on File, Inc., New York, 1979.
2. Frank Snepp, *Decent Interval*, copyright © 1977 by Frank W. Snepp III, Random House, Inc., New York, 1977.
3. Tiziano Terzani, *Giai Phong! The Fall and Liberation of Saigon*, translated from the Italian by John Shepley, St. Martin's Press, Inc., New York, 1976.
4. Terzani, *op. cit.*
5. UNHCR statistics are based on registrations by the agency rather than actual arrivals; in practice, they amount to almost the same thing. For a variety of reasons, UNHCR periodically revises its figures, though the adjustments are for the most part minor.
6. *Boat People*, Asian Relations Center, Socio-Economic Institute, Sophia University, Tokyo, 1978.
7. "A Prayer for Land," *Boat People* (reproduced from *Nguoi Viet Tu Do* magazine).
8. Ben Kiernan, an Australian historian who spent four months in Kampuchea in 1980 and conducted 400 interviews, provided the most authoritative independent assessment. He concluded that 1.5 million to 2 million people died as a result of Angka's policies.
9. François Ponchaud, *Cambodia Year Zero*, Penguin Books, London, 1978.
10. *Ibid.*
11. *Asia 1977 Yearbook*, Far Eastern Economic Review, Hong Kong.
12. Details of nationalization measures in southern Vietnam are drawn largely from reports by Nayan Chanda in the issues of *Far Eastern Economic Review* of April 14 and May 26, 1978.
13. Stephen FitzGerald, in *China and the Overseas Chinese*, Cambridge University Press, London, 1972, cites figures showing the number of ethnic Chinese in Vietnam in 1965 at 1,050,000, more than 80 percent of them in the South.

272

Various estimates have been given for the community's strength in 1975, ranging from 1.2 million to 2 million. Hanoi's figure is 1.5 million.

CHAPTER THREE

1. Details drawn mainly from K. Das, "The Tragedy of the KG-0729," *Far Eastern Economic Review*, December 22, 1979.
2. "MacLehose: A First-Hand Account of the Refugee Dilemma," *The Asian Wall Street Journal*, July 10, 1979.
3. Nayan Chanda, "Vietnam Puts Its Case to the Test," *Far Eastern Economic Review*, June 16, 1978.
4. John Barron and Anthony Paul, *Murder of a Gentle Land*, copyright © 1977 by The Reader's Digest Association, Inc., Reader's Digest Press, New York, 1977.

CHAPTER FOUR

1. Much of this chapter is compiled from the debriefing of refugees by security and intelligence organizations, as well as personal interviews conducted by the author and others. It is supported by witnesses, both Vietnamese and foreign, who were in the country at the time, and by defecting Communist cadres.
2. "Pointing the Finger at Hanoi," *Far Eastern Economic Review*, August 3, 1979. Tran Quoc Hoan was removed from the Interior portfolio in a leadership reshuffle in February 1980.

CHAPTER SIX

1. Cynthia H. Enloe, "The Nature of Ethnic Politics in Southeast Asia," *Diversity and Development in Southeast Asia*, 1980s Project/Council on Foreign Relations, McGraw-Hill Book Co., New York, 1979.
2. "The Refugee Resettlement Problem in Thailand," U.S. Central Intelligence Agency, National Foreign Assessment Center, May 1978.
3. Peter A. Poole, *The Vietnamese in Thailand*, Cornell University Press, New York, 1970.

4. Halinah Bamadhaj, "Unwanted Guests in a Once Tranquil Society," *New Straits Times*, May 17, 1979.
5. Barry Came, "On China's Frontier," *Newsweek*, September 17, 1979.

CHAPTER SEVEN

1. Wilfred Burchett, "Between Devil and Deep Blue Sea," *The Guardian*, July 22, 1979.
2. Interview with Seymour M. Hersh, *The New York Times*, August 7, 1979.
3. Document No. 2-22 "Vietnam's Refugee Machine," Department of State, Washington, D.C., July 20, 1979.
4. See the author's "The Indochina Refugee Crisis," *Foreign Affairs*, Fall 1979, Vol. 58, No. 1.

CHAPTER EIGHT

1. David Jenkins, "Forming Distant Friendships," *Far Eastern Economic Review*, September 29, 1978.
2. Nayan Chanda, "The Timetable for a Takeover," *Far Eastern Economic Review*, February 23, 1979.

CHAPTER NINE

1. Testimony by Albert Shanker, president of the American Federation of Teachers, to the House Subcommittee on Asian and Pacific Affairs, August 15, 1978.
2. "1979 World Refugee Assessment," Office of the U.S. Coordinator for Refugee Affairs, March 14, 1979.
3. *Ibid.*
4. Report dated April 30, 1979, submitted by a congressional delegation that visited Southeast Asia from December 28, 1978, to January 13, 1979.
5. "1979 World Refugee Assessment."

CHAPTER TEN

1. Mahathir never publicly disowned any of the local reports of his comments. He said he would not "withdraw any-

274

thing." But his aides complained privately to the management of the Bernama news agency that he had been misquoted. They insisted the Deputy Premier had not talked of shooting on sight but had said that shooting would be a last resort and would be carried out only with the backing of the legislature. Mahathir himself volunteered to a U.S. congressional delegation that he had been "misunderstood." What he had really said was that "we will do everything short of shooting them, for which we would need the approval of Parliament." Perhaps explaining his refusal to retract or clarify his comments, he said that in any case they had served a purpose in drawing the world's attention to the severity of the refugee problem in Southeast Asia.

2. "The Khmers Who Couldn't Look Back," *The Economist,* London, July 21, 1979.

CHAPTER ELEVEN

1. Simon Barber, "Sanctioning a Tough Course," *Far Eastern Economic Review,* July 6, 1979.

AFTERWORD

1. Astri Surki, "Indochinese Refugees: The Impact on First Asylum Countries and Implications for American Policy," a study prepared for the use of the Joint Economic Committee of the U.S. Congress, November 25, 1980.
2. Kathleen Newland, "Refugees: The New International Politics of Displacement," Worldwatch Paper 43, Worldwatch Institute, March 1981.
3. *Ibid.*
4. "Overview of World Refugee Situation," Office of the U.S. Coordinator for Refugee Affairs, August 1980.
5. Newland, *op. cit.*

INDEX

277

Minh, Ngoc, 92
Mondale, Walter, 126, 156, 177, 178, 228

National Association for the Advancement of Colored People, 189
National Liberation Front, 212
National Security Council, U.S., 190
National United Front for the Salvation of Kampuchea, 74, 166
National Urban League, 189
Neang Sotha, 239
Netherlands, 183
New Economic Zones:
border war disruptions in, 42
businessmen relocated in, 61
defectors from, 68
in early reform programs, 40–41, 142–43
ethnic Chinese in, 77, 79, 97, 98, 147
New Straits Times, 135, 166
Newsweek, 130, 139
New York Times, 184, 189, 190
New Zealand, 183
Nikitas F, 221–23
Nixon, Richard, 174
Nong Khai refugee camp, 257, 258
Northwest Nine refugee camp, 244, 258
Norway, 183

Oakley, Robert, 66–67, 193
Observer, 237
Organization of African Unity, 266–67
Oxfam, 242

Partai Islam, 202
Pathet Lao, 6, 55, 56, 57, 58, 76, 134, 251
Paul, Anthony, 82
Pentagon Papers, 180

People's Daily, 147
People's Liberation Armed Forces, 51
Philippines, 111
refugee policies of, 125, 198, 218
UNHCR funds for, 127
Vietnam's relations with, 160, 161
Phoenix program, 37, 68
piracy, 42–43, 69–73, 202, 204, 228
Pol Pot, 6, 9, 36n, 41, 54, 134, 241
Prasong Soonsiri, 133–34
Pulau Bidong refugee camp, 9, 212, 249, 265
Pura, Raphael, 8

Quan Doi Nhan Dan, 41

Rajaratnam, Sinnathamby, 156, 167, 169, 178
Red Crescent, 130
Red Cross, 212, 241
reeducation programs:
in Laos, 6, 56, 59–60, 76
Vietnamese camps for, 7, 40, 68, 90, 143, 178
in Vietnamese unification plans, 39–40
Refugee Act (1980), U.S., 214, 259, 260
refugee camps:
conditions in, 9, 59, 127–28, 265
local problems created by, 128, 129–30, 134
in Malaysia, 9, 73, 127, 128, 129–30, 197, 198, 212, 228, 249, 265
population figures for, 176, 195, 213
potential permanency of, 123, 127–28
in Thailand, 9, 59, 81, 127–28, 134, 193, 244–46, 247, 248, 257, 258

283